BIPLANES, TRIPLANES
AND SEAPLANES

BIPLANES, TRIPLANES AND SEAPLANES

MICHAEL SHARPE

BARNES
&NOBLE
BOOKS
NEW YORK

This edition published by Barnes & Noble, Inc.,
by arrangement with Amber Books Ltd
2000 Barnes & Noble Books

M 10 9 8 7 6 5 4 3 2

ISBN: 0-7607-1993-4

Editorial and design by
Amber Books Ltd
Bradley's Close
74–77 White Lion Street
London N1 9PF

Design: Sarah Williams

Printed in Singapore

PICTURE CREDITS
TRH Pictures

ARTWORK CREDITS
Aerospace Publishing

CONTENTS

Introduction

This book provides a comprehensive guide to the most significant biplane, triplane and seaplane aircraft of period between 1900 and 1945, an era often recalled as the 'golden age' of aviation. By far the most prolific type of aircraft of this period, and hence most strongly represented in this book, is the biplane. Although the single wing configuration was pioneered at an early stage, the most popular designs of the pioneering age used a biplane wing for strength and rigidity. In the mid-1920s the first really successful monoplanes were built and flown, and from the mid-1930s the biplane entered a terminal decline. This era also witnessed some extraordinary experiments with multi-winged designs, but the only one that met with consistent success was the triplane, also represented in this book.

The term seaplane may of course encompass an aircraft with any wing configuration, and the category may be further divided into floatplanes and flying boats. Floatplanes are ordinary landplanes that are fitted with float gear or else are designed to operate from water, with integral float gear. The flying boat has a boat-type hull that forms the fuselage, and aircraft-type flying surfaces. Those aircraft that have the capability to land on both land and water are termed amphibians.

The Sopwith Camel was one of the best Allied fighters of World War I, and helped to swing the air war decisively towards the Allies when it was introduced in 1917.

History records that the first flight in a fixed wing aircraft was undertaken in 1849 by a unnamed 'small boy' in a glider designed and built by Sir George Cayley. Up until this time balloons had been the only means by which man had successfully flown and, despite Cayley's significant advance, in the ensuing four decades the most notable research focused on lighter-than-air craft. Cayley helped to establish the principles of flight and pointed the way for the future development of the airfoil, but it was generally accepted that to achieve true flight in a heavier-than-air machine some means of propulsion was required; this research was the dominate the second half of the century. But by 1890 the internal combustion engine was still very much in its infancy and of the other options only steam was deemed remotely practical. In the latter part of the century emerged an extraordinary collection of steam-powered 'aerial carriages', which were all handicapped by a lack of power and excessive weight. Simply, until piston engines could be developed that produced greater power or lighter aircraft built, aviation could advance no further.

BREAKTHROUGH AT KITTYHAWK

It has been suggested that the most remarkable thing about the December 17 1903 flight at Kittyhawk by the Wright brothers in the Flyer was not the design of the aircraft itself, but its engine, which was the first such unit to successfully overcome the overriding thrust-to-weight ratio problems. The aircraft itself was a flimsy biplane of wood and fabric with a basic wing-warping control system, but by marrying this to a lightweight engine the Wright brothers created the first practical heavier-than-air flying machine.

The problem of developing powerful and reliable aero engines continued to dog engineers for many years; the relatively poor performance of available engines was the key influence on aircraft design and construction until the end of the war. The earliest aircraft were little more than a thin timber airframe within a fabric covering, with added rigidity lent by bracing wires and struts. Single and multiple-wing designs were trialled by the pioneers with varying degrees of success; Louis Blériot, Alberto Santos-Dumont and Anthony Fokker were among the most successful exponents of monoplanes before the war, but their designs were extremely fragile and accident-prone.

However it should be remembered that in the Edwardian era the aeroplane represented the an extraordinary technological marvel. Aeronautics represented the very white heat of technology and its exponents, the pioneer pilots, were the astronauts of their day, fêted by press and public alike. But this age of innocence lasted only briefly, before the aircraft was applied to the pursuit of war.

By the outbreak of war in Europe in 1914 all of the major powers had established a military air service equipped with heavier-than-air machines. The few aircraft available to these early military aviators were in no sense combat machines; they had been conceived during the pioneering days, and were not equipped for offensive or defensive use. The first tentative air operations over the Western Front were reconnaissance and artillery-spotting flights, utilising frail, slow and unarmed machines of limited range such as the Royal Aircraft Factory B.E.2c and Albatros B.II biplanes.

But the warplane proper came into being with the adoption of the machine gun and the development of effective interrupter gear allowing it to be fired forward through the arc of the propeller. First seen on the Fokker E.III monoplane, this was one of the most significant advances in military aviation.

Aerial combat became increasingly frequent from mid-1915. Interestingly, after the Fokker E.III, few monoplanes were built by either side. Experience proved that violent manoeuvrings necessary in aerial combat induced stresses that contemporary monoplanes could not withstand. They were therefore deemed unsuitable for the rigours of military aviation. The widespread adoption of the biplane configuration for military aircraft and post-war civil aircraft was a direct result of the greater strength that this layout afforded, and not, as is sometimes assumed, a desire for greater lift.

Captain Eddie Rickenbacker, the leading American ace of World War I with 26 victories, poses in front of his squadron's famous 'Hat in the Ring' insignia.

The de Havilland DH.82a Tiger Moth was a very popular civil aircraft produced between the wars. Many examples are still flying today around the world.

The Great War proved a powerful catalyst for developments in aircraft technology and laid the foundations for the future use of air power. By 1918 combat aircraft were flying at 200mph+, armed with two machine guns firing through the propeller arc. Speed, firepower, ceiling and other performance measurements increased dramatically. Innovation was not restricted to aircraft design, for as performance increased so the number of roles in which aircraft were employed expanded. The role of aircraft progressed from the original 1914 concept, aerial observation, to a wide tactical application and strategic design, as seen in the German Air Service's long range bomber offensive against Britain. Tactics had evolved from primitive, limited means of fighting, to the use of large formations organised for high altitude, controlled combat.

Germany led the way in other fields. In the March 1918 Kaiser Offensive on the Western Front its commanders pioneered the use of *Schlactstaffeln* (specialised ground-attack air units) in support of advancing troops. Armed with light bombs, anti-personnel darts, machine-guns for strafing (from the German word *strafe*, meaning strike) and controlled by a rudimentary ground-air signalling system these units proved highly effective. In the closing months of the war Britain refined these tactics, using aircraft to attack field artillery in the path of advancing tanks. In 1939 the German forces used similar tactics in its Blitzkreig offensive on Poland, and again in the Low Countries, in France and during Operation Barbarossa.

The seaplane, which grew out of naval commander's desire to use aircraft to spot for their ship's gunners, saw a similar expansion in roles. Torpedo bombing, convoy escort, anti-submarine and carrier operations were all pioneered during the war and at its conclusion it was generally accepted that the aircraft had a very important role to play in warfare.

THE INTER-WAR YEARS

Post-war defence cutbacks forced widespread reductions in European and US military air fleets, and military aircraft design developed little. But while military aviation stagnated, civil aviation, which prior to the war had been in its infancy, took advantage of advances made in the war years and became the catalyst for technological progress. Commercial pressures now stimulated aircraft production. The 1920s and 1930s were a golden age in civil aviation. It was in these two decades that air travel became accessible to the common man and in which intercontinental air travel became a reality.

In the early 1920s, a huge surplus of ex-military aircraft flooded onto the market. At last private ownership became a practical reality for thousands of would-be airmen, prompting prompting many to learn to fly. The marked downturn in military market encouraged manufacturers to produce truly affordable light aircraft for the general public and this market grew enormously. Ex-military aircraft and pilots formed the backbone of the joy-riding enterprises catering for a new-found enthusiasm for aerial adventure that sprang up in Europe and in the US in the early 1920s; in the latter country military pilots satisfied their passions for aerial derring-do through 'barnstorming' antics that wowed audiences across the land.

THE FIRST AIRLINES

Aircraft also had some rather more serious applications in peacetime. In both the US and Europe, the potential of the aircraft for official mail-carrying duties was soon exploited, paving the way for an great expansion in the commercial transport industry. From the early 1920s the network of routes expanded rapidly, pioneered by the airlines of Britain, Germany, the United States and Italy. From those countries emerged the first generation of airliners and passenger flying-boats. The expansion continued apace throughout the following two decades, encompassing the great age of the China Clipper flying boats and of the Imperial Air routes, until the outbreak of World War II brought it to an abrupt halt, just as Germany was preparing to inaugurate the first non-stop transatlantic commercial route.

RECORD BREAKERS

Another interesting development was a reawakening in the pioneer spirit through competition. Airmen strove to fly faster, higher and for longer than their competitors, compelled by national pride and the promise of international recognition. Aircraft manufacturers, for their part, saw record-breaking flights as an effective way of publicising their latest products. Aside from the numerous long-distance flights mounted during the period, the greatest indication of the advances made in this period are the aircraft that competed for the Schneider Trophy and in the National Air Races. These two events attracted great interest among the public and stimulated manufacturers to research and develop ever more powerful engines, materials and airframes. Metal replaced wood for airscrews, undercarriage became retractable in response to the need for clean aerodynamic lines, and most importantly, the biplane came to replaced by the monoplane.

Military aviation was slow to adopt these advances. Funding for aircraft development was drastically cut after the Versailles Treaty and in many areas of military aircraft design progress was slow. In general, there was a very marked but ultimately damaging faith in the primacy of offence in aerial operations throughout the inter-war years, one that prompted the British, French and US air forces to build small numbers of inadequate bombers whilst holding true to the belief that well-regimented formations of bombing aircraft with defensive armament held the key to the projection of air power. Much effort was concentrated into the development of strategic bombers, while in many instances the needs of the fighter, reconnaissance and naval air forces were neglected.

Thus in 1930, in almost every field save for the bomber, military aircraft were remarkably unchanged from the form in which they had emerged from World War I. Performance had improved, but in essence they were the same, with a biplane wing, taildragger landing gear and light armament. Metal skinning and structure was beginning to replace the fabric and wood of previous generations. The biplane soldiered on well into the late 1930s, when it was rapidly becoming obsolete, as aircraft manufacturers turned their attentions to stressed-skin monoplane designs. However, as late as

The Short Sunderland flying boat, seen here on the point of take off, served with distinction for RAF Coastal Command in a variety of roles during World War II.

1936, Britain introduced its last biplane fighter, the Gloster Gladiator, into service; development of the biplane continued in Italy even after this date.

TWILIGHT OF THE GOLDEN AGE

Despite its apparent obsolescence, the fact remains that in 1939 the biplane still equipped many of the front-line units in Britain, Germany, France, Belgium, Holland and the Netherlands. As the war progressed it was rapidly relegated to secondary roles, and aside from a few notable exceptions such as the Fairey Swordfish the biplane was well and truly defunct by 1945. Only Antonov has successfully reprised the biplane with the extraordinary An-2.

The flying boat served with distinction in its intended role of long-range maritime reconnaissance patrol long after 1945, but grandiose plans for a rebirth of the flying boat in the long-range passenger carrying role fell by the wayside after post-war development was overtaken by a new generation of long-range landplane airliners. Floatplanes and flying boats continue to serve in some numbers across the globe, notably in Canada and the Caribbean, but their role has been diminished by the helicopter.

Fortunately, many of the aircraft in this book survive in the hands of collectors and with preservation groups. Of the others, only pictures and memories remain. This book will provide a useful guide or perhaps rekindle those memories for enthusiasts both old and new.

AEG C.IV

Allgemeine Elektrizitäts Gesellschaft (AEG) began building aircraft in 1910 and from the outset of World War I was required to build military aircraft for both German air services. The AEG 'C' series began with the C.I, introduced in March 1915 as a two-seat biplane armed reconnaissance aircraft powered by a 150hp (112kW) Benz Bz.III inline engine. Most important of the series was the C.IV, which was fitted with a Mercedes D.III inline engine and a fixed forward-firing machine gun for the pilot. It was built in numbers totalling some 400 aircraft. Development of the C.IV included the IV.N night bomber with increased span wings and Benz Bz.III power, the C.V two-seat reconnaissance prototype and the C.VIII.Dr triplane. Pictured is a C.IV of Fliegerabteilung 'A' (Artillery Cooperation) 224, flying from Chateau Bellingchamp during the spring of 1917.

Country of origin:	Germany
Type:	two-seat armed reconnaissance biplane
Powerplant:	one 160hp (119kw) Mercedes D.III inline piston engine
Performance:	maximum speed 115km/h (71mph); service ceiling 5000m (16,400ft); endurance 4hrs
Weights:	empty 800kg (1764lb); maximum take-off weight 1120kg (2469lb)
Dimensions:	span 13.45m (44ft 1in); length 7.15m (23ft 5in); height 3.35m (10ft 10in); wing area 39 sq m (420 sq ft)
Armament:	one fixed forward-firing 7.92mm LMG 08/15 machine gun; one 7.92mm Parabellum machine gun on ring mounting for observer in rear cockpit

AEG G.IV

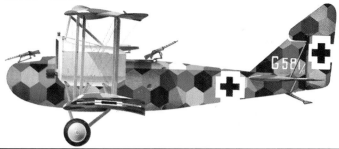

A EG undertook development of bomber aircraft for the German *Kampfstaffel* (battle squadrons) early in World War I. The first of the 'G' series, the G.I, was rather underpowered and only a single example was constructed. The following G.II and G.III suffered from the same problem and were therefore built in very small numbers. Marrying the powerplant of twin Mercedes D.IV engines to the airframe produced a far more effective aircraft in the form of the G.IV, but this did not enter service until the end of 1916. The four crew positions within the steel tube, fabric- and plywood-skinned aircraft were interconnected, enabling crew members to change position in flight as necessary. However, with a maximum bomb load and a crew of three, range was limited. Pictured is a G.IV of Bogohl 4, Staffel 19, stationed at Bazuel in the summer of 1918.

Country of origin:	Germany
Type:	four-seat bomber/reconnaissance biplane
Powerplant:	two 260hp (194kW) Mercedes D.IVa inline engines
Performance:	maximum speed 165km/h (103mph); service ceiling 4500m (14,765ft); endurance 5hrs
Weights:	empty 2400kg (5291lb); maximum take-off weight 3630kg (8003lb)
Dimensions:	span 18.40m (60ft 3in); length 9.7m (31 8in); height 3.9m (12ft 8in); wing area 67 sq m (721 sq ft)
Armament:	one 7.92mm Parabellum machine gun on ring mounting in forward cockpit; one 7.92mm Parabellum machine gun on rail mounting in aft cockpit; underwing pylons for maximum bomb load of 400kg (882lb)

Aero A.18

Aero Tovarna Letadel Dr Kabes was formed in Prague just after World War I, at a time when the majority of European aircraft manufacturers were closing down. The A.18 was the company's successful submission to a Czech Air Force competition for a new single-seat fighter aircraft. The A.18 was a smaller, single-seat version of the A.11, and followed that aircraft's single-bay, unequal-span biplane wing planform. The powerplant was sourced from the Bayerne MotorischeWerke and the twin machine guns, synchronised to fire through the propeller disc, came from Vickers. Some 20 aircraft were supplied to the Czech Air Force; development continued with the A.18B with a reduced wing span, victor by default of a national aircraft race in 1923 when the two other competitors crashed, and the A.18C with a 300hp (224kW) Walter W-IV engine. Shown here is an A.18 of the 2nd Air Regiment, Czech Air Force, stationed at Oloumouc in the mid-1920s.

Country of origin:	Czechoslovakia
Type:	single-seat fighter biplane
Powerplant:	one 185hp (138kW) BMW IIIa inline piston engine
Performance:	maximum speed 229km/h (142mph); service ceiling 9000m (29,530ft); range 400km (249 miles)
Weights:	empty 637kg (1404lb); maximum take-off weight 862kg (1900lb)
Dimensions:	span 7.6m (24ft 11in); length 5.9m (19ft 4in); height 2.9m (9ft 6in); wing area 15.9 sq m (171 sq ft)
Armament:	two fixed forward-firing synchronised machine guns

Aero A.100

The success of its A.11 encouraged Aero to fund further development of the basic airframe. However, installing a more powerful 450hp (336kW) Lorraine-Dietrich engine proved unsatisfactory and substantial revisions to the structure were necessary before the resulting A.30 could enter production. From the A.30 was spawned the A.430 prototype, a single example of which was built with a 650hp (485kW) Avia engine and oleo-pneumatic shock-struts for the main landing gear units. This aircraft offered significantly improved performance over the A.30. Redesignated as the A.100, it was offered to the Czech Air Ministry and selected for production in 1933. Some 44 aircraft were produced for the Czech Air Force. Two bomber versions were the A.101 with an 800hp (596kW) Praga engine, and the Ab.101, with a 750hp (559kW) Hispano-Suiza 12Ydrs engine. Pictured is an A.100 of the 3rd Air Regiment, Czech Air Force, based at Piestany in the mid-1930s.

Country of origin:	Czechoslovakia
Type:	two-seat long-range reconnaissance biplane
Powerplant:	one 650hp (485kW) Avia Vr-36 inline piston engine
Performance:	maximum speed 270km/h (168mph); service ceiling 6500m (21,325ft); endurance 4hrs
Weights:	empty 2040kg (4497lb); maximum take-off weight 3220kg (7099lb)
Dimensions:	span 14.7m (48ft 2in); length 10.6m (34ft 9in); height 3.5m (11ft 5in); wing area 44.3 sq m (477 sq ft)
Armament:	two fixed forward-firing 0.303in Vickers machine guns; two Lewis guns on flexible mount in rear cockpit; external pylons for a maximum bomb load of 600kg (1322lb)

Aichi D1A2 'Susie'

Like many of its contemporaries, Aichi Tokei Denki Kabushiki Kaisha was a successful industrial manufacturing company in its own right before branching out into aircraft design and production. Aichi gained experience in this field through close association with Ernst Heinkel, whose design staff produced a prototype aircraft (the He 66) for Aichi in 1931 to meet a Japanese Navy requirement for a carrier-based dive bomber. Under Japanese manufacture with a Nakajima engine this aircraft was designated Navy Type 94 Carrier Bomber (Aichi D1A1). From it was developed the Aichi D1A2, which appeared in 1936 with a more powerful Nakajima Hikari engine, spatted wheels and more streamlined windscreens. Production totalled some 428 aircraft but by the time of Japan's entry into World War II in December 1941 the 70 that remained had been relegated to second-line duties.

Country of origin:	Japan
Type:	two-seat carrier-based biplane dive bomber
Powerplant:	one 730hp (544kW) Nakajima Hikari 1 radial piston engine
Performance:	maximum level speed 310km/h (193mph); climb to 3000m (9845ft) in 7 mins 50 secs; service ceiling 7000m (22,965ft); range 930km (578 miles)
Weights:	empty 1516kg (3342lb); maximum take-off weight 2610kg (5754lb)
Dimensions:	span 11.4m (37ft 4in); length 9.3m (30ft 6in); height 3.41m (11ft 2in); wing area 34.7 sq m (373 sq ft)
Armament:	two fixed forward-firing 7.7mm Type 97 machine guns and one 7.7mm Type 92 machine gun on flexible mount in rear cockpit; plus external pylons for one 250kg (551lb) and two 30kg (66lb) bombs

Aichi E13A 'Jake'

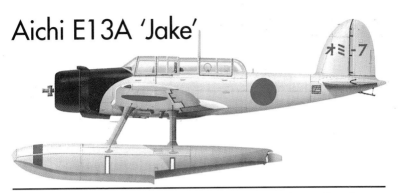

The Aichi concern produced a number of excellent reconnaissance floatplanes for the Imperial Japanese Navy. The best known and most successful of these is the E13A. In 1937 the navy issued a requirement calling for a long-range reconnaissance floatplane that could operate from both surface vessels and shore bases, and provide escort for the merchant convoys that were Japan's lifeblood. The Aichi submission was ordered into production as the Navy Type 0 Reconnaissance Seaplane Model 11, and the first of an eventual 1273 aircraft entered service in late 1941. A number flew reconnaissance patrols during the attack on Pearl Harbor. One of the best features of the aircraft – which saw service throughout the Pacific theatre – was its endurance; the three-man crews regularly undertook patrols of anything up to 15 hours.

Country of origin:	Japan
Type:	long-range reconnaissance floatplane
Powerplant:	one 1080hp (805kW) Mitsubishi Kinsei 43 radial piston engine
Performance:	maximum speed 375km/h (233mph); service ceiling 8370m (27,460ft); endurance 15 hrs; range 2090km (1299 miles)
Weights:	empty 2642kg (5825lb); maximum take-off weight 3640kg (8025lb)
Dimensions:	span 14.5m (47ft 6in); length 11.3m (37ft); height 7.4m (24ft 3in); wing area 36 sq m (387 sq ft)
Armament:	one Type 92 7.7mm machine gun on flexible mount in rear cockpit; external pylons for up to 250kg (551lb) of bombs; optional Type 99 20mm cannon on flexible mount in ventral position

Airco D.H.2

The Aircraft Manufacturing Company (Airco) was established at Hendon in early 1912 and while still in its infancy nurtured the talents of one of Britain's greatest aircraft designers, Geoffrey de Havilland. De Havilland designed the D.H.2 as a smaller version of the earlier D.H.1, a single-seat pusher reconnaissance/fighter biplane of wood-and-fabric construction. With no interrupter gear available to British aircraft designers the unusual pusher layout was considered essential. The D.H.2 mounted a Lewis gun in the front cockpit, its field of fire unencumbered by the need to avoid the propeller. Controlling the aircraft while operating the gun was tricky, but the D.H.2 was the best fighter available to the British in mid-1916 and did much to counter the superiority of the Fokker monoplanes. A total of 400 were built, but by early 1917 the D.H.2 had been eclipsed by the Albatros D.I and D.II and was withdrawn from service on the Western Front and reallocated to less demanding theatres.

Country of origin:	United Kingdom
Type:	single-seat scout fighter biplane
Powerplant:	one 100hp (75kW) Gnome Monosoupape rotary piston engine; later examples had 110hp (82kW) Le Rhône rotary
Performance:	maximum speed 150km/h (93mph); service ceiling 1300m (4265ft); endurance 2hrs 45mins
Weights:	empty 428kg (943lb); maximum take-off weight 654kg (1441lb)
Dimensions:	span 8.61m (28ft 3in); length 7.68m (25ft 2in); height 2.91m (9ft 6½in); wing area 23.13 sq m (249 sq ft)
Armament:	one forward-firing .303in Lewis gun on flexible mounting (pilots often fixed this to fire straight ahead, preferring instead to bring the gun to bear by aiming the aircraft)

Airco D.H.4

De Havilland designed the Airco D.H.4 around the 200 BHP (Beardmore-Halford-Pullinger) engine in response to an Air Ministry request for a new day bomber. In this role the D.H.4 was the best aircraft in its class during the war. Using an inline piston engine, de Havilland employed a clean tractor layout, breaking away from the traditional use of the rotary engine, but the wide separation between pilot and observer was a controversial and potentially dangerous feature as it hampered communication in the air. The 1449 British-built aircraft was manufactured by various sub-contractors, although delayed production of the BHP engine meant that other engines were employed on production aircraft. By spring 1918 the D.H.4 equipped nine RAF squadrons and was also in service with the Royal Naval Air Service. D.H.4s were engaged in the destruction of the flagship Zeppelin L.70. Pictured is a Rolls Royce Eagle VI-engined aircraft of No 5 (Naval) Squadron, RNAS.

Country of origin:	United Kingdom
Type:	two-seat day bomber biplane (Westland-built, Eagle VI engine)
Powerplant:	one 250hp (186kW) Rolls-Royce Eagle VI inline piston engine
Performance:	maximum speed 230km/h (143mph); service ceiling 6705m (22,000ft); endurance 3hrs 45mins
Weights:	empty 1083kg (2387lb); maximum take-off weight 1575kg (3742lb)
Dimensions:	span 12.92m (42ft 4in); length 9.35m (30ft 8in); height 3.35m (11ft); wing area 40.32 sq m (434 sq ft)
Armament:	two fixed forward-firing .303in Vickers machine guns and two .303in Vickers machine guns in rear cockpit; external pylons; provision for 209kg (460lb) of bombs

Airco D.H.4

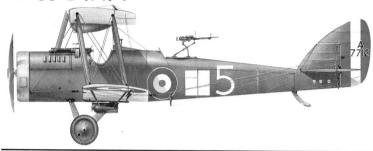

Seven different engines of between 200hp (149kW) and 275hp (205kW) output were fitted to production D.H.4 aircraft, and a further 15 were trialled. These were the Royal Aircraft Factory RAF 3a 200hp (149kW), the 230hp (171kW) BHP, the 230hp (171kW) Siddeley Puma, the 250hp (186kW) Rolls Royce Mk III, the 250hp (186kW) Rolls Royce Mk IV, the 260hp (194kW) Fiat and the 275hp (205kW) Rolls Royce Eagle VI. The best D.H.4s had a 375hp (280kW) Eagle VIII from Rolls Royçe, but this was expensive to produce and because of its larger propeller needed longer landing gears. The Airco-built example pictured has the more common RAF 3a engine, distinguishable by the frontal radiator that is tapered slightly from top to bottom and single exhaust stack. The aircraft was delivered to No 18 Squadron, RFC, in summer 1917. Note also the Scarff ring-mounted Lewis gun and underwing bombs.

Country of origin:	United Kingdom
Type:	two-seat day bomber biplane (early RAF 3a engine)
Powerplant:	one 200hp (149kW) RAF 3a inline piston engine
Performance:	maximum speed 230km/h (143mph); service ceiling 5000m (17,400ft); endurance 3hrs 45mins
Weights:	empty 1083kg (2387lb); maximum take-off weight 1575kg (3742lb)
Dimensions:	span 12.92m (42ft 4in); length 9.35m (30ft 8in); height 3.35m (11ft); wing area 40.32 sq m (434 sq ft)
Armament:	one fixed forward-firing .303in Vickers machine gun and one .303in Lewis machine gun in rear cockpit; external pylons with provision for 209kg (460lb) of bombs

Airco DH-4 'Liberty Plane'

America showed great interest in the D.H.4, and from mid-1917 licensed manufacture of the aircraft was undertaken by three US companies – Dayton-Wright (3106 aircraft), Fisher Body Corporation (1600 aircraft) and the Standard Aircraft Corporation (140 aircraft). The first American-manufactured machines had the baseline American Liberty 12 engine that produced some 400hp (298kW). Many of the aircraft passed to civilian operators after the war and in post-war USA the D.H.4 (as it was known locally) flourished. No fewer than 60 separate versions were evolved for roles as diverse as crop-dusting and aerial mapping, using developments of the Liberty engine. Pictured is a DH-4B that served with the 168th Aero Squadron as part of the American Expeditionary Force, one of 13 squadrons equipped with the aircraft. The winged skull badge adopted by the squadron is painted on the fuselage.

Country of origin:	USA (United Kingdom)
Type:	two-seat day bomber biplane (US-built American Liberty engine)
Powerplant:	one 400hp (298kW) Packard Liberty 12 inline piston engine
Performance:	maximum speed 230km/h (143mph); service ceiling 5000m (17,400ft); endurance 3hrs 45mins
Weights:	empty 1083kg (2387lb); maximum take-off weight 1575kg (3742lb)
Dimensions:	span 12.92m (42ft 4in); length 9.35m (30ft 8in); height 3.35m (11ft); wing area 40.32 sq m (434 sq ft)
Armament:	one fixed forward-firing .303in Vickers machine gun and one .303in Lewis machine gun in rear cockpit; external pylons with provision for 209kg (460lb) of bombs

Airco D.H.9A

Persistent German raids on Britain during World War I prompted a doubling in the size of the Royal Flying Corps, with most of the new squadrons equipped with day bombers. The D.H.4 was the expected type, but de Havilland had already attempted to rectify a glaring weakness of this aircraft by designing a modified version designated D.H.9 with the pilot and observer accommodated in back-to-back seating. This had a Siddeley Puma engine that could only produce 230hp (172kW), and performance of the early production D.H.9s was decidedly inferior to the D.H.4. In service with the RNAS and RFC from December 1917, the Puma engine was chronically unreliable and, furthermore, the new aircraft that it powered had a much reduced ceiling of 3960m (13,000ft). A much improved version of the aircraft, the D.H.9A, with a 400hp (298kW) Liberty engine was produced after the war and became an important tool of RAF operations in the Middle East during the 1920s.

Country of origin:	United Kingdom
Type:	two-seat day bomber biplane (American Liberty engine)
Powerplant:	one 420hp (313kW) Packard Liberty 12 vee-12 piston engine
Performance:	maximum speed 198km/h (123mph); service ceiling 5105m (16,750ft); endurance 5hrs 15mins
Weights:	empty 1270kg (2800lb); maximum take-off weight 2107kg (4645lb)
Dimensions:	span 14.01m (45ft 11in); length 9.22m (30ft 3in); height 3.45m (11ft 4in); wing area 45.22 sq m (487 sq ft)
Armament:	one fixed forward-firing .303in Vickers machine gun and one or two .303in Lewis machine guns on Scarff ring in rear cockpit; external pylons with provision for 299kg (660lb) of bombs

Airco D.H.9C

In the years following the World War I there was something of a boom in the civil
aviation industry and de Havilland was one of a number of firms to adapt
surplus military aircraft for peacetime roles. There were two different variants of
the D.H.9 for the passenger-carrying role, the 9B and the 9C. The 20 9B aircraft on
the British civil register could carry two passengers, one in front of and one
behind the pilot. The 9C provided accommodation for three passengers. One was
carried in an open cockpit forward of the pilot, while the others benefitted from
the protection of a faired dorsal canopy aft of the pilot. A total of 19 aircraft were
produced – 13 for operators in the UK, three for Australia, and the remaining three
for Spain. Pictured is the last aircraft in service, a D.H.9C operated by Northern Air
Lines in 1932 at Barton. Note the cut-down engine cowling and radiator for the
water-cooled Packard Liberty engine.

Country of origin:	United Kingdom
Type:	three-seat passenger biplane (American Liberty engine)
Powerplant:	one 420hp (313kW) Packard Liberty 12 vee-12 piston engine
Performance:	maximum speed 198km/h (123mph); service ceiling 5105m (16,750ft); endurance 5hrs 15mins
Weights:	empty 1270kg (2800lb); maximum take-off weight 2107kg (4645lb)
Dimensions:	span 14.01m (45ft 11in); length 9.22m (30ft 3in); height 3.45m (11ft 4in); wing area 45.22 sq m (487 sq ft)

Airco D.H.10 Amiens

In 1916 de Havilland produced his first twin-engine aircraft for Airco, a bomber powered by two pusher Beardmore engines mounted midway between the biplane wings. This D.H.3 was never put into production, but during 1917 de Havilland redesigned it for greater power in response to the urgent need for a retaliatory weapon to counter German bomber raids. The first prototype D.H.10 Amiens flew in March 1918 with 230hp (171kW) BHP pusher engines, however the other two prototypes – the Amiens II with 360hp (268kW) Rolls Royce Eagle VIII and Amiens III with 400hp (298kW) Liberty 12 engines – had their engines installed in a tractor configuration. The fourth prototype mounted the engines directly on to the lower wing, and in this form was produced as the Amiens D.H.10A. A total of 1291 were ordered by 7 manufacturers but were delivered too late to see service in World War I. At least 220 were completed for the RAF and these served with distinction in Britain, Egypt and India until 1927.

Country of origin:	United Kingdom
Type:	three-seat day bomber biplane
Powerplant:	one 400hp (313kW) Packard Liberty 12 vee-12 piston engine
Performance:	maximum speed 180km/h (112mph); service ceiling 5030m (16,500ft); endurance hrs 45mins
Weights:	empty 2533kg (5585lb); maximum take-off weight 4082kg (9000lb)
Dimensions:	span 19.96m (65ft 6in); length 12.08m (39ft 7in); height 4.42m (14ft 6in); wing area 77.79 sq m (837 sq ft)
Armament:	single or twin .303in Lewis guns on Scarff ring mounting in nose and midships cockpits; external pylons with provision for a maximum bomb load of 408kg (900lb)

Albatros B.III

Albatros Flugzeugwerke GmbH was established in early 1909 and in 1913 collaborated with Ernst Heinkel to produce the B.I, a two-seat reconnaissance aircraft for the German Air Service. Development of the aircraft continued with the B.II series that had reduced span wings and various engines in the 100–120hp (75–89kW) range. This aircraft established Albatros' name as an aircraft manufacturer, and was built in some numbers. Accommodation for the pilot and observer was in tandem cockpits with the pilot seated aft, a configuration that somewhat hampered the downward view of the observer. The B.II-W (Albatros W.1) was a floatplane variant and the B.IIa a trainer with slightly increased span and either a Mercedes D.II or Argus As.II. Pictured is a B.III, a variant built in small numbers in 1915, that served with Fliegersatzabteilung (FEA) 1 at Döberitz during the winter of 1916–17.

Country of origin:	Germany
Type:	two-seat reconnaissance biplane
Powerplant:	one 120hp (89kW) Mercedes D.II inline piston engine
Performance:	maximum speed 120km/h (75mph); service ceiling 3000m (9840ft); endurance about 4hrs
Weights:	empty 723kg (1594lb); maximum take-off weight 1071kg (2361lb)
Dimensions:	span 11m (36ft 1in); length 7.8m (25ft 7in); height 3.15m (10ft 4in); wing area (B.II) 40.12 sq m (432 sq ft)

Albatros C.III

A natural development of the B.III was the C.I, which had a more powerful engine and revised accommodation which placed the observer aft of the pilot where he was provided with a machine gun on a movable mount. The C.II never reached production, but the Albatros C.III, which first entered service in late 1916, was the company's most prolific two-seater of the war. This followed a generally similar configuration to the C.I series, but had a number of important revisions including a redesigned tail, which prefigured the more rounded versions of later Albatros types. Later aircraft were equipped with a synchronised forward-firing machine gun and had a small bay between the two crew for the stowage of small bombs. These features greatly increased the offensive capabilities of the aircraft. Pictured is the C.III of Lieutenant Bruno Maas (hence the stylised insignia on the fuselage) of Fliegerabteilung 14, flying on the Eastern Front in January 1917.

Country of origin:	Germany
Type:	two-seat general purpose biplane
Powerplant:	one 150hp (112kW) Benz Bz.III or 160hp (119kW) Mercedes D.III inline piston engine
Performance:	maximum speed 140km/h (87mph); service ceiling 3350m (11,000ft); endurance about 4hrs
Weights:	empty 851kg (1876lb); maximum take-off weight 1353kg (2983lb)
Dimensions:	span 11.69m (38ft 4in); length 8.0m (26ft 3in); height with Benz engine 3.07m (10ft); Mercedes engine 3.10m (10ft 2in); wing area 36.91 sq m (397.31 sq ft)
Armament:	one 7.92mm Parabellum machine gun on flexible mount in rear cockpit; later aircraft had one 7.92mm LMG 08/15 fixed forward-firing machine gun, plus a small internal bomb bay

Albatros D.V

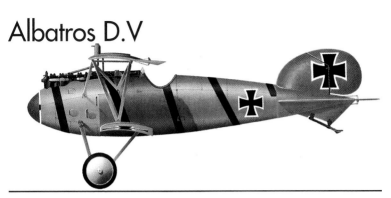

First of the 'D' series of Albatros fighter scouts, the D.I was introduced in early 1917 and was for some time the best aircraft in its class. Designed by Robert Thelen and first demonstrated in prototype form in August 1916, the D.I followed a familiar single-bay, staggered biplane wing planform but introduced the distinctive elliptical fuselage of monocoque structure that is characteristic to all of the 'D' series aircraft. This proved expensive to produce but the aircraft became the favoured mount of Böelcke and Richtofen. For the improved D.II the wing was remounted nearer to the top fuselage to facilitate a better view for the pilot. The D.III was the result of Thelen's attempt to improve the manoeuvrability of the D.II, by revising the wing configuration to a lower-chord lower and increased-chord upper wing. However rapid improvements in Allied fighter capability prompted the development of the D.V, pictured above.

Country of origin:	Germany
Type:	single-seat scout fighter
Powerplant:	one 180/200hp (134/149kW) Mercedes D.II inline piston engine
Performance:	maximum speed 186km/h (116mph); service ceiling 5700m (18,700ft); endurance about 2hrs
Weights:	empty 687kg (1515lb); maximum take-off weight 937kg (2066lb)
Dimensions:	span 9.05m (29ft 7in); length 7.33m (24ft); height 2.70m (8ft 10in); wing area 21.20 sq m (228 sq ft)
Armament:	two fixed forward-firing 7.92mm LMG 08/15 machine guns

Albatros D.Va

Development of the D.IV began in early 1917, in response to the emergence of much improved Allied fighters, but was plagued by problems associated with the experimental Mercedes D.III engine chosen for the powerplant and never entered production. The D.V reverted to the D.IIIa engine mounted in a deeper fuselage that improved streamlining and thus reduced drag. The gap between the wing and upper fuselage was further reduced, rudder area was increased and the aileron controls were revised. The D.V entered service in May 1917 and was quickly followed by the D.Va which reverted to the the upper wing and aileron control system of the D.III. Production of the two versions was in excess of 3000 aircraft, with 1512 in service on the Western Front in May 1918, by which time they had been outclassed by the latest scout aircraft of both sides. Pictured is the D.Va of Lieutenant H.J. von Hippel, serving with Jagdstaffel 5 in the spring of 1918.

Country of origin:	Germany
Type:	single-seat scout fighter
Powerplant:	one 180/200hp (134/149kW) Mercedes D.II inline piston engine
Performance:	maximum speed 186km/h (116mph); service ceiling 5700m (18,700ft); endurance about 2hrs
Weights:	empty 687kg (1515lb); maximum take-off weight 937kg (2066lb)
Dimensions:	span 9.05m (29ft 8in); length 7.33m (24ft); height 2.70m (8ft 10in); wing area 21.20 sq m (228 sq ft)
Armament:	two fixed forward-firing 7.92mm LMG 08/15 machine guns

Albatros J.I

Infantry close support was pioneered by the German Army Air Service in 1916 with the introduction of *Infantrie-flieger* (infantry contact patrol) units for the Battle of Verdun. This role became an increasingly important aspect of air operations and in response Albatros developed the J.I which adopted the wing of the C.XII two-seat reconnaissance aircraft mated to a fuselage of completely new design.The hazards associated with low-level operations called for some measure of armoured protection to the cockpit floor and sides, but the added weight (490kg/1080lb) of this armour, coupled with the decision to use the Benz Bz.IV engine rather than the more powerful Mercedes D.IVa of the Albatros C.XII, had an inevitably detrimental effect on performance. Entering service in late 1917, the J.I enjoyed some measure of success despite its shortcomings and may be considered as a truly pioneering aircraft. Pictured is a J.I of the post-war Polish Air Force.

Country of origin:	Germany
Type:	two-seat close-support biplane
Powerplant:	one 200hp (149kW) Benz Bz.IV inline piston engine
Performance:	maximum speed 140km/h (87mph); service ceiling 4000m (13,120ft); endurance about 2hrs 30mins
Weights:	empty 1398kg (3082lb); maximum take-off weight 1808kg (3986lb)
Dimensions:	span 14.14m (46ft 4in); length 8.83m (28ft 11in); height 3.37m (11ft); wing area 42.82 sq m (461 sq ft)
Armament:	two fixed downward-firing 7.92mm LMG 08/15 machine guns; one 7.92mm Parabellum machine gun on movable mount in rear cockpit

Antonov An-2 'Colt'

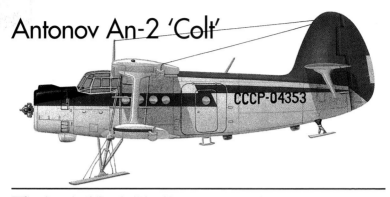

First flown in 1947 and still in widespread use today, Oleg Antonov's An-2 (NATO designated it 'Colt', while in Russia and the former Soviet republics it is more affectionately known as 'Annushka') can rightly claim its status as one of the world's greatest aircraft. The Antonov Bureau was formed in 1946 for the express purpose of building an all-purpose utility aircraft for the Ministry of Agriculture and Forestry to replace the Polikarpov Po-2. The An-2 is the largest single-engine biplane in history but its physical size belies outstanding short take-off and landing (STOL) capabilities and the overall simplicity of design has been instrumental in the successful export of the aircraft to developing nations. Pictured above is a ski-equipped civil aircraft, probably in Aeroflot's Northern or Artic Directorate markings. although Aeroflot titling is absent. The colour scheme is intended to stand out against the snow.

Country of origin:	USSR
Type:	12-seat transport biplane
Powerplant:	one 1000hp (746kW) Shvetsov ASh-62IR 9-cylinder radial piston engine
Performance:	maximum speed 258km/h (160mph); service ceiling 4500m (14,763ft); range 845km (525 miles)
Weights:	empty 3450kg (7605lb); maximum take-off weight 5500kg (12,125lb)
Dimensions:	span 18.18m (59ft 7in); length 12.4m (40ft 8in); height 4.13m (13ft 6in); wing area 71.6 sq m (770 sq ft)

Antonov An-2TD 'Colt'

The An-2 has been readily adapted for a wide variety of roles, including multi-role utility transport (An-2T), crop-spraying (An-2SKh), fire-fighting (An-2L), medivac (An-2S), atmospheric sampling (An-2ZA), artillery correction (An-2RK), and as a floatplane water-bomber (An-2PP). A special parachute trainer designated An-2TD was created by Antonov with static lines, removable cargo door and folding bench seats along the sides. For many years it was a staple workhorse of the DOSAAF, the Soviet Union's paramilitary training organisation, and continued in licensed production after 1960, when manufacture of the An-2 switched to WSK-PZL of Poland. Production at the WSK-PZL factory continued well into the 1980s and encompassed a further six derivative versions. Some estimates of the total number of aircraft completed by Polish, Russian, Chinese and East German sources are in excess of 23,000.

Country of origin:	USSR
Type:	12-seat parachute training biplane
Powerplant:	one 1000hp (746kW) Shvetsov ASh-62IR 9-cylinder radial piston engine
Performance:	maximum speed 258km/h (160mph); service ceiling 4500m (14,763ft); range 845km (525 miles)
Weights:	empty 3450kg (7605lb); maximum take-off weight 5500kg (12,125lb)
Dimensions:	span 18.18m (59ft 7in); length 12.4m (40ft 8in); height 4.13m (13ft 6in); wing area 71.6 sq m (770 sq ft)

Antonov An-2T Antek

First in the long line of An-2 variants was the An-2T (*Transportnyi*) which became available in October 1948 and remained in almost constant production for 40 years, accounting for nearly half of the output of this airframe. Other passenger-carrying versions of the An-2 are the An-2P (100 built in East Germany under licence in the late 1950s), the more refined An-2TP, and the PZL-Mielec-built An-2PK five-seat executive transport. One of the few vices common to all aircraft in the An-2 family is tail-heaviness with the resulting tendency to pitch up, but in general they are simple aircraft to fly. Although the Soviet Union took the vast majority (at least 8400 of 10,000) of Polish-built An-2 aircraft, and others were exported around the world, some were retained. Of note on this Polish An-2T Antek built at Mielec is the AV-2 propeller without spinner and the dielectric domes under the rear fuselage enclosing the radio altimeter aerials.

Country of origin:	USSR
Type:	12-seat transport/utility aircraft
Powerplant:	one 1000hp (746kW) Shvetsov ASh-62IR 9-cylinder radial piston engine
Performance:	maximum speed 258km/h (160mph); service ceiling 4500m (14,763ft); range 845km (525 miles)
Weights:	empty 3450kg (7605lb); maximum take-off weight 5500kg (12,125lb)
Dimensions:	span 18.18m (59ft 7in); length 12.4m (40ft 8in); height 4.13m (13ft 6.5in); wing area 71.6 sq m (770 sq ft)

Antonov An-3

In the early 1970s the Soviet Ministry of Agriculture began the difficult task of finding a replacement for its vast, hard-worked fleet of An-2SKh and An-2R crop-spraying aircraft. After rejecting the extraordinary turbofan-powered PZL-Mielec Lala-1 biplane (an experimental twin-boom development of the An-2), the Ministry opted instead for an updated version of the An-2 developed by Antonov in the late 1970s. This An-3 was virtually a standard An-2 with a 1450hp (1081kW) Glushenkov TVD-20 turboprop installed. The structure of the An-3, like that of the An-2, is almost entirely of metal, save for the wings aft of the main spar and the tailplane, which are covered with fabric. Mielec subsequently converted many An-2s to An-3 standard, with the TVD-20 turboprop and a 2200-litre (484-gallon) chemical hopper in the fuselage. Pictured is one of the first production aircraft. Note the underwing dusting duct.

Country of origin:	USSR
Type:	12-seat agricultural utility/crop-spraying biplane
Powerplant:	one 1450hp (1081kW) Glushenkov TVD-20 turboprop
Performance:	maximum speed 258km/h (160mph); service ceiling 4500m (14,763ft); range 845km (525 miles)
Weights:	empty 3450kg (7605lb); maximum take-off weight 6356kg (14,015lb)
Dimensions:	span 18.18m (59ft 7in); length 12.4m (40ft 8in); height 4.13m (13ft 6in); wing area 71.6 sq m (770 sq ft)

Arado Ar 65F

Arado Handelgessellschaft GmbH was founded in 1925 from the remnants of the wartime AGO company, and took over the premises of the Werft Warnemünde der Flugzeugbau Friedrichhafen GmbH. Because of the ban on military aircraft production imposed by the Armistice, development of the SD I and II fighter aircraft in the late 1920s for the *Reichswehrministerium* was undertaken under great secrecy. These aircraft formed the basis for the Ar 64, intended as a replacement for the Fokker DXIII then equipping the secret German flying training school at Lipetsk in the Soviet Union. This aircraft gestated into the Ar 65, modelled closely on the 64 but with a more powerful engine. The first production version was the Ar 65E, which was followed by the 65F with improved communications equipment. Used only for a short time in the fighter role, Ar 65Es and Ar 65-Fs were used as fighter trainers until 1936.

Country of origin:	Germany
Type:	single-seat fighter trainer
Powerplant:	one 750hp (560kW) BMW V1 7.3 Vee-12 piston engine
Performance:	maximum speed 300km/h (186mph); service ceiling 7600m (24,935ft)
Weights:	empty 1550kg (3418lb); maximum take-off weight 1970kg (4344lb)
Dimensions:	span 11.2m (36ft 9in); length 8.4m (27ft 6in); height 3.42m (11ft 2in); wing area 23 sq m (248 sq ft)
Armament:	two fixed forward-firing 7.92mm MG 17 machine guns with 500 rpg

Arado Ar 68E

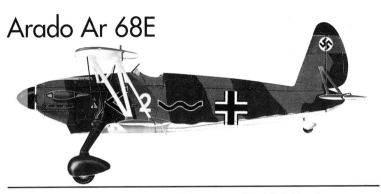

In 1933 the Nazi party gained control of Germany and rapidly initiated a programme of re-armament. Arado and Heinkel were charged with urgently building a first-line fighter aircraft for the new Luftwaffe and this resulted in the Ar 68A prototype, a single-seat fighter biplane with an oval-section fuselage of steel tube construction, wood-and-fabric single-bay wings, and a 550hp (410kW) BMW VId engine. The Ar 68B and 68C prototypes were fitted with the 610hp (455kW) Junkers Jumo 210, the latter with a redesigned chin radiator. The Ar 68D and 68E had BMW VI and Jumo 210 power respectively, and although this last engine was chosen for the E-1 production model, delays in delivery of the Jumo engine meant that the BMW Ar 68F with an upright BMW V1 was first to come into service with the Luftwaffe in the summer of 1936, followed in spring 1937 by the Ar 68E-1. Pictured is the Ar 68E of Lieutenant Riegel, Gruppe Adjutant of III/JG 141 based at Fürstenwalde during 1938.

Country of origin:	Germany
Type:	single-seat fighter
Powerplant:	one 690hp (515kW)Junkers Jumo 210Da inverted inline piston engine
Performance:	maximum speed 305km/h (190mph); service ceiling 8100m (26,575ft); range 415km (258 miles)
Weights:	empty 1840kg (4057lb); maximum take-off weight 2475kg (5457lb)
Dimensions:	span 11m (36ft 1in); length 9.5m (31ft 2in); height 3.28m (10ft 9in); wing area 27.3 sq m (294 sq ft)
Armament:	two fixed forward-firing 7.92mm MG 17 machine guns with 500 rpg

Arado Ar 68F

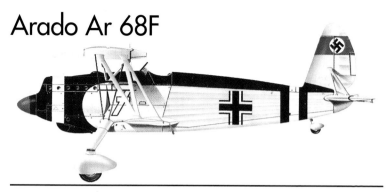

Despite its good engines the Ar 68 was never an outstanding machine, and ran second in both timing and performance to the Heinkel He 51 that was its great rival. The Ar 68 proved to be something of an anachronism. Almost as soon as it had entered service it was made obsolete by the Messerschmitt Bf 109, and by the outbreak of the war almost all had been relegated to advanced fighter-trainer status with the *Jagdfliegerschulen* (fighter pilot schools). A proposed development that was built only in prototype form was the AR 68H with an 850hp (634kW) BMW 132 9-cylinder radial engine, a sliding cockpit canopy, and two additional MG 17 machine guns located in the upper wing. Developed in parallel with the Ar 68H and sharing many of that aircraft's features was the Ar 197, a single-seat naval fighter/bomber for Germany's still-born aircraft carrier programme. Pictured is an Ar 68F of 2./JG 131 based at Seerappen in the summer of 1937.

Country of origin:	Germany
Type:	single-seat fighter
Powerplant:	one 750hp (570kW) BMW VI Vee-12- piston engine
Performance:	maximum speed 305km/h (190mph); service ceiling 8100m (26,575ft); range 415km (258 miles)
Weights:	empty 1840kg (4057lb); maximum take-off weight 2475kg (5457lb)
Dimensions:	span 11m (36ft 1in); length 9.5m (31ft 2in); height 3.28m (10ft 9in)
Armament:	two fixed forward-firing 7.92mm MG 17 machine guns

Arado Ar 68F Night Fighter

The Ar 68F was the last biplane to see service with the Luftwaffe. The oval-section fuselage was of steel tube construction, with metal panels covering the rear decking and forward sections, while the wings were made of wood with a plywood and fabric covering. By 1939 most Ar 68s had been relegated to advanced fighter trainers, the only examples remaining in the front line serving with night-fighter units (*Nachtgeschwader*). A small number of the Ar 68F aircraft were converted for the night-fighting role by fitting flame dampers to the exhaust stubs and applying a low-visibility paint scheme. These remained in service with the Luftwaffe *Nachtgeschwader* long after the day-fighter units had converted to the Messerschmitt Bf 109. The aircraft pictured wears a matt olive paint scheme and was operated by 10.(Nacht)/JG 53 based at Oedheim/Heilbronn in September 1939. Note the owl clutching a spade symbol, just visible under the forward outer strut.

Country of origin:	Germany
Type:	single-seat fighter
Powerplant:	one 750hp (570kW) BMW VI Vee-12 piston engine
Performance:	maximum speed 305km/h (190mph); service ceiling 8100m (26,575ft); range 415km (258 miles)
Weights:	empty 1840kg (4057lb); maximum take-off weight 2475kg (5457lb)
Dimensions:	span 11m (36ft 1in); length 9.5m (31ft 2in); height 3.28m (10ft 9in)
Armament:	two fixed forward-firing 7.92mm MG 17 machine guns

Arado Ar 95A-1

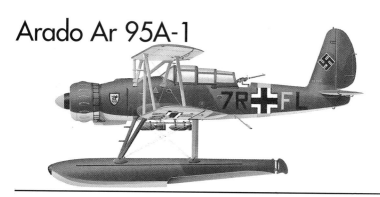

A rado Chief Engineer Walter Blume designed the Ar 95 two-seat twin-float seaplane in 1935 to meet a Luftwaffe requirement for a coastal patrol and light-attack aircraft. Two prototypes had, respectively, the 880hp (656kW) BMW 132De 9-cylinder radial engine and 690hp (515kW) Junkers Jumo 210 12-cylinder inline piston engine, and the first of these flew in 1937. After evaluation with the Focke-Wulf Fw 62 seaplane, the BMW-powered Ar 95V2 was further developed. Twelve aircraft were sent to Spain for evaluation, but the Luftwaffe showed a marked indifference to the aircraft and Arado offered it for export as the Ar 95W, and with fixed landing gear as the Ar 95L. A Turkish order for the Ar 95W was diverted to the Luftwaffe *Seeaufklärungsgruppe* (coastal reconnaissance units) at the outbreak of World War II and given the designation Ar 95A. Pictured is aircraft F, an Ar 95A-I of the 3rd Staffel of Seeaufklärungsgruppe 125 operating in the Baltic during 1941.

Country of origin:	Germany
Type:	two-seat coastal patrol and light attack aircraft
Powerplant:	one 880hp (656kW) BMW 132De 9-cylinder radial engine
Performance:	maximum speed 310km/h (193mph); service ceiling 7300m (23,945ft); range 1100km (683 miles)
Weights:	empty 2450kg (5402lb); maximum take-off weight 3560kg (7870lb)
Dimensions:	span 12.5m (41ft); length 11.1m (36ft 5in); height 3.6m (11ft 9in); wing area 45.40 sq m (489 sq ft)
Armament:	one fixed forward-firing 7.92mm MG 17 machine gun, one 7.92mm MG 15 on flexible mounting in rear cockpit; underfuselage rack with provision for an 800kg (1764lb) torpedo or 500kg (1102lb) bomb

Arado Ar 196A-1

One of the few float seaplanes to be used outside the Pacific theatre during World War II, the Ar 196 was designed to replace the He 60 biplane used as a catapult-launched reconnaissance aircraft on German capital ships. Four prototypes were built with various float configurations, all of them powered by the 880hp (656kW) BMW 132Dc engine (derived in Germany from the Pratt & Whitney Hornet). The 196V1 flew in May 1938, and the type entered production in 1939 as the Ar 196A-1. Some 20 aircraft were built and these were deployed on board the *Admiral Graf Spee, Lützow, Gneisenau, Scharnhorst, Deutschland, Prince Eugen* and *Admiral Hipper*, coming under the command of Bordfliegerstaffeln 1./196 and 5./196 which were based at the major naval bases of Wilhelmshaven and Kiel-Holtenau. The first ship to take its Ar 196A-1 to sea was the *Admiral Graf Spee*.

Country of origin:	Germany
Type:	two-seat shipborne reconnaissance aircraft
Powerplant:	one 960hp (716kW) BMW 132K 9-cylinder radial engine
Performance:	maximum speed 310km/h (193mph); service ceiling 7000m (22,960ft); range 1070km (665 miles)
Weights:	empty 2990kg (6593lb); maximum take-off weight 3730kg (8223lb)
Dimensions:	span 12.4m (40ft 8in); length 11m (36ft 1in); height 4.45m 14ft 7in); wing area 28.40 sq m (306 sq ft)
Armament:	two fixed forward-firing 20mm MG FF cannon in wings; one fixed forward-firing 7.92mm MG 17 machine gun in starboard side of fuselage; one fixed forward-firing 7.92mm MG 15 machine gun on flexible mounting in rear cockpit; underwing racks with provision for two 50kg (110lb) bombs

Arado Ar 196A-3

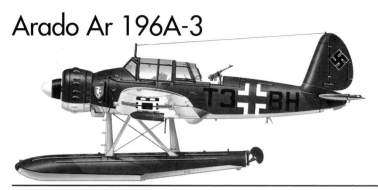

$\mathbf{T}$he success of the Ar 196A-1 prompted Arado to develop the aircraft further. The A-2 was equipped for coastal patrol duties and had armament increased by the addition of two 20mm MG FF cannon in the wings and a fuselage-mounted forward-firing 7.92mm MG 17 machine gun, adding some 227kg (500lb) to the empty weight. This was followed by the A-3, a structurally strengthened version with additional radio equipment and three-blade variable pitch propeller. The A-3 was the most extensively built of all the variants with 401 aircraft built. It was a versatile multi-role warplane operated mainly on sea patrols from bases on the Bay of Biscay and islands in the Mediterranean. Batches were built by SNCA at St Nazaire in Vichy France and by Fokker in Amsterdam. Pictured is an Arado Ar 196A-3 of 1./Bordfliegergruppe 196 based in the Lofoten Islands during February 1944.

Country of origin:	Germany
Type:	two-seat coastal patrol aircraft
Powerplant:	one 960hp (716kW) BMW 132K 9-cylinder radial engine
Performance:	maximum speed 310km/h (193mph); service ceiling 7000m (22,960ft); range 1070km (665 miles)
Weights:	empty 2990kg (6593lb); maximum take-off weight 3730kg (8223lb)
Dimensions:	span 12.4m (40ft 8in); length 11m (36ft 1in); height 4.45m (14ft 7in); wing area 28.40 sq m (306 sq ft)
Armament:	two fixed forward-firing 20mm MG FF cannon in wings; one fixed forward-firing 7.92mm MG 17 machine gun in starboard side of fuselage; one fixed forward-firing 7.92mm MG 15 machine gun on flexible mounting in rear cockpit; underwing racks with provision for two 50kg (110lb) bombs

Arado Ar 196A-5

The Ar 196A-4 was a catapult-launched version of the A-3 produced to replace the A-1s serving on German capital ships, although very few were to serve at sea, as the ships remained in port after the loss of the *Tirpitz* and German naval action was limited to the U-boats and E-boats. The final production example was the Ar 196A-5, with 91 completed by Fokker during 1943–4 with improved radio equipment and twin 7.92mm MG 81Z machine guns in the rear cockpit. The last aircraft was completed in August 1944. Total production of all types was in excess of 500 aircraft. This Ar 196A-5 served with 2./Seeaufklärungsgruppe 125 in the eastern Mediterranean and Aegean Seas during 1943, alongside Blohm und Voss Bv 138. The unit later became 4./Seeaufklärungsgruppe 126 under the control of Luftwaffenkommando Südost.

Country of origin:	Germany
Type:	two-seat coastal patrol aircraft
Powerplant:	one 960hp (716kW) BMW 132K 9-cylinder radial engine
Performance:	maximum speed 310km/h (193mph); service ceiling 7000m (22,960ft); range 1070km (665 miles)
Weights:	empty 2990kg (6,593lb); maximum take-off weight 3730kg (8223lb)
Dimensions:	span 12.4m (40ft 8in); length 11m (36ft 1in); height 4.45m (14ft 7in); wing area 28.40 sq m (306 sq ft)
Armament:	two fixed forward-firing 20mm MG FF cannon in wings; one fixed forward-firing 7.92mm MG 17 machine gun in starboard side of fuselage; one fixed forward-firing 7.92mm MG 15 machine gun on flexible mounting in rear cockpit; underwing racks with provision for two 50kg (110lb) bombs

Armstrong Whitworth Argosy Mk 1

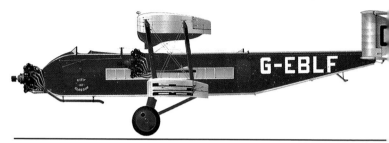

Alongside the de Havilland Hercules, the Armstrong Whitworth Argosy was developed specifically to meet Imperial Airways' need for a comfortable, reliable and efficient passenger airliner, and equally importantly to provide postal and freight transport on European and Empire routes. The first example of this tri-engine biplane flew in March 1926 and the first of an initial order of three aircraft for the airline opened the Croydon–Paris route on 16 July 1926. The Argosy became famous operating Imperial Airways' de luxe 'Silver Wing' service on the Croydon–Paris route from May 1927, in competition with the LeO 212 flights of Air Union. A later version was the Argosy II with Armstrong Siddeley Jaguar IVA engines. This aircraft was also used on the Empire mail link to India from 1929, and continued in service until December 1936. Pictured above is the City of Glasgow, a Mk I of Imperial Airways.

Country of origin:	United Kingdom
Type:	20-seat commercial transport biplane
Powerplant:	three 385hp (287kW) Armstrong Siddeley Jaguar IIIA 14-cylinder radial engines
Performance:	maximum speed 177km/h (110mph); range 652km (405 miles)
Weights:	empty 5443kg (12,000lb); maximum take-off weight 8165kg (18,000lb)
Dimensions:	span 27.64m (90ft 8in); length 20.07m (65ft 10in); height 6.05m (19ft 10in); wing area 175.22 sq m (1886 sq ft)

Armstrong Whitworth F.K.3

The talented Dutchman Frederick Koolhoven began designing aircraft in 1910, and in 1914 joined Armstrong Whitworth of Coventry. He produced a number of designs for the company that bore his initials, the first of them the Royal Aircraft Factory B.E.2C-derived F.K.3. The prototype for this aircraft had a 70hp (52kW) Renault engine, although production models had a more powerful Royal Aircraft Factory IA which considerably improved performance. The F.K.3 and B.E.2C were evaluated at Upavon with the former aircraft demonstrating speed and height advantage. Production totalled some 493 aircraft, 150 by Armstrong Whitworth and a further 300 by Hewlett & Blondeau Ltd. The aircraft, dubbed 'Little Ack' by servicemen, served at Salonika with No 47 Squadron, but was used mainly for training duties until replaced by the Avro 504K.

Country of origin:	United Kingdom
Type:	two-seat general purpose aircraft
Powerplant:	one 90hp (67kW) Royal Aircraft Factory. IA inline piston engine
Performance:	maximum speed 143km/h (89mph); service ceiling 3660m (12,000ft); endurance 3 hours
Weights:	empty 629kg (1,386lb); maximum take-off weight 983kg (2,056lb)
Dimensions:	span 12.19m (40ft); length 8.84m (29ft); height 3.63m (11ft 11in); wing area 42.46 sq m (457 sq ft)
Armament:	one .303 Vickers machine gun on flexible mount in rear cockpit

Armstrong Whitworth F.K.8

The increasing importance of the army co-operation role from 1916 prompted development of a larger version of the F.K.3 designated the F.K.8. Koolhoven designed this with a sturdier fuselage to accommodate a more powerful engine, allowing for a bomb load of up to 72kg (160lb). The F.K.8 is roughly comparable to the Royal Aircraft Factory R.E.8 that was produced at the same time and although a superior aircraft, for political reasons it was never produced in the same numbers. Armstrong Whitworth built 700 between August 1916 and July 1918, and thereafter production passed to the Angus Sanderson & Co. company which built a further 700 aircraft. The 'Big Ack' gained a reputation for being strong and reliable, and did every kind of reconnaissance, bombing and strafing mission on the Western Front, in Macedonia and in Palestine. Two aircraft were used in Australia post-war by Queensland and Northern Territory Aerial Services Ltd (later QANTAS).

Country of origin:	United Kingdom
Type:	two-seat general-purpose aircraft
Powerplant:	one 160hp (119kW) Beardmore, 150hp (112kW) Lorraine-Dietrich or 150hp (112kW) Royal Aircraft Factory.4A inline piston engine
Performance:	maximum speed 153km/h (95mph); service ceiling 3690m (13,000ft); endurance 3hrs
Weights:	empty 869kg (1916lb); maximum take-off weight 1275kg (2811lb)
Dimensions:	span 13.26m (43ft 6in); length 9.58m (31ft 5in); height 3.33m (10ft 11in); wing area 50.17 sq m (540 sq ft)
Armament:	one fixed forward-firing .303in Vickers machine gun; one .303in Lewis machine gun on flexible mount in rear cockpit

Armstrong Whitworth Siskin IIIA

This aircraft has its origins in the Siddeley S.R.2 Siskin, produced by the Siddeley-Deasy Motor Car Company in 1918 for the 300hp (224kW) Royal Aircraft Factory RAF.8 engine but which in fact first flew with the 320hp (239kW) ABC Dragonfly. The poor performance of this latter engine prompted Armstrong Siddeley to equip the aircraft with its own 325hp (242kW) Jaguar engine, and after the aircraft had been redesigned in line with Air Ministry policy with an all-metal structure it was ordered for the RAF in 1923 as the Siskin Mk IIIA. Some 360 were delivered by Armstrong Whitworth Aircraft at Coventry, and by Bristol, Vickers, Gloster and Blackburn. This superbly aerobatic aircraft formed the vanguard of Britain's home-defence squadrons from March 1927 but faded swiftly in the 1930s as technology developed and newer types such as the Bristol Bulldog. Pictured is a Siskin IIIA of No 43 Squadron in 1929.

Country of origin:	United Kingdom
Type:	single-seat fighter biplane
Powerplant:	one 420hp (313kW) Armstrong Siddeley Jaguar IV radial engine
Performance:	maximum speed 251km/h (156mph); service ceiling 8230m (27,000ft); endurance 3hrs
Weights:	empty 935kg (2061lb); maximum take-off weight 1366kg (3012lb)
Dimensions:	span 10.11m (33ft 2in); length 7.72m (25ft 4in); height 3.10m (10ft 2in); wing area 27.22 sq m (293 sq ft)
Armament:	two fixed forward-firing .303in Vickers machine guns in forward fuselage; underwing racks with provision for up to four 9kg (20lb) Cooper practice bombs

Avia B.534-IV

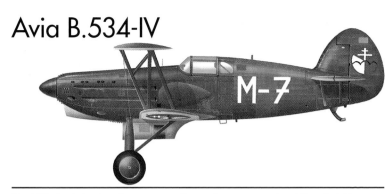

In 1930 the Avia aircraft company at Prague-Letnany appointed Frantisek Novotny as its chief engineer. His first design was the B.34 fighter that was re-engined with a Hispano-Suiza 12Ydrs engine and eventually gelled into the B.534-I prototype. The first production model of this outstanding fighter was the B.534-I, which had a wooden screw to replace the metal unit of the prototype, an open cockpit, and twin fuselage machine guns with two more carried in lower-wing fairings. The B.534-II carried all four machine guns in fuselage blisters, and also had underwing racks for light bombs. The B.534-III had mainwheel fairings and revised carburettor air intake, and the definitive B.536-IV had an enclosed cockpit and revised aft fuselage decking. Pictured is one of the three B.534-IVs of the Slovak Air Force, used with limited success during the Slovak National Uprising of September 1944. The aircraft operated from the airfield at Tri Duby.

Country of origin:	Czechoslovakia
Type:	single-seat fighter biplane
Powerplant:	one 850hp (634kW) Hispano-Suiza HS 12Ydrs inline piston engine
Performance:	maximum speed 394km/h (245mph); service ceiling 10,600m (34,775ft); range 580km (360 miles)
Weights:	empty 1460kg (3219lb); maximum take-off weight 2120kg (4674lb)
Dimensions:	span 9.4m (30ft 10in); length 8.2m (26ft 10in); height 3.1m (10ft 2in); wing area 23.56 sq m (254 sq ft)
Armament:	four fixed forward-firing 7.7mm Model 30 machine guns in forward fuselage; underwing Pantof racks with provision for up to six 20kg (44lb) bombs

Avia B.534-IV

The B.534 proved to be the outstanding fighter of the 1937 Zürich International Flying Meet and is widely regarded as the finest fighter of its day, until inevitably outclassed by low-wing monoplanes. At the time of the Munich crisis in September 1938 the B.534 had been in large scale production for three years and around 300 of the eventual total of 445 were in service with 21 Czech fighter squadrons. After the occupation of Czechoslovakia in March 1939 a large number of aircraft passed to the Luftwaffe, and also to Hungary and Bulgaria, the latter's only combat outing being against the Consolidated B-24 Liberators that bombed the Ploesti oilfields in 1943. Pictured is an Avia B.534-IV of 3.Staffel, Jagdgeschwader 71, based at Eutlingen near Stuttgart in late 1939. The unit only operated the B.534 for a short time before re-equipping with Messerschmitt Bf 109s. Note the spatted mainwheels and fuselage blisters covering the machine gun breeches.

Country of origin:	Czechoslovakia
Type:	single-seat fighter biplane
Powerplant:	one 850hp (634kW) Hispano-Suiza HS 12Ydrs inline piston engine
Performance:	maximum speed 394km/h (245mph); service ceiling 10,600m (34,775ft); range 580km (360 miles)
Weights:	empty 1460kg (3219lb); maximum take-off weight 2120kg (4674lb)
Dimensions:	span 9.4m (30ft 10in); length 8.2m (26ft 10in); height 3.1m (10ft 2in); wing area 23.56 sq m (254 sq ft)
Armament:	four fixed forward-firing 7.7mm Model 30 machine guns in forward fuselage; underwing Pantof racks with provision for up to six 20kg (44lb) bombs

Avia BH.21

The Avia company (Avia ack. spolecnost pro prumsyl letecky) was founded in 1919 and established workshops near Cakovice in the newly-formed republic of Czechoslovakia. The chief engineers of the company, until their move to Praga in 1927, were Pavel Benes and Miroslav Hajn. The BH.21 traced its lineage to the BH-17 biplane fighter of 1924, and had revised forward upper fuselage for improved pilot view, single underfuselage radiator to replace the twin mainwheel leg mounted units of the BH.17, and single-bay 'N' interplane struts. Some 137 aircraft were acquired by the Czech Air Force and, with the designation B.21, these served until the early 1930s when they were replaced in service by the Avia B.33. After a competition in 1925 SABCA and SEGA in Belgium licence-built 44 and 39 respectively for the Belgian Air Force. Pictured above is a B.21 of the 3rd Air Regiment of the Czech Air Force.

Country of origin:	Czechoslovakia
Type:	single-seat fighter biplane
Powerplant:	one 310hp (231kW) Avia (license-built Hispano-Suiza) 8Fb inline piston engine
Performance:	maximum speed 245km/h (152mph); service ceiling 5500m (18,045ft); range 550km (342 miles)
Weights:	empty 720kg (1587lb); maximum take-off weight 1084kg (2390lb)
Dimensions:	span 8.9m (29ft 2in); length 6.87m (22ft 6in); height 2.74m (8ft 11in); wing area 21.96 sq m (236 sq ft)
Armament:	two fixed forward-firing .303in Vickers machine guns in forward fuselage

Avia BH.25

Avia entered the burgeoning commercial transport market in 1928 with the Benes-Hajn designed BH.25, a single-engine single-bay biplane of wood-and-fabric construction that flew in prototype form in July 1936 with a 450hp (335kW) Skoda-built Lorraine-Dietrich inline engine. Unusually for a biplane, the lower wing was of greater span than the upper. Forward of the wings was an open cockpit, with side-by-side seating for the captain and his co-pilot. The enclosed passenger cabin had seats for six people and space for up to 100kg (220lb) of baggage. After flight testing, a number of major airframe modifications were made and a Walter-built 420hp (313kW) Bristol Jupiter engine was substituted. Eight of the twelve production aircraft served with CLS of Czechoslovakia, and the remainder with SNNA of Romania.

Country of origin:	Czechoslovakia
Type:	six-seater commercial transport biplane
Powerplant:	one 420hp (313kW) Walter (licence-built Bristol Jupiter IV) 9-cylinder radial piston engine
Performance:	maximum speed 180km/h (112mph); service ceiling 4000m (13,125ft); range 600km (373 miles)
Weights:	empty 1840kg (4057lb); maximum take-off weight 3100kg (6834lb)
Dimensions:	span 15.3m (50ft 2in); length 12.82m (42ft); wing area 62.5 sq m (673 sq ft)

Avia BH.26

The prototype for the BH.26 two-seat fighter reconnaissance aircraft first flew in 1927. In common with previous Benes and Hajn designs the aircraft had a slab-sided fuselage, single-bay unequal-span biplane wing planform, a rudder but no fixed vertical tail fin. Early flight testing revealed the inadequacy of this configuration and the design was revised to include the fin and rudder assembly that appeared on production aircraft. Only a very limited production run of eight aircraft was completed for the Czech Air Force, and these served under the designation B.26. A development of the BH.26 was the BH.28 with the powerplant of a single 385hp (287kW) Armstrong Siddeley Jaguar radial engine, but this did not progress beyond the prototype stage. Pictured is an Avia B.26 of the Czech Central Flying School.

Country of origin:	Czechoslovakia
Type:	two-seater fighter reconnaissance biplane
Powerplant:	one 450hp (336kW) Walter (licence-built Bristol Jupiter IV) 9-cylinder radial piston engine
Performance:	maximum speed 242km/h (150mph); service ceiling 8500m (27,885ft); range 530km (329 miles)
Weights:	empty 1030kg (2721lb); maximum take-off weight 1630kg (3594lb)
Dimensions:	span 10.8m (35ft 5in); length 8.85m (29ft); height 3.35m (10ft 11in); wing area 31 sq m (334 sq ft)
Armament:	two fixed forward-firing .303in Vickers machine guns in forward fuselage; two .303in Lewis machine guns on Skoda mount over rear cockpit

Aviatik B.II

The early products of Automobil und Aviatik AG were copies of French designs, however with the experience gained the Mulhausen-based company was soon able to produce its own original designs. The B.I two-seat reconnaissance aircraft that appeared in service in 1914 was developed from a 1913 design for a racing biplane, and in common with contemporary unarmed reconnaissance machines the observer was accommodated in the forward cockpit. Power for this three-bay reconnaissance biplane was provided by a 100hp (75kW) Mercedes D.I engine, and the cooling was provided by a radiator mounted on the lower wing inboard of the inner starboard strut. The B.II appeared in 1915 and had a lightened and stronger rudder and elevator structure, as well as a more powerful Mercedes engine. Pictured is an Aviatik B.II of the *Beobachterschule* (Observers' School) based at Köln-Butzweilerhof in 1916.

Country of origin:	Germany
Type:	two-seat reconnaissance biplane
Powerplant:	one 120hp (89kW) Mercedes D.III 6-cylinder inline piston engine
Performance:	maximum speed 100km/h (62mph); endurance 4hrs
Weights:	1088kg (2400lb)
Dimensions:	span 13.97m (45ft 10in); length 7.97m (26ft 2in); height 3.3m (10ft 10in)

Aviatik C.Ia

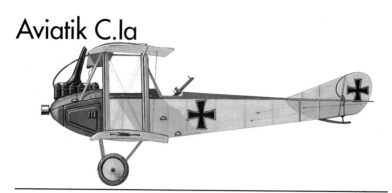

The first Aviatik aircraft designed from the outset for military use was the C.I. This aircraft bore a marked resemblance to the earlier B series, and although the observer in the forward cockpit was provided with a machine gun, his field of fire was severely restricted. In the C.Ia this layout was reversed and resulted in a much more potent aircraft. Construction was of wood and fabric, with an aluminium engine bay and tailskid landing gear. Power was provided by a Mercedes D.III producing some 160hp (119kW). Only a small number of C.Ia aircraft were built before production switched to the C.II with 200hp (149kW) Benz Bz.IV power and significantly revised tail surfaces. Most widely produced was the C.III, which had reduced span wings, streamlined nose, improved exhaust system, and armament uprated to two machine guns. Pictured above is a C.Ia aircraft serving on the Eastern Front.

Country of origin:	Germany
Type:	two-seat reconnaissance biplane
Powerplant:	one 120hp (89kW) Mercedes D.II 6-cylinder inline piston engine
Performance:	maximum speed 142km/h (89mph); service ceiling 3500m (11,480ft) endurance 3hrs
Weights:	empty 980kg (2161lb); maximum take-off weight 1340kg (2954lb)
Dimensions:	span 12.5m (41ft); length 7.92m (26ft); height 2.95m (9ft 8in)
Armament:	one 7.92mm Parabellum machine gun on flexible mount in rear cockpit

Avions Fairey Fox VI

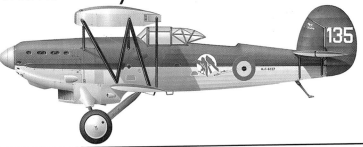

After a thrilling programme of competitive fly-offs with rival designs, the Belgian Government selected an all-metal version of the Fairey Fox for licensed manufacture by Belgian subsidiary Avions Fairey at Gosselies as the Fox IIM . This aircraft was powered by a 480hp (385kW) engine, and the first of 31 examples entered service in 1933 with the Aéronautique Militaire. Avions Fairey developed a number of versions, including the Fox III reconnaissance fighter with Armstrong Siddeley Serval radial power, Fox IIIC with enclosed cockpits and Rolls Royce Kestrel engine (47 aircraft built), Fox IIICS dual-control variant (1), Fox IIIS dual-control trainer (4), Fox V prototype for the Fox VI with Hispano-Suiza 12Ydrs engine (1), and the Fox VI with this latter engine (94). Pictured is a Fox VI of 6/III, 2e Regiment d'Aéronautique, based at Le Zoute on the eve of the German invasion on 10 May 1940.

Country of origin:	Belgium
Type:	two-seat reconnaissance fighter biplane
Powerplant:	one 860hp (641kW) Hispano-Suiza 12Ydrs inline piston engine
Performance:	maximum speed 365km/h (227mph); service ceiling 11,200m (36,745ft); range 600km (373 miles)
Weights:	empty 1361kg (3000lb); maximum take-off weight 2245kg (4950lb)
Dimensions:	span 11.58m (38ft); length 9.17m (30ft 1in); height 3.35m (9ft 8in)
Armament:	two fixed forward-firing 7.5mm FN machine guns in forward fuselage; one .303in Lewis on flexible mount in rear cockpit; underwing racks with provision for 240kg (528lb) bomb load

Avro Type D

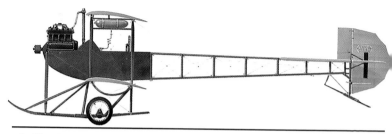

Alliot Verdon Roe was one of the first generation of British aeronautical pioneers. He built his first full-scale flying machine in 1907. The experience that Roe gained with the early Avro Triplanes, and the financial support of his brother, was to prove invaluable and helped to set one of Britain's most famous aircraft manufacturers on course. The Type D marked a breakaway from the triplane configuration employed on his earlier machines. The first of an eventual six machines was flown at Brooklands on 1April 1911, and was powered by a 35hp (26kW) Green engine. The aircraft rapidly gained a reputation for viceless handling. A float-equipped version became the first successful British seaplane when it took off from water on 18 November 1911. The six aircraft built were variously equipped with 45hp (34kW) Green, 35hp (26kW) Viale and 50hp (37kW) Isaacson engines until the three survivors were withdrawn from use in 1913.

Country of origin:	United Kingdom
Type:	two-seat biplane
Powerplant:	one 35hp (26kW) Green 4-cylinder inline piston engine
Performance:	maximum speed 78km/h (49mph)
Weights:	maximum take-off weight 227kg (500lb)
Dimensions:	span 9.45m (31ft); length 8.53m (28ft); height 2.79m (9ft 2in); wing area 28.8 sq m (310 sq ft)

Avro 504K

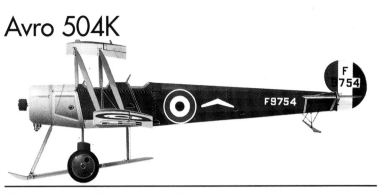

When A.V. Roe built the first Avro 504 in the pioneer days more than a year before World War I, he could not have envisaged that the aircraft would still be in production in 1933. Production in wartime alone totalled around 8340 aircraft. In the summer of 1913 the War Ministry placed an order for 12 of the Avro 504 production aircraft for the Royal Flying Corps, and these were followed into service by examples for the Royal Naval Air Service. Sixty-three of the basic version were produced and although these saw limited active service, including the famous raid on the Zeppelin sheds at Friedrichshafen on 21 November 1914, the type saw far more widespread use in the training role. Some 504Ks were used for testing at RAE Farnborough. Pictured is a 504K built by Hewlett & Blondeau, of No 8 Training Squadron, Royal Air Force, in 1918. Other major sub-contractors were Harland & Wolff, Frederic Sage, Humber Motor Co, and Sunbeam.

Country of origin:	United Kingdom
Type:	(504K) two-seat elementary trainer
Powerplant:	one 110hp (82kW) Le Rhône rotary piston engine
Performance:	maximum speed 153km/h (95mph); service ceiling 4875m (16,000ft); range 402km (250 miles)
Weights:	empty 558kg (1230lb); maximum take-off weight 830kg (1829lb)
Dimensions:	span 10.97m (36ft); length 8.97m (29ft 5in); height 3.17m (10ft 5in); wing area 30.66 sq m (330 sq ft)

Avro 504K

Principal wartime production versions of the Avro 504 were the 504A with smaller ailerons and broader struts (455 aircraft built), the naval 504B with bomb racks, larger fin, tailskid, and a Lewis gun for the observer (240), single-seat 504C and 504D for anti-Zeppelin patrols, 504E for the Royal Naval Air Service with a 100hp (75kW) Gnome Monosoupape engine (10), and 504G gunnery trainer (10 newly built plus unknown number modified from 504Bs). The 504F and 504H were built only in prototype form. Undoubtedly the most important were the 504J, essentially a 504A with a 100hp (76kW) Gnome Monosoupape engine in a lobed cowling (1050) and the main production variant, the 504K (6350). This last aircraft was little changed from the 504J and was equipped with any one of 12 different engines on a universal engine mounting. Pictured is one of the 30 504Ks with Le Rhône engines supplied to Portugal between November 1923 and May 1924.

Country of origin:	United Kingdom
Type:	two-seat elementary trainer
Powerplant:	one 110hp (82kW) Le Rhône rotary piston engine
Performance:	maximum speed 153km/h (95mph); service ceiling 4875m (16,000ft); range 402km (250 miles)
Weights:	empty 558kg (1230lb); maximum take-off weight 830kg (1829lb)
Dimensions:	span 10.97m (36ft); length 8.97m (29ft 5in); height 3.17m (10ft 5in); wing area 30.66 sq m (330 sq ft)

Avro 504R

By the time the 24-year production run of the Avro 504 ended in October 1937, the aircraft had been exported to all corners of the globe, from Thailand to Finland. Licensed manufacture accounted for a significant percentage of the production total and was undertaken in Argentina, Australia, Belgium, Canada, and Japan. The final variant of the Avro 504 was the 504R Gosport. This was an attempt to produce a less-costly version of the 504N by installing a cheaper engine of lower power but without degrading performance. Several engines were tried, including the 90hp (67kW) Avro Alpha, 100hp (75kW) Gnome Monosoupape, and 150hp (112kW) Mongoose. The most successful installation was the Mongoose and in this form ten were sold to Argentina, six to Estonia, and an unknown number to Peru. Pictured is one of the Estonian machines in November 1928, some of which were to survive into the 1940s.

Country of origin:	United Kingdom
Type:	two-seat elementary trainer
Powerplant:	one 150hp (112kW) Mongoose rotary piston engine
Performance:	maximum speed 153km/h (95mph); service ceiling 4875m (16,000ft); range 402km (250 miles)
Weights:	empty 558kg (1230lb); maximum take-off weight 830kg (1829lb)
Dimensions:	span 10.97m (36ft); length 8.97m (29ft 5in); height 3.17m (10ft 5in); wing area 30.66 sq m (330 sq ft)

Avro 504N

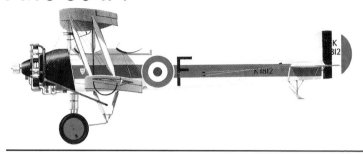

In the aftermath of World War I, an enterprising businessman could pick up a surplus Avro 504 for a song and, unsurprisingly, the type became the ubiquitous mount of barnstorming circuses and joy-riding enterprises, surviving in various guises well into the 1930s. The RAF had vast stocks of the aircraft and continued to use it as a trainer for many years. The main peacetime version of the aircraft was the 504N, the first of which were produced by converting Avro 504Ks. These had redesigned landing gear, which did away with the central skid, tapered ailerons, and a variety of engine fits. The first two new-build 504Ns were ordered in 1925 by the Air Ministry with a 100hp (75kW) Bristol Lucifer engine and 180hp (134kW) Armstrong Siddeley Lynx respectively. The latter engine was selected for series production aircraft, of which 598 were completed between 1925 and 1932, when they were replaced in the training role by the Avro Tutor.

Country of origin:	United Kingdom
Type:	two-seat elementary trainer
Powerplant:	one 160hp (112kW) Armstrong Siddeley Lynx IV rotary piston engine
Performance:	maximum speed 161km/h (100mph); service ceiling 4450m (14,600ft); range 402km (250 miles)
Weights:	empty 718kg (1584lb); maximum take-off weight 1016kg (2240lb)
Dimensions:	span 10.97m (36ft); length 8.69m (28ft 6in); height 3.33m (10ft 11in); wing area 29.73 sq m (320 sq ft)

Avro 504N

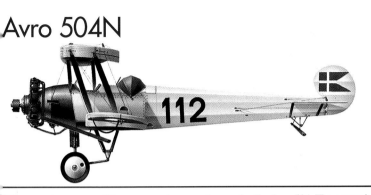

Denmark was one of the many post-war customers for the Avro 504. The example pictured was sold as a 504K to the Danish Government in 1920 and was operated by the Danish Navy. It was subsequently converted to 504N standard in 1928 and used in the training role. It was sold in July 1936 to Czechoslovakia and in 1940 was seized by the Germans. Note the blind flying hood enclosing the rear cockpit, used to develop instrument flying skills. Denmark purchased a single new-build 504N and then licence-built five more. In Britain the aircraft soldiered on in military service into World War II, seven ending their days as glider tugs with the Special Duty Flight at Christchurch, Hampshire, testing the reflectiveness of wooden aircraft to radar, while others were used at Ringway to develop glider towing techniques for the airborne forces. University Air Squadron and Auxilary Air Force 504Ns were gradually replaced by Avro Tutors and Hawker Tomtits.

Country of origin:	United Kingdom
Type:	two-seat elementary trainer
Powerplant:	one 160hp (112kW) Armstrong Siddeley Lynx IV rotary piston engine
Performance:	maximum speed 161km/h (100mph); service ceiling 4450m (14,600ft); range 402km (250 miles)
Weights:	empty 718kg (1584lb); maximum take-off weight 1016kg (2240lb)
Dimensions:	span 10.97m (36ft); length 8.69m (28ft 6in); height 3.33m (10ft 11in); wing area 29.73 sq m (320 sq ft)

Avro 529A

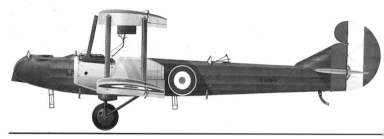

A fter failing to win a production order from the Admiralty for the promising Avro 523 Pike long-range escort/reconnaissance aircraft, Avro was requested to construct a modified and enlarged version for evaluation in the long-range bombing role. Roy Chadwick, the Avro chief designer who had designed the 523 and went on to lead the Lancaster team, created a prototype for the new aircraft, designated Avro 529, by simply stretching the dimensions of his original design. Other changes were wings that hinged outboard of the engines, revised tail unit, and twin Rolls Royce Falcon engines in a tractor rather than pusher installation. The second prototype (pictured) substituted 230hp (172kW) BHP engines and had a revised fuel system. Communication between the crew positions by the Gosport tube system was an innovative feature, but no production order was made.

Country of origin:	United Kingdom
Type:	three-seat long-range bomber
Powerplant:	two 230hp (172kW) BHP inline piston engines
Performance:	maximum speed 153km/h (95mph); service ceiling 4115m (13,500ft); endurance 5hrs
Weights:	empty 2148kg (4736lb); maximum take-off weight 2862kg (6309lb)
Dimensions:	span 19.2m (63ft); length 12.09m (39ft 8in); height 3.96m (13ft); wing area 85.7 sq m (922 sq ft)
Armament:	one .303in Lewis gun on Scarff ring mounting in front cockpit; one .303in Lewis gun on Scarff ring mounting in rear cockpit; internal bay with provision for up to twenty 23kg (50lb) bombs

Avro 533 Manchester Mk I

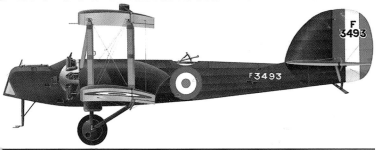

Rather less famous than the later Manchester Mk II, the Avro 533 Manchester of 1918 represented the final development of the 523/529 concept. The new design incorporated a number of changes including deeper fuselage, balanced ailerons, larger fin and horizontal stabiliser, and enlarged bomb aimer/front gunners position. It was designed around the ABC Dragonfly, the engine that was supposed to bring some measure of standardisation to the wartime British aircraft industry, but protracted development problems with this engine meant that Avro was forced to substitute 300hp (224kW) Siddeley Puma engines to produce the Avro 533 Manchester Mk II. By the time this flew in December 1918, a month after the Armistice, the 533 was an aircraft without a purpose. A year later the Mk I, pictured here, finally flew under the power of the much delayed and troublesome Dragonfly engines. No production orders were received.

Country of origin:	United Kingdom
Type:	three-seat long-range bomber
Powerplant:	two 320hp (239kW) ABC Dragonfly radial piston engines
Performance:	maximum speed 185km/h (115mph); service ceiling 5790m (19,000ft); endurance 5hrs 45 mins
Weights:	empty 2217kg (4887lb); maximum take-off weight 3352kg (7390lb)
Dimensions:	span 18.29m (60ft); length 11.28m (37ft); height 3.81m (12ft 6in); wing area 75.90 sq m (817 sq ft)
Armament:	one .303in Lewis gun on Scarff ring mounting in front cockpit; one .303in Lewis gun on Scarff ring mounting in rear cockpit; internal bay with provision for up to 339kg (880lb) of bombs

Avro 536

In response to the enormous growth in the post-war pleasure-flying market, Avro modified the fuselage of a number of its extensive stock of surplus 504K models so that the aft cockpit could accommodate four passengers seated in two pairs. The first conversion of an eventual 25 aircraft flew from Avro's Hamble factory on the south coast of England in April 1919. One was completed as a two-seater with a long-range fuel tank; another with float gear. A four-seater cabin version, the last of ten aircraft built at Hamble, was designated the Avro 546, although it flew very little and its registration was cancelled after a year. During the 1920s countless thousands of first-time fliers were carried aloft in the small fleet of 536s. The three surviving aircraft, fitted with 130hp (112kW) Clerget engines, were finally withdrawn from service with Surrey Flying Services in 1930.

Country of origin:	United Kingdom
Type:	five-seat open cockpit biplane
Powerplant:	one 150hp (112kW) Bentley BR1 rotary piston engine
Performance:	maximum speed 145km/h (90mph); service ceiling 3660m (12,000ft); range 322km (200 miles)
Weights:	empty 649kg (1431lb); maximum take-off weight 1010kg (2226lb)
Dimensions:	span 11.20m (36ft 9in); length 9.02m (29ft 5in); height 3.17m (10ft 5in); wing area 31.12 sq m (335 sq ft)

Avro 549 Aldershot III

In 1920 Avro and de Havilland submitted proposals to Air Ministry Specification 2/20, which called for a long-range day bomber. Avro's submission, the Type 549 Aldershot, was the company's first post-war military aircraft, a three-bay unequal-span biplane with all-metal fuselage (the first built by the company) and Rolls Royce Condor engine. After competitive trials with the de Havilland Derby the Type 549 won an order for two prototypes. The first of these flew at Hamble in 1922 and after a 1.8m (6-ft) fillet had been added to the fuselage the aircraft was demonstrated at the Hendon RAF display in June 1922. In 1923 this aircraft was ordered as the Aldershot III. Around 15 were supplied and all were operated by No 99 Squadron, from April 1924, until they were replaced by the Handley Page Hyderabad at the end of 1925.

Country of origin:	United Kingdom
Type:	three-seat heavy bomber
Powerplant:	one 650hp (485kW) Rolls Royce Condor III inline piston engine
Performance:	maximum speed 177km/h (110mph); service ceiling 4420m (14,500ft); range 1006km (625 miles)
Weights:	empty 649kg (1431lb); maximum take-off weight 1010kg (2226lb)
Dimensions:	span 11.20m (36ft 9in); length 9.02m (29ft 5in); height 3.17m (10ft 5in); wing area 31.12 sq m (335 sq ft)

Avro 555 Bison

A vro produced very few naval aircraft, a notable exception being the Type 555 Bison of 1921. This aircraft was designed to Admiralty Specification 3/11 that called for a carrier-based fleet spotter and reconnaissance aircraft. The first prototype was flown in 1921, followed by a second with raised upper wing, and a third in 1923. The first production aircraft were built to the standard of the second prototype and became Bison IAs in Royal Navy service. Orders for a further 35 aircraft (Bison II) were received between July 1924 and February 1927. The Bison IA entered service with No 3 Squadron, Royal Air Force, at Gosport, and it first went to sea with No 423 Fleet Spotter Flight embarked on HMS *Eagle*, on patrol in the Mediterranean. After serving aboard several other Royal Navy carriers and with shore-based units the Bison was replaced by the Fairey IIIF and retired in 1929. An attempted seaplane conversion was not a success.

Country of origin:	United Kingdom
Type:	three/four-seat fleet spotter biplane
Powerplant:	one 450hp (336kW) Napier Lion inline piston engine
Performance:	maximum speed 177km/h (110mph); service ceiling 4265m (14,000ft); range 547km (340 miles)
Weights:	empty 1887kg (4160lb); maximum take-off weight 2631kg (5800lb)
Dimensions:	span 14.02m (46ft); length 10.97m (36ft); height 4.22m (13ft 10in); wing area 57.6 sq m (620 sq ft)
Armament:	one .303 Lewis machine gun on flexible mount in aft cockpit

Avro 561 Andover

In June 1921 the Cairo–Baghdad mail link pioneered by the RAF was formally inaugurated by Nos 30 and 47 Squadrons flying twin-engine de Havilland D.H.10 Amiens III bombers. Although a fine aircraft, the route rapidly expanded and a more specialised replacement was sought. The single-engine Avro 561 Andover was ordered, having an empty weight some 25 per cent higher than the D.H.10. The design borrowed the wings, tail and landing gear of the earlier Type 549 Aldershot, but had a substantially larger fuselage with accommodation for 12 passengers, or six litters. The order was cut to just three aircraft when in July 1922 the British Government contracted the operation out to Imperial Airways. The three RAF aircraft were subsequently used as air ambulances and based at Halton. A single 12 passenger airliner variant, the Avro 563, was ordered and loaned to Imperial Airways before joining the other three Andovers.

Country of origin:	United Kingdom
Type:	12-seat ambulance/transport biplane
Powerplant:	one 650hp (485kW) Rolls Royce Condor III inline piston engine
Performance:	maximum speed 177km/h (110mph); service ceiling 4115m (13,500ft); range 740km (460 miles)
Weights:	empty 3166kg (6980lb); maximum take-off weight 5216kg (11,500lb)
Dimensions:	span 20.73m (68ft); length 15.72m (51ft 7in); height 4.91m (16ft 1in); wing area 98.66 sq m (1062 sq ft)

Avro 581E Avian

The Avro 594 Avian two-seat touring biplane derived from the 581 prototypes did not achieve the same sales success as the contemporary de Havilland D.H.60 Moth, but nonetheless has its own place in aviation history. The prototype appeared in April 1921 and was entered in the Daily Mail two-seat light aeroplane trials in September. Magneto problems hastened the aircraft's departure from the competition and it was modified as the 581E with an 80hp (60kW) ADC Cirrus engine. This was the aircraft flown by Squadron Leader Bert Hinkler in numerous racing and endurance events, culminating in his 15½-day flight from Croydon, England, to Darwin, Australia, in 1928 (albeit in much modified form with a de Havilland Gipsy II engine). The first production version was designated the Type 594 Avian Mk II. More powerful engines, revised landing gear, and strengthened interplane struts were fitted to the later Mks II–IV.

Country of origin:	United Kingdom
Type:	(581E G-EBOV) single-seat biplane
Powerplant:	one 80hp (60kW) ADC Cirrus inline piston engine
Performance:	maximum speed 113km/h (70mph); service ceiling 4115m (13,500ft); range 740km (1000 miles)
Weights:	empty 340kg (750lb); maximum take-off weight 717kg (1580lb)
Dimensions:	span 9.75m (32ft); length 7.47m (24ft 6in); height 2.59m (8ft 6in); wing area 27.30 sq m (294 sq ft)

Avro 621 Tutor

Roy Chadwick, the Avro designer, realised that the aircraft built to succeed the Avro 504N would have to be special, and in the 621 Tutor he designed an aircraft with the excellent handling characteristics of its predecessor. The prototype was evaluated at the Aircraft and Armament Experimental Establishment at Martlesham Heath in December 1929 before being selected for production in 1930. The production aircraft had the 240hp (179kW) Armstrong Siddeley Lynx IVC radial piston engine. Delivery of the first of an eventual 394 aircraft (from the production total of 795) for the RAF flying schools was made in 1933. Export orders to Canada (7 aircraft), Eire (3), Greece (30), Denmark (3) and China (5) were fulfilled before the line closed in 1936; licensed manufacture was undertaken in South Africa (57). In the late 1930s the Tutor was phased out from its position as main Royal Air Force elementary trainer in favour of the Miles Magister, a low-wing monoplane.

Country of origin:	United Kingdom
Type:	two-seat elementary trainer biplane
Powerplant:	one 240hp (179kW) Armstrong Siddeley Lynx IVC radial piston engine
Performance:	maximum speed 196km/h (122mph); service ceiling 4940m (16,200ft); range 402km (250 miles)
Weights:	empty 839kg (1844lb); maximum take-off weight 1115kg (2458lb)
Dimensions:	span 10.36m (34ft); length 8.08m (26ft 6in); height 2.92m (9ft 7in); wing area 27.96 sq m (301 sq ft)

Avro 626 Prefect

In an attempt to wring the maximum potential from the Avro 621 Tutor airframe and to maximise its sales potential to foreign clients, Avro developed the 626 specifically for export. This involved a number of changes to the basic airframe to incorporate a tailwheel and a gunner's position behind the aft cockpit. As supplied to foreign clients with special conversion kits the 626 could be used for a wide variety of training roles. A successful tour of South America was undertaken in 1931, and the aircraft subsequently served with the air arms of Argentina, Belgium, Brazil, Canada, Chile, China, Eire, Egypt, Estonia, Greece, Lithuania, New Zealand, Portugal, and the UK. The Royal Air Force and Royal New Zealand Air Force aircraft was known as the Prefect. Pictured here is one of the RNZAF aircraft, as can be seen from its registration number.

Country of origin:	United Kingdom
Type:	two/three-seat elementary trainer biplane
Powerplant:	one 240hp (179kW) Armstrong Siddeley Lynx IVC radial piston engine
Performance:	maximum speed 180km/h (112mph); service ceiling 4510m (14,800ft); range 354km (220 miles)
Weights:	empty 801kg (1765lb); maximum take-off weight 1247kg (2750lb)
Dimensions:	span 10.36m (34ft); length 8.08m (26ft 6in); height 2.92m (9ft 7in); wing area 27.87 sq m (300 sq ft)

Avro 643 Mk II Cadet

Essentially a scaled-down version of the Avro 621 Tutor, the Cadet was produced in three versions for civilian and military customers. The 631 Cadet first flew in 1931, and 35 aircraft were eventually built for private customers and the Irish Air Corps. In 1934 the 634 Cadet was introduced, retaining the uncowled 135hp (101kW) Armstrong Siddeley Genet Major of the 631. A sub-variant, the 643 Mk II, had minor modifications and an uprated 150hp (112kW) Genet. This was the most extensively produced model with 4 supplied to private clients, 20 to Air Service Training and 34 for the Royal Australian Air Force. These last aircraft soldiered on until the 1950s under civilian ownership. One was converted as a single-seat crop-spraying aircraft with a chemical hopper in the forward cockpit and a 220hp (164kW) Jacobs R-755 radial piston engine.

Country of origin:	United Kingdom
Type:	two-seat elementary trainer biplane
Powerplant:	one 150hp (112kW) Armstrong Genet Major IA radial piston engine
Performance:	maximum speed 187km/h (116mph); service ceiling 3660m (12,000ft); range 523km (325 miles)
Weights:	empty 839kg (1844lb); maximum take-off weight 1115kg (2458lb)
Dimensions:	span 9.19m (30ft 2in); length 7.54m (24ft 9in); height 2.69m (8ft 10in); wing area 24.34 sq m (262 sq ft)

Barling XNBL-1

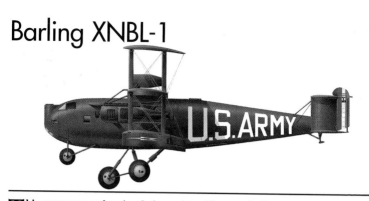

This enormous and curiously formed machine was designed by Walter Barling of the Army Air Services' Engineering Division in response to a request from US Chiefs of Staff for a strategic bomber. It was built by the Witteman-Lewis Aircraft Corporation of Newark, New Jersey. The XNBL-1 (Experimental Night Bomber Long-range), which first flew in August 1923, was at that time the world's largest aircraft with triplane wings spanning some 36.6m (120ft), ten wheel main gear, and positions for seven machine guns in five separate locations around the capacious fuselage. All this made for a heavy aircraft, and during flight testing the six Liberty engines driving a total of ten propellers (including four pushers) proved insufficient for the excessive demands placed on them. Development was abandoned in 1925, and no funds were made available for the improved XNBL-2.

Country of origin:	United States
Type:	experimental long-range bomber
Powerplant:	six 420hp (313kW) Liberty inline piston engines
Performance:	maximum speed 154km/h (96mph); service ceiling 2355m (7725ft); range with 2268kg (5000lb) 274km (170 miles)
Weights:	empty 12,566kg (27,703lb); maximum take-off weight 19,309kg (42,569lb)
Dimensions:	span 36.58m (120ft); length 19.81m (65ft); height 8.23m (27ft); wing area 390.18 sq m (4200 sq ft)
Armament:	seven .3in machine guns on flexible mountings, plus up to 2268kg (5000lb) of bombs

BAT F.K.23 Bantam

In 1917 Frederick Koolhoven left Armstrong Whitworth and took his services to the British Aerial Transport Co Ltd (BAT). His first design for the company was the F.K. 22, a single-seat two-bay biplane of wooden construction and monocoque fuselage housing a 170hp (127kW) ABC Wasp I. Six prototypes were constructed under the development contract, the final three designated F.K. 23 Bantam I. Flight tests of the Bantam I commenced in May 1918 and revealed unsatisfactory spin characteristics. Development of a further two slightly larger prototypes and nine pre-production aircraft was undertaken, and by the time the aircraft was ready for production the problems had been eradicated. In the event, a combination of a lengthy development process and post-war contraction of the Royal Air Force meant that no orders for the aircraft were forthcoming, although at least one ended up substantially modified for the air races at Hendon.

Country of origin:	United Kingdom
Type:	single-seat fighter biplane
Powerplant:	one 170hp (127kW) ABC Wasp I radial piston engine
Performance:	maximum speed 206km/h (128mph); service ceiling 6100m (20,000ft); endurance 2hrs 30mins
Weights:	empty 378kg (833lb); maximum take-off weight 599kg (1321lb)
Dimensions:	span 7.62m (25ft); length 5.61m (18ft 5in); height 2.06m (6ft 9in); wing area 17.19 sq m (185 sq ft)

Beardmore W.B.III

One of the many licensed wartime manufacturers of the Sopwith Pup was William Beardmore and Co Ltd of Balmuir, which developed a prototype version, the Beardmore W.B.III, for carrier operations. This had folding landing gear, folding, unstaggered wings, a lengthened fuselage carrying emergency flotation gear, a modified interplane strut configuration, and rod-operated ailerons with inter-aileron struts fitted to the upper and lower mainplanes. Some 100 production aircraft were ordered under the designation Beardmore S.B.3, and a number served aboard the carriers HMS *Furious*, *Nariana* and *Pegasus*. The first 13 aircraft (S.B.D.3F) had a tripod-mounted Lewis gun fired upwards through a centre section cut-out; in later S.B.D. aircraft the Lewis gun was mounted above the wing-centre section, the rod-operated ailerons were replaced by a conventional cable system, the wing-root interplane struts were deleted and a jettisonable undercarriage was provided.

Country of origin:	United Kingdom
Type:	single-seat shipboard fighter
Powerplant:	one 80hp (60kW) Le Rhône 9C or Clerget rotary piston engine
Performance:	maximum speed 166km/h (103mph); service ceiling 3780m (12,400ft); endurance 2hrs 45mins
Weights:	empty 404kg (890lb); maximum take-off weight 585kg (1289lb)
Dimensions:	span 7.62m (25ft); length 6.16m (20ft); height 2.47m (8ft 1in); wing area 22.57 sq m (243 sq ft)
Armament:	one .303in Lewis machine gun

Bellanca C-27 (Airbus)

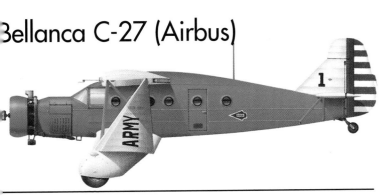

Italian-born American Guiseppe Bellanca began designing aircraft during World War I and in 1925 produced the Wright-Bellanca WB-2 that carried Chamberlin and Levine on their epic flight across the Atlantic to Germany. In 1927 he parted company with Wright and in 1930 introduced the Model P-100 Airbus, a 14-seat commercial monoplane with a 600hp (447kW) Curtiss Conqueror engine. An interesting feature of the aircraft was the concept of using the interplane struts as lifting surfaces. However, its potential was only realised when the unreliable Curtiss engine was substituted for a 650hp (485kW) Pratt & Whitney unit, and in this form the aircraft was ordered by the Army Air Corps as the Bellanca C-27A Airbus. These were later re-engined with a 675hp (504kW) Wright R-1820-17 Cyclone and redesignated C-27C. Total production of the Airbus and its derivative the Aircruiser, in the depressed US commercial aircraft market of the 1930s, was just 23.

Country of origin:	USA
Type:	11- to 14-seat transport aircraft
Powerplant:	one 650hp (485kW) Pratt & Whitney Hornet S3D1-G radial piston engine
Performance:	maximum speed 259km/h (161mph); service ceiling 4875m (16,000ft); range 1046km (650 miles)
Weights:	empty 2449kg (5400lb); maximum take-off weight 4613kg (10,170lb)
Dimensions:	span 19.81m (65ft); length 13.03m (42ft 9in); height 3.52m (11ft 6in); wing area 60.57 sq m (652 sq ft)

Beriev KOR-2 (Be-4)

In the mid-1930s a pressing need for a catapult-launched reconnaissance floatplane to equip the Soviet Navy's capital ships prompted Beriev to design the KOR-1 (Be-2) single-float biplane, which entered service with the Russian Navy in 1938. Developed in conjunction with the Be-2, and a considerable improvement on this hasty design, was the KOR-2 (Be-4), an inverted-gull parasol wing reconnaissance flying-boat with a single Shvetsov M-62 radial engine mounted on a pylon above the wing. The engine was mounted as high as possible to provide adequate clearance for the three-bladed controllable-pitch propeller. The first flight was made in 1940 and only a small number had been delivered to the Soviet Navy before the factory was overrun in September 1941. Production from an as yet unknown factory beyond the Urals resumed in June 1942, but no final production figures are available. Pictured is a KOR-2 of the Soviet Navy.

Country of origin:	Soviet Union
Type:	two-seat reconnaissance flying-boat
Powerplant:	one 900hp (671kW) Shvetsov M-62 radial piston engine
Performance:	maximum speed 360km/h (223mph); service ceiling 8100m (26,575ft); normal range 950km (590 miles)
Weights:	empty 2055kg (4530lb); maximum take-off weight 2760kg (6085lb)
Dimensions:	span 12m (39ft 4in); length 10.5m (34ft); height 4.05m (13ft 3in); wing area 25.5 sq m (274 sq ft)
Armament:	one 7.62mm machine gun on flexible mount in rear cockpit; underwing racks with provision for up to 300kg (661lb) of bombs

Beriev MBR-2

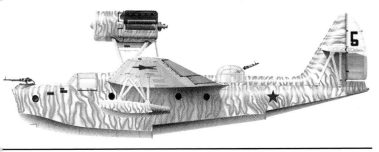

The bureau of Georgi M. Beriev, at Taganrog on the Azov Sea, was for many years the centre of Soviet marine aircraft design and manufacture. Beriev's first design, Aircraft No.25, was for a reconnaissance flying-boat that went on to achieve production success as the MBR-2. Deliveries of this aircraft began in 1934. It was a shoulder-wing cantilever monoplane with a two-step plywood fuselage, overwing strut-mounted engine and partly enclosed cockpit. The definitive MBR-2AM-34 had a fully enclosed cockpit, glazed mid-ship gunners position, and a redesigned fin and rudder. Some 1300 were built and these saw considerable service with all four Soviet fleets from the Winter War of 1939–40 until 1945. After the war the MBR-2 served for nearly a decade on fishery protection duties, and received the NATO codename 'Mote'. Pictured is a MBR-2 with sea green streaking camouflage, in the service of the Soviet Navy.

Country of origin:	Soviet Union
Type:	short-range reconnaissance/patrol flying-boat
Powerplant:	one 680hp (507kW) M-17B inline piston engine
Performance:	maximum speed 200km/h (124mph); service ceiling 4400m (14,435ft); normal range 650km (404 miles)
Weights:	empty 2475kg (5456lb); maximum take-off weight 4100kg (9039lb)
Dimensions:	span 19m (62ft 4in); length 13.5m (44ft 3in); wing area 55 sq m (592 sq ft)
Armament:	one 7.62mm ShKAS machine gun on ring mount in bow cockpit; one 7.62mm ShKAS machine gun on flexible mount in mid-ship cockpit; underwing racks with provision for up to 500kg (1102lb) of bombs or depth charges

Berliner-Joyce OJ-2

The US Bureau of Aeronautics, established in 1921, was able to win for the Naval Flying Corps a healthy portion of the scant resources allocated by the Department of Defence to military flying in the interwar years. In 1930 the Bureau announced a competition for a lightweight observation aircraft for the US Navy and after trials the Berliner-Joyce XOJ-1 prototype was selected over the Keystone Aircraft Corporation submission. The winning design was a conventional two-seat biplane with fabric-covered fuselage, staggered wings and strut-braced tailplane, powered by a Pratt & Whitney Wasp radial engine. Catapult launch gear was fitted to a number of the 39 OJ-2 aircraft delivered to the US Navy, the first of them entering service with VS-5B and VS-6B in 1933. They were in service for only a short time, as the type was withdrawn in 1935. Pictured is is an OJ-2 of VS-6B, based in Cincinnati in 1933.

Country of origin:	USA
Type:	two-seat observation biplane
Powerplant:	one 400hp (298kW) Pratt & Whitney R-985-A Wasp radial piston engine
Performance:	maximum speed 243km/h (151mph)
Weights:	maximum take-off weight 1646kg (3629lb)
Dimensions:	span 10.26m (33ft 8in); length 7.82m (25ft 8in)

Berliner-Joyce P-16

The Berliner-Joyce Aircraft Corporation was established in February 1929 with the intention of producing the Berliner Monoplane, but when the Army announced its intention to purchase a new two-seat fighter the company entered the competition. Boeing and Curtiss also submitted designs and in June a prototype contract was awarded for the Berliner-Joyce XP-16. This gull-winged biplane had tandem open cockpits and was powered by a supercharged Curtiss V-1570-25 Conqueror engine. Flight trials commenced in October 1929, and 25 service-test aircraft were ordered in March 1931. The production PB-16 (later PB-1), with three-blade airscrew and unsupercharged engine, entered service in 1933 with the 27th and 94th Pursuit Squadrons (pictured). However, it exhibited a number of defects, including a tendency to nose-over on landing and poor manoeuvrability, and was withdrawn at the end of January 1934.

Country of origin:	USA
Type:	two-seat fighter biplane
Powerplant:	one 600hp (447kW) Curtiss V-1570-25 Conqueror vee piston engine
Performance:	maximum speed 282km/h (175mph); service ceiling 6588m (21,600ft); range 1046km (650 miles)
Weights:	empty 1271kg (2803lb); maximum take-off weight 1813kg (3996lb)
Dimensions:	span 10.36m (34ft); length 8.59m (28ft 2in); height 2.74m (9ft); wing area 25.92 sq m (279 sq ft)
Armament:	two fixed forward-firing .3in machine guns; one .3in machine gun on flexible mount in rear cockpit; underwing racks with provision for up to 102kg (224lb) of bombs

Besson MB.35

French aviation pioneer Marcel Besson collaborated with Georges Lévy from 1915 to produce a series of flying boats that appeared between 1917 and 1919 with the LB designation. The partnership did not endure the war, although Besson continued to produce new designs for marine aircraft throughout the 1920s and early 1930s. The ungainly MB.35 twin-float reconnaissance and observation monoplane-winged floatplane was intended for service on board a proposed new class of French ocean-going submarines, and was by necessity of compact, easily disassembled design to allow it to be accommodated in a sealed deck hangar. This can clearly be seen in the 'upside-down' tailplane, to allow the hangar roof to be as low as possible. The first flight was made in 1926, but the two machines that were built served on surface vessels during their short service careers, and failed to win export orders.

Country of origin:	France
Type:	two-seat spotter and observation floatplane
Powerplant:	one 120hp (89kW) Salmson 9Ac radial piston engine
Performance:	maximum speed 160km/h (99mph); service ceiling 4800m (15,750ft); range 300km (186 miles)
Weights:	empty 540kg (1190lb); maximum take-off weight 765kg (1687lb)
Dimensions:	span 9.82m (32ft 2in); length 7m (22ft 11in); height 2.45m (8ft); wing area 16.5 sq m (178 sq ft)
Armament:	(intended) one light machine gun on ring mounting in rear cockpit

Besson MB.411

Clearly derived from the earlier Besson MB.35, the MB.410 of 1932 substituted the twin floats of the earlier aircraft for a single mainfloat and two outriggers, cowled engine, a more streamlined fuselage and revised tail surfaces. The prototype was lost in a fatal accident during flight tests. However, the French Navy had recently taken delivery of the cruiser submarine *Surcouf* and had a requirement for a spotter aircraft. As a result it ordered a developed version of the prototype designated the MB.411. The first of two aircraft (pictured above) was embarked on the *Surcouf* in September 1935 as a spotter plane for the submarine's 8in (203mm) guns. The second aircraft went to Aéronavale Escadrille 7-S-4, based at St Mandrier. After escaping to Plymouth in 1940, *Surcouf* was lost with all hands off the West Indies in February 1942, although the aircraft was not embarked and its fate is something of a mystery.

Country of origin:	France
Type:	two-seat spotter and observation floatplane
Powerplant:	one 175hp (130kW) Salmson 9Nd radial piston engine
Performance:	maximum speed 190km/h (118mph); service ceiling 5000m (16,405ft); range 400km (249 miles)
Weights:	empty 760kg (1676lb); maximum take-off weight 1140kg (2513lb)
Dimensions:	span 12m (39ft 4in); length 8.25m (27ft); height 2.85m (9ft 4in); wing area 22 sq m (237 sq ft)

Blackburn B-5 Baffin

The lineage of this aircraft may be traced back to the T.1 Swift, built by Blackburn as a private venture single-seat carrier-based torpedo bomber in 1920. From this were developed the T.2 Dart, T.3 Velos, T.5 Ripon, B-5 Baffin and finally the B-6 Shark, each a progressive improvement on its predecessor. The emergence of lighter, more efficient radial engines and the successful use of a radial engine in the Ripons supplied to Finland, prompted Blackburn to develop the Baffin privately. Two Fleet Air Arm Ripon V airframes were trialled with Armstrong Siddeley Tiger I (Blackburn B-4) and Bristol Pegasus I.MS engines (Blackburn B-5). The latter version was selected by the Fleet Air Arm for service, powered by the Pegasus I.M3 engine. More than 80 FAA Ripon IICs were converted on the production line, or re-engined to Baffin standard, serving from 1934 until 1937. Three squadrons of Baffins later served with the Royal New Zealand Air Force.

Country of origin:	United Kingdom
Type:	two-seat torpedo bomber
Powerplant:	one 565hp (421kW) Bristol Pegasus I.M3 radial piston engine
Performance:	maximum speed 219km/h (136mph); service ceiling 4570m (15,000ft); range 869km (450 miles)
Weights:	empty equipped 1444kg (3184lb); maximum take-off weight 3452kg (7610lb)
Dimensions:	span 13.88m (45ft 6in); length 11.68m (38ft 3in); height 3.91m (12ft 10in); wing area 63.45 sq m (683 sq ft)
Armament:	one fixed forward-firing .303in Vickers machine gun; one .303in Lewis machine gun on flexible mounting in rear cockpit; underfuselage rack for one torpedo or up to 907kg (2000lb) of bombs

Blackburn R.B.1 Iris

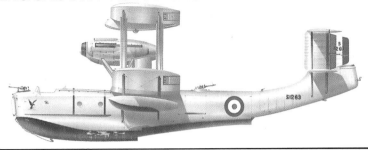

Robert Blackburn was among the first generation of British aviation pioneers, and produced his first aircraft, a monoplane, in April 1909. There followed a successful series of monoplanes and military biplanes before Blackburn responded to Air Ministry Specification R.14/24, which called for a long-range reconnaissance aircraft, with the R.B.1 design. The wooden-hulled prototype first flew in June 1926 and undertook flying and sea trials at Felixstowe that summer. Refitted at the factory with a metal hull and Rolls Royce Condor IIIA engines the aircraft undertook a successful overseas tour and in this form was ordered as the Blackburn R.B.1B Iris Mk III. The first of three aircraft was delivered in November 1929, all of which served with No 209 Squadron. The survivors were re-engined with 825hp (615kW) Rolls-Royce Buzzard IIMS engines in 1932, becoming R.B.1D Iris Vs.

Country of origin:	United Kingdom
Type:	five-seat long-range reconnaissance flying-boat
Powerplant:	three 675hp (503kW) Rolls Royce Condor IIIB inline piston engines
Performance:	maximum speed 190km/h (118mph); service ceiling 3230m (10,600ft); range 1287km (800 miles)
Weights:	empty 8640kg (19,048lb); maximum take-off weight 13,376kg (29,489lb)
Dimensions:	span 29.57m (97ft); length 20.54m (67ft 4in); height 7.77m (25ft 6in); wing area 207.07 sq m (2229 sq ft)
Armament:	one .303in Lewis machine gun in nose position; one .303in Lewis machine gun in mid-ships position; one .303in Lewis machine gun in tail position; underwing racks with provision for up to 907kg (2000lb) of bombs

Blériot-SPAD S.51-4

André Herbemont, the Blériot-SPAD chief designer, gleaned his knowledge of single-seat fighter design during World War I and applied it to a succession of post-war fighter aircraft. The S.51 was built to a French Aéronautique Specification of 1924 that called for a replacement for the Nieuport-Delage 29 C.1 then in service. The first of four prototypes flew in June 1924, and followed Herbemont's familiar unequal-span biplane with a swept back upper wing and straight lower formula, with faired interplane struts, wooden monocoque fuselage and Gnome-Rhône Jupiter engine. Fifty production examples of the S.51-2 prototype were supplied to Poland. The other prototypes were the S.51-3 with variable pitch propeller, and the S.51-4 of 1928 with a supercharged Jupiter engine. Twelve of the latter were built, one of which went to Turkey (pictured above).

Country of origin:	France
Type:	single-seat fighter biplane
Powerplant:	one 600hp (447kW) Gnome-Rhône Jupiter radial piston engine
Performance:	maximum speed 231km/h (143mph); service ceiling 9000m (29,530ft); endurance 2hrs
Weights:	empty equipped 838kg (1843lb); maximum take-off weight 1311kg (2890lb)
Dimensions:	span 9.47m (31ft); length 6.45m (21ft 2in); height 3.1m (10ft 2in); wing area 23.95 sq m (258 sq ft)
Armament:	two fixed forward-firing .303in Vickers machine guns

Blériot-SPAD S.56-5

The Société Anonyme Pour L'Aviation et ses Derivés, or SPAD, became a subsidiary of the famous Blériot company in August 1914. The post-war designs of André Herbemont, who succeeded Louis Béchereau as chief designer in the spring of 1917, dominated the post-war European light transport market until the outbreak of World War II. The S.33 of 1920 was a great success and was later modified to produce the S.46 of 1921 (41 built), and the S.56 of 1923. This was a basic S.33 airframe with additional modifications including metal wings, revised cabin layout for four passengers, and an uprated engine. It first flew in prototype form in 1923. In 1928 Six S.56-3 (380hp/283kW Gnome-Rhône Jupiter engine) aircraft of the CIDNA company were converted to the S.56-5 standard (pictured circa 1930), with accommodation for six in wicker armchairs, plus a limited amount of freight.

Country of origin:	France
Type:	six-seat commercial transport
Powerplant:	one 380hp (283kW) Gnome-Rhône Jupiter radial piston engine
Performance:	maximum speed 200km/h (124mph); service ceiling 5050m (16,568ft); endurance 800km (497 miles)
Weights:	loaded 2400kg (5292lb)
Dimensions:	span 13.08m (42ft 11in); length 9.05m (29ft 9in); height 3.2m (10ft 6in)

Blériot-SPAD S.510

The S.510 was the last SPAD fighter to enter production before the company became part of the SNCASO group in 1941, and was the only biplane entry to the French fighter competition of 1930. The aircraft followed André Herbemont's familiar wing planform, married to an oval section fuselage of Duralumin and steel. The prototype S.510.01 flew in January 1931 and, although it subsequently lost the design competition to the Dewoitine D.500 monoplane, it proved sufficiently impressive to gain an order for 60 aircraft from the French Air Minister in 1935. Deliveries of the S.510 production aircraft to the II/7 Groupe began in April 1937, but these had been relegated to flying schools and regional defence squadrons by the outbreak of war in 1939. Details of their combat record remain sketchy, and rumours that some served in the Spanish Civil War are unconfirmed. Pictured is an S.510 of ERC 4/561, based at Havre-Octeville in October 1939.

Country of origin:	France
Type:	single-seat fighter biplane
Powerplant:	one 690hp (515kW) Hispano-Suiza 12Xbrs inline piston engine
Performance:	maximum speed 372km/h (231mph); service ceiling 9950m (32,645ft); range 700km (435 miles)
Weights:	empty equipped 1250kg (2756lb); maximum take-off weight 1677kg (3697lb)
Dimensions:	span 8.84m (29ft); length 7.46m (21ft 5in); height 3.41m (11ft 2in); wing area 22 sq m (237 sq ft)
Armament:	four fixed forward-firing 7.5mm Chatellerault machine guns in underwing gondolas

Blohm und Voss Bv 138C-1

The aircraft subsidiary of the Blohm und Voss shipyard, Hamburger Flugzegbau, was founded in 1933. Its most important product for the emerging Luftwaffe was the Ha 138 series of reconnaissance flying-boats. Chief Engineer Richard Vogt designed the aircraft in the mid-1930s for twin-engines, but development problems necessitated redesign to accept three 650hp (485kW) Junkers Jumo 205Cs diesel engines. The first of two prototypes (Ha 138V1) flew in July 1937, followed by a second (Ha 138V2) with a radically redesigned hull. During testing at Travemünde the aircraft demonstrated an inherent instability both on the water and in the air, and a convoluted development programme followed before the 138A series aircraft was accepted for production. Pictured is a Bv 138C-1, the main production variant introduced in March 1941 with uprated engines and additional armament, of 2/KüFlGr. 406 based in northern Norway.

Country of origin:	Germany
Type:	five-man reconnaissance flying-boat
Powerplant:	three 880hp (656kW) Junkers Jumo 105D inline diesel piston engines
Performance:	maximum speed 275km/h (171mph); service ceiling 5000m (16,405ft); range 5000km (3107 miles)
Weights:	empty 8100kg (17,857lb); maximum take-off weight 14,700 kg (32,408lb)
Dimensions:	span 27m (88ft 7in); length 19.9m (65ft 3in); height 6.6m (21ft 8in); wing area 112 sq m (1205 sq ft)
Armament:	one 20mm MG151 cannon in bow turret; one 20mm MG151 in rear hull position; one 13mm MG131 machine gun in rear of centre nacelle; provision for three 50kg (110lb) understarboard wing root, or (Bv 138C1-U1) six 50kg (110lb) bombs, or four 150kg (331lb) depth charges

Blohm und Voss Bv 138 MS

The first 25 Bv 138A-1 boats were intended to be ocean reconnaissance platforms, but they were underpowered and ended up as transports in the Norwegian Campaign. In late 1940 the B-1 entered service with the 880hp (656kW) Jumo, modified tail and a 20mm turret at each end of the hull. Twenty-one were built before production switched to the Bv 138C-1, of which some 227 were delivered between 1941 and 1943. Until the end of the war the C-1 served in the front line in all theatres of German operations. A mine-sweeping version designated Bv 138MS was produced by converting the Bv 138B-0 series prototype aircraft to accept a degaussing loop and electrical field-generating equipment. All armament was deleted, as the aircraft was intended to operate in friendly waters and such a measure would save weight. Shown here is a Bv 138MS of 6./MSGr.1, based at Grossenbrode in the winter of 1944–5.

Country of origin:	Germany
Type:	five-man mine-sweeping flying-boat
Powerplant:	three 880hp (656kW) Junkers Jumo 105D inline diesel piston engines
Performance:	maximum speed 275km/h (171mph); service ceiling 5000m (16,405ft); range 5000km (3107 miles)
Weights:	empty 8100kg (17,857lb); maximum take-off weight 14,700 kg (32,408lb)
Dimensions:	span 27m (88ft 7in); length 19.9m (65ft 3in); height 6.6m (21ft 8in); wing area 112 sq m (1205 sq ft)

Blohm und Voss Bv 222 Wiking

The Bv 222 was designed before World War II for a proposed transatlantic service by Deutsche Lufthansa. Three aircraft powered by six 1000hp (746kW) BMW-Bramo Fafnir 323R radial engines were ordered in September 1937. The prototype's first flight was in September 1940, when it was seconded for military transport operations in Norway and the Mediterranean. Armament was fitted to the second and third prototypes and to all subsequent prototypes (V2–V8). To strengthen the Luftwaffe's long-range reconnaissance forces, four of its Bv 222 aircraft were modified to carry airborne radars and additional armament, but unsuccessful in this role they were withdrawn from their bases on the French coast. The seventh prototype was used as a development aircraft for the C-series production standard; it first flew in April 1943, with 980hp (731kW) Jumo diesels. Only four Bv 222C-0 pre-production examples were completed, serving in the Atlantic, Baltic and Arctic regions.

Country of origin:	Germany
Type:	(Bv 222C) transport and maritime reconnaissance flying-boat
Powerplant:	six 1000hp (746kW) Junkers Jumo 207C 12-cylinder vertically opposed diesel engines
Performance:	maximum speed 390km/h (242mph); service ceiling 7300m (23,950ft); range 6100 km (3790 miles)
Weights:	empty 30,650kg (67,572lb); maximum take-off weight 49,000kg (108,025lb)
Dimensions:	span 46m (150ft 11in); length 37m (121ft 5in); height 10.90m (35ft 9in)
Armament:	one 20mm trainable cannon in the dorsal turret; one 20mm trainable cannon in each of the two power-operated wing turrets; one 13mm trainable forward-firing machine gun in the bow position; one 13mm trainable lateral-firing machine gun in each of the four lateral hull positions

Boulton & Paul P.64 Mailplane

During World War I the Air Department of Boulton & Paul manufactured Sopwith 1½ Strutters and Camels and subsequently undertook the design and production of their own machines. In 1939 the company built the P.64 Mailplane (pictured) for Imperial Airways, which had issued a requirement for an aircraft that could carry a 454kg (1000lb) payload over a 1609km (1000 mile) range. The aircraft proved costly to develop and barely six months after the flight of the first prototype at Mousehold, Norwich, it was destroyed in a fatal accident. The lighter, more streamlined P.71A was developed from this airframe and two examples were delivered to Imperial Airways at Croydon in February 1935. They never saw service in their intended role and were converted for passenger carrying with 13 seats (seven if carrying VIPs). Both aircraft were lost in accidents, in October 1935 and September 1936.

Country of origin:	United Kingdom
Type:	(P.71A) mailplane/light transport
Powerplant:	two 490hp (365kw) Armstrong Siddeley Jaguar VIA radial piston engines
Performance:	maximum speed 314km/h (195mph); range 966km (600 miles)
Weights:	empty 2767kg (6100lb); maximum take-off weight 4309kg (9500lb)
Dimensions:	span 16.46m (54ft); length 13.46m (44ft 2in); height 4.62m (15ft 2in); wing area 66.75 sq m (718 sq ft)

Boulton Paul P.75 Overstrand

The Boulton & Paul P.75 Overstrand prototype was developed on the production line from the airframe of the eighth production P.29 Sidestrand, a twin-engined medium bomber designed to meet an Air Ministry specification of 1924. The first three conversions were designated Sidestrand Mk V, but the name Overstrand was adopted in March 1934. The aircraft shared the general configuration of its predecessor, but had a number of innovative features. Principal among them was the power-operated nose turret, one of the first to be fitted to a production aircraft, an enclosed cockpit, three-axis autopilot, and the luxury of a heating system that supplied hot air to all crew positions. The 27 Overstrands were the last aircraft built at Boulton Paul's (as the company became in 1933) Norwich factory, which moved to Wolverhampton during the production cycle. Bicester-based No 101 Squadron received its first aircraft in January 1935, operating the aircraft until late 1938.

Country of origin:	United Kingdom
Type:	five-seat medium bomber
Powerplant:	two 580hp (433kW) Bristol Pegasus IIM.3 radial piston engines
Performance:	maximum speed 246km/h (153mph); service ceiling 6860m (22,500ft); range 877km (545 miles)
Weights:	empty 3600kg (7936lb); maximum take-off weight 5443kg (12,000lb)
Dimensions:	span 21.95m (72ft); length 14.02m (46ft); height 4.72m (15ft 6in); wing area 91.04 sq m (980 sq ft)
Armament:	one .303in Lewis gun in nose turret; one .303in Lewis gun in each of the two dorsal ventral positions; internal bay with provision for up to 726kg (1600lb) of bombs

Breguet Bre.14 A.2

L ouis Breguet established his aircraft manufacturing company at Douai in 1909, but was forced to relocate to Villacoublay in 1914 in front of the rapid German advance. In the summer of 1916 his Chief Engineer Louis Vullierme began the design of Breguet's most successful wartime product, the Bre. 14. The prototype of this two-seat reconnaissance/light bomber aircraft made its first flight barely five months later, and the first Bre.14 A2 production aircraft entered service with the Aéronautique Militaire the following spring. The Bre.14 quickly established a reputation for toughness and reliability, and by the end of the year orders for some 2650 aircraft had been placed with the five licensees. The B.2 bomber, with trailing edge flaps, was the next version, followed by the Bre.14S ambulance. Military and civil versions of this outstanding aircraft were in production until 1926. Pictured is a Breguet Bre. 14 A.2 of the 15e Escadrille, 5e Groupe, French Air Force, in 1921.

Country of origin:	France
Type:	two-seat reconnaissance/light bomber biplane
Powerplant:	one 300hp (224kW) Renault 12Fe inline piston engine
Performance:	maximum speed 184km/h (114mph); service ceiling 6000m (19,690ft); endurance 3hrs
Weights:	empty 1030kg (2271lb); maximum take-off weight 1565kg (3450lb)
Dimensions:	span 14.36m (47ft 1in); length 8.87m (29ft 1in); height 3.3m (10ft 10in); wing area 47.50 sq m (530 sq ft)
Armament:	one fixed forward-firing .303 machine gun; twin .303in Lewis machine guns on ring mounting in rear cockpit; underwing racks with provision for up 40kg (88lb) of bombs

Breguet Bre.19.8

The interest generated by successive record-breaking flights in the special long-range Bidon and Super Bidon versions of the Bre.19 prompted Breguet to develop a similar type for export as the Bre.19.7. Yugoslavia had already shown a remarkable faith in the Bre.19 design and acquired five of these machines. A licence was negotiated and 125 further machines were produced at the Kraljevo plant. Many of these were in the front line when Germany attacked on 6 April 1941. Among the aircraft captured and then turned on the Yugoslav partisan forces by Axis and co-belligerent Croatian forces after the Axis invasion of Yugoslavia were a number of the 50 Bre.19.8 aircraft (pictured here in Croatian colours around 1943) that Yugoslavia completed in November 1937 with a Wright Cyclone GR-1820-F56 radial engine.

Country of origin:	Yugoslavia (France)
Type:	two-seat reconnaissance aircraft
Powerplant:	one 450hp (336kW) Wright-Cyclone Gr-820-F56 radial piston engine
Performance:	maximum speed 235km/h (146mph); service ceiling 7000m (22,970ft); endurance 1200km (746 miles)
Weights:	empty 1722kg (3796lb); maximum take-off weight 3110kg (6856lb)
Dimensions:	span 14.83m (48ft 7in); length 9.51m (31ft 2in); height 3.69m (12ft 1in); wing area 50 sq m (538 sq ft)
Armament:	one fixed forward-firing .303in Vickers machine gun; two .303 Lewis machine guns on Scarff ring mount on rear cockpit; one ventral .303in Lewis machine gun

Breguet Bre.19A.2

Yugoslavia was one of the first nations to express an interest in the Bre.19 after an aircraft was displayed at an international competition organised by the Spanish War Ministry in 1923 and a pre-production aircraft was delivered to the country for evaluation. Successful flight trials prompted an order for 100 A.2s and B.2s (as the bomber version was designated), to be powered by the Lorraine-Dietrich 12Db and 12Eb respectively. Deliveries were completed during 1925–6. From October 1927 Yugoslavia imported a further 85 complete and 25 disassembled aircraft from France, built some parts of another 15, and gained a licence to manufacture another 175 in two batches, the last with Yugoslav-built Gnome-Rhône Jupiter 9AB radial engines. Manufacture of the aircraft was undertaken at the State Aircraft factory at Kraljevo, while engine construction took place at a factory at Rakovica.

Country of origin:	Yugoslavia (France)
Type:	two-seat reconnaissance aircraft
Powerplant:	one 420hp (313kW) Gnome-Rhône 9AB radial piston engine
Performance:	maximum speed 235km/h (146mph); service ceiling 7000m (22,970ft); endurance 1200km (746 miles)
Weights:	empty 1722kg (3796lb); maximum take-off weight 3110kg (6856lb)
Dimensions:	span 14.83m (48ft 7in); length 9.51m (31ft 2in); height 3.69m (12ft 1in); wing area 50 sq m (538 sq ft)
Armament:	one fixed forward-firing .303in Vickers machine gun; two .303 Lewis machine guns on Scarff ring mount on rear cockpit; one ventral .303in Lewis machine gun; plus (B.2) maximum internal bomb load of 400kg (882lb) with underwing racks for a further 400kg (882lb)

Breguet Bre.19A.2

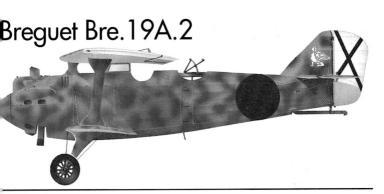

In 1923 Breguet test pilot Robert Thiery demonstrated the Bre.19 at an international fighter contest in Spain and swept the opposition from the board. Spain immediately signed a licensees contract and three pattern aircraft were delivered, together with components for 26 other aircraft for assembly by CASA. At the same time Elizalde acquired a licence to build the Lorraine-Deitrich 12Ebs as the A.4. The crisis in Spanish Morocco in 1925 prompted Spain to import another 16 complete aircraft as no domestically manufactured aircraft had been completed. By 1935 a total of 177 Bre.19s had been built in Spain, and saw front-line service with both Nationalist and Republican forces in the early stages of the Civil War. The Nationalists even bought 20 reconditioned examples from Poland. By mid-1937 however both sides had withdrawn the Bre. 19 from front-line service. Pictured is an Elizalde A-4 powered Bre.19 of the Nationalist Observers' school in 1938.

Country of origin:	Spain (France)
Type:	two-seat reconnaissance aircraft
Powerplant:	one 450hp (336kW) Elizalde A-4 (license-built Lorraine-Dietrich 12Ebs) inline piston engine
Performance:	maximum speed 235km/h (146mph); service ceiling 7000m (22,970ft); endurance 1200km (746 miles)
Weights:	empty 1722kg (3796lb); maximum take-off weight 3110kg (6856lb)
Dimensions:	span 14.83m (48ft 7in); length 9.51m (31ft 2in); height 3.69m (12ft 1in); wing area 50 sq m (538 sq ft)
Armament:	one fixed forward-firing .303in Vickers machine gun; two .303 Lewis machine guns on Scarff ring mount on rear cockpit; one ventral .303in Lewis machine gun

Breguet Bre.19 A.2

Louis Vullierme rested on the success of the Bre.14, and in 1920 began designing its natural successor, the Bre. 19. This was not an ideal time for European aircraft manufacturers, with thousands of surplus military aircraft on the market. Nevertheless, the company showed great faith in the design and after the prototype Bre.19 A.2 No 01 made a promising showing at the 1921 Paris Air Salon the company built 11 pre-production aircraft. These were already under construction when the prototype made its first flight. It had been intended to power the prototype with a 16-cylinder 450hp (336kW) Breguet-Bugatti Vee engine, but this proved troublesome in ground tests and was replaced with the Renault 12Kb for the maiden flight in March 1922. The pre-production aircraft had a fuselage some 0.5m (2ft) shorter than the prototype, and a variety of engine fits. The first of 112 A.2 aircraft ordered by the Aéronautique Militaire were delivered in October 1924.

Country of origin:	France
Type:	two-seat reconnaissance aircraft
Powerplant:	one 513hp (383kW) Renault 12Kd water-cooled Vee engine
Performance:	maximum speed 235km/h (146mph); service ceiling 7000m (22,970ft); endurance 1200km (746 miles)
Weights:	empty 1722kg (3796lb); maximum take-off weight 3110kg (6856lb)
Dimensions:	span 14.83m (48ft 7in); length 9.51m (31ft 2in); height 3.69m (12ft 1in); wing area 50 sq m (538 sq ft)
Armament:	one fixed forward-firing .303in Vickers machine gun; two .303 Lewis machine guns on Scarff ring mount on rear cockpit; one ventral .303in Lewis machine gun; plus (B.2) maximum internal bomb load of 400kg (882lb) with underwing racks for a further 400kg (882lb)

Breguet Bre.19 GR

Numerous record-breaking flights were undertaken in specially developed versions of the Bre.19, which of course did nothing to harm the sales and kept the type in the public eye. The first of these special versions was the Bre.19 Grand Raid, essentially a Bre.19 with increased fuel tankage. Following this came the Bre.19GR Bidon (fuel can) aircraft, Nos 1685, 1686 and 1687 rebuilt with 2915-litre (641-gallon) fuel capacity (over the 440-litre/97-gallon capacity of the standard aircraft). The first was fitted with a Hispano-Suiza 12Ha and then 12Hb engine, and the second and third had the Renault 12Kb. One was built for Belgium, another for Greece, and two were built by CASA in Spain. Pictured is No 1685 flown by Commandants Grizier and Weiss on 25 May 1929 to establish a world speed record of 188.1km/h (116.8mph) over a distance of 5000km (3107 miles).

Country of origin:	France
Type:	two-seat long-range test aircraft
Powerplant:	one 500hp (373kW) Hispano-Suiza 12Lb inline piston engine
Performance:	maximum speed 235km/h (146mph); service ceiling 7000m (22,970ft); range 3500km (2174 miles)
Weights:	empty 1722kg (3796lb); maximum take-off weight 3110kg (6856lb)
Dimensions:	span 16.5m (54ft 1in); length 9.51m (31ft 2in); height 3.69m (12ft 1in); wing area 50 sq m (538 sq ft)
Armament:	one fixed forward-firing .303in Vickers machine gun; two .303 Lewis machine guns on Scarff ring mount on rear cockpit; one ventral .303in Lewis machine gun

Breguet Bre.19 Super Bidon

The most illustrious of the Breguet 19 family was the French-built Super-Bidon *Point d'Interrogation*. The fuel capacity was raised to 5170 litres (1137 gallons) to enable a series of record-breaking flights. Powered by a Hispano-Suiza 12Lb engine, this aircraft established a new distance record of 7905km (4912 miles) when it was flown by Dieudonné Costes and Maurice Bellonte from Le Bourget in France and Tsitsihkar in Manchuria between 27 and 29 September 1929. It was subsequently re-engined with a 650hp (485kW) Hispano-Suiza 12Nb engine, made the first direct flight from Paris to New York, and thereafter embarked on a *Tour d'Amitié* (Voyage of Friendship) of the USA. Its landing points are recorded on the rear fuselage tricolour chevron. CASA in Spain built one of these aircraft that was named Cuatro Vientos, and subsequently lost in the Caribbean between Cuba and Mexico.

Country of origin:	France
Type:	two-seat long-range test aircraft
Powerplant:	one 650hp (485kW) Hispano-Suiza 12Nb inline piston engine
Performance:	maximum speed 235km/h (146mph); service ceiling 7000m (22,970ft); range 3500km (2174 miles)
Weights:	empty 1722kg (3796lb); maximum take-off weight 3110kg (6856lb)
Dimensions:	span 16.5m (54ft 1in); length 9.51m (31ft 2in); height 3.69m (12ft 1in); wing area 50 sq m (538 sq ft)

Breguet 393T

Breguet developed the 393T three-engine passenger transport aircraft from the earlier 390T of 1931 (prototype destroyed in a fatal accident in July 1931) and 392T (single example built that was completed as a freight carrier). The 393T differed from this latter aircraft in having seated accommodation for ten passengers in armchairs next to large windows, a fabric- rather than metal-covered fuselage, modified interplane struts, and tailwheel landing gear. The prototype 393T first flew in 1933 and the first production example was delivered to national carrier Air France in July 1934. A further five aircraft were delivered to this customer by the end of 1935, and were operated on North African services and the Mediterranean leg of the route to South America. Pictured is one of the aircraft employed on the Air France Toulouse–Casablanca route in 1934. It was later operated from Paris to numerous European cities.

Country of origin:	France
Type:	10-seat passenger transport
Powerplant:	three 350hp (261kW) Gnome-Rhône 7Kd Titan Major radial piston engines
Performance:	maximum speed 249km/h (155mph); service ceiling 5850m (19,190ft); range 975km (606 miles)
Weights:	empty 3966kg (8743lb); maximum take-off weight 6000kg (13,228lb)
Dimensions:	span 20.71m (67ft 11in); length 14.76m (48ft 5in); wing area 66.46 sq m (715 sq ft)

Breguet 521 Bizerte

Breguet acquired a licence to build the Short Calcutta and with minor modifications built this as the Bre.521 Bizerte to a French Air Ministry requirement for a long-range flying-boat. The prototype first flew in September 193? with three uncowled 845hp (630kW) Gnome-Rhône 14Kdrs radials, which were enclosed for the official trials beginning in January 1934. Three pre-production aircraft were built, the second with minor modifications that were standard to production aircraft. Deliveries to the first of five Aéronautique Maritime squadrons began in 1935 and production continued until 1940, by which time 35 had been built. Two of the five squadrons served with the Vichy French Air Force until November 1942, when they were seized by the Luftwaffe and thereafter used for North Atlantic air-sea-rescue operations. Pictured is an example based in north-wes? France in the winter of 1943–4.

Country of origin:	France
Type:	eight-seat long-range maritime flying-boat
Powerplant:	three 900hp (671kW) Gnome-Rhône 14Kirs or 14N-11 radial piston engines
Performance:	maximum speed 245km/h (152mph); service ceiling 6000m (19,685ft); maximum range 3000km (1864 miles)
Weights:	empty 9470kg (20,878lb); maximum take-off weight 16,600kg (36,597lb)
Dimensions:	span 35.15m (115ft 4in); length 20.50m (67ft 3in); height 7.45m (24ft 5in); wing area 162.60 sq m (1750 sq ft)
Armament:	two 7.5mm Darue machine guns on flexible mounts in port and starboard lateral positions; one 7.5mm Darue machine gun on flexible mount in tail position; underwing racks with provision for up to 300kg (661lb) of bombs

Bristol Type 22 F.2B

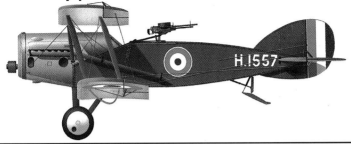

Frank Barnwell designed the Type 9 R.2A as a two-seat reconnaissance aircraft, but by August 1916 this had been re-engined and redesignated as the Type 12 F.2A, to denote its new fighter role. The first production F.2As were delivered in February 1917 and, although their early operational tactical employment as a gun platform was naive and resulted in heavy casualties, pilots soon adopted single-seat fighter tactics and the aircraft went on to become one of the most successful and prolific British fighters of World War I. The F.2B was the main production variant and incorporated modified upper longerons for improved pilot visibility, enlarged fuel tank and a variety of engines. Production total was 5308 aircraft, with licensed manufacture by eight subcontractors. Post-war, the aircraft was operated by Australia, Belgium, Canada, the Irish Free State, Greece, Mexico, New Zealand, Norway, Peru, and Spain, and remained in RAF service until 1932.

Country of origin:	United Kingdom
Type:	two-seat fighter/army cooperation aircraft
Powerplant:	one 275hp (205kW) Rolls Royce Falcon III inline piston engine
Performance:	maximum speed 198km/h (123mph); service ceiling 5485m (18,000ft); endurance 3hrs
Weights:	empty 975kg (2150lb); maximum take-off weight 1474kg (3250lb)
Dimensions:	span 11.96m (39ft 3in); length 7.87m (25ft 10in); height 2.97m (9ft 9in); wing area 37.62 sq m (405 sq ft)
Armament:	one fixed forward-firing .303in Vickers machine gun, plus one or two .303 Lewis guns on flexible mount in rear cockpit; underwing racks with provision for up to 12 9kg (28lb) of bombs

Bristol Type 26 Pullman

First flown in August 1918, the Bristol Type 24 Braemar triplane bomber never saw service in its intended role and was scrapped in 1920. The second prototype, which flew in February 1919, was designated the Type 25 Braemar II and shared the same basic configuration, although the inadequate original powerplant of four 230hp (172kW) Armstrong Siddeley Puma engines was replaced by four Liberty engines. The Armistice ended the Air Ministry's requirement for long-range bomber aircraft and the third prototype Braemar was completed as the Type 26 Pullman 14-seat passenger transport. This was exhibited and well-received at the International Air Show at Olympia in 1920, whilst engaged in a programme of testing at the British test facility at Martlesham Heath, but was dismantled without ever entering production.

Country of origin:	United Kingdom
Type:	triplane heavy bomber
Powerplant:	four 400hp (298kW) Liberty 12 inline piston engines
Performance:	maximum speed 196km/h (122mph); absolute ceiling 5180m (17,000ft)
Weights:	empty 5084kg (11,208lb); maximum take-off weight 7490kg (16,512lb)
Dimensions:	span 24.89m (81ft 8in); length 15.7m (51ft 6in); height 6.3m (20ft 8in); wing area 176.97 sq m (1905 sq ft)

Bristol Type 32 Bullet

An unequal-span stagger-wing biplane with circular-section fuselage, the Type 32 Bullet was designed primarily as a company demonstrator for the Cosmos Jupiter engine. Great things were expected for this attractive little fighter, which first flew in the Aerial Derby of 1920, but the early performance estimates proved to be somewhat optimistic, and despite a continual series of revisions the Bullet never achieved its hoped-for potential. Only one was ever built and it is shown here in the configuration in which it flew into second place at the 1921 Aerial Derby at Croydon. For the next year's Aerial Derby the 380hp (283kW) Jupiter II engine was fitted, and in this trim the Bullet achieved its final racing success – second place at the hands of Rollo A. de Haga Haig. Although the Bullet was scrapped in 1924, the Jupiter engine became one of the most important engines of the inter-war period.

Country of origin:	United Kingdom
Type:	single-seat racing biplane
Powerplant:	one 450hp (336kW) Bristol Jupiter radial piston engine
Performance:	maximum speed 249km/h (155mph)
Weights:	empty 816kg (1800lb); maximum take-off weight 998kg (2200lb)
Dimensions:	span 9.51m (31ft 2in); length 7.35m (24ft 1in); height 2.95m (9ft 8in); wing area 27.41 sq m (295 sq ft)

Bristol Type 62 Ten-Seater

Pictured here in its original configuration with four-wheel main landing gear, the Type 62 Ten-Seater was designed for the newly established, government-subsidised post-war British air transport industry. The design was revised on the drawing board to accommodate nine passengers, as opposed to the proposed six, and although the plan was to power the aircraft with the Bristol Jupiter engine, the first prototype had a Napier Lion unit. The basic parts for four airframes were built, and the first assembled aircraft flew in June 1921. The front set of wheels was removed before the aircraft undertook flight trials at Croydon and Martlesham Heath during the summer. The Air Council procured the aircraft in December and sold it on to the Instone Air Line on the London–Paris route. Instone also purchased the second and fourth airframes, designated Type 75s, operating them until 1926. The fourth airframe became the Type 79 Brandon air ambulance.

Country of origin:	United Kingdom
Type:	ten-seat passenger transport biplane
Powerplant:	one 450hp (336kW) Napier Lion radial piston engine
Performance:	maximum speed 177km/h (110mph); service ceiling 2590m (8500ft); endurance 5hrs 30mins
Weights:	empty 1814kg (4000lb); maximum take-off weight 3064kg (6755lb)
Dimensions:	span 17.07m (56ft); length 12.34m (40ft 6in); height 3.35m (11ft); wing area 65.03 sq m (700 sq ft)

Bristol Type 105A Bulldog Mk IIA

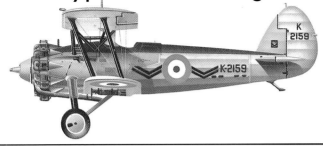

In September 1926 the British Air Ministry issued a requirement for a new single-seat day/night fighter aircraft powered by a radial air-cooled engine and armed with two .303 Vickers machine guns, to equip the RAF. No fewer than nine submissions were received, most of them powered by Bristol's Jupiter radial engine. The field was narrowed down to the Bristol Type 105 and the Hawker Hawfinch, designed by Sidney Camm, and after a stiff competition the Bristol design was selected for development. The prototype Bulldog Mk I flew for the first time in May 1927, and after the fuselage had been lengthened entered production as the Bulldog Mk II. The first aircraft was delivered to No 3 Squadron, RAF, in June 1929, powered by a 440hp (328kW) Bristol Jupiter engine. Pictured is the main production variant, Mk IIA (213 aircraft built), with larger fin, wider track main gear, bigger tyres, and an improved oil system.

Country of origin:	United Kingdom
Type:	single-seat biplane fighter
Powerplant:	one 490hp (365kW) Bristol Jupiter VIIF radial piston engine
Performance:	maximum speed 280km/h (174mph); service ceiling 8940m (29,300ft); range 482km (300 miles)
Weights:	empty 1008kg (2222lb); maximum take-off weight 1583kg (3490lb)
Dimensions:	span 10.3m (33ft 10in); length 7.7m (25ft 2in); height 2.7m (8ft 9in); wing area 28.47 sq m (307 sq ft)
Armament:	two fixed forward-firing .303in Vickers machine guns; underwing racks with provision for up to four 9kg (20lb) bombs

Bristol Type 105A Bulldog Mk IVa

Bristol built a private-venture Bulldog Mk IIIA in 1931 with a Mercury IVA radial engine and flew this unsuccessfully against the Gloster SS.19B in the competition to find a replacement for the Bulldog Mk IIA. In the event the SS.19B (Gauntlet) was selected for production, but Bristol remained faithful to the design and adapted it for four guns under Specification F.7/30 requirements with the designation Mk IV. Again, the company lost out to a Gloster submission, the SS.37 (Gladiator), primarily because of the superior top speed of the Gloster aircraft. A further Mk IV prototype was built and flown as the Mk IVA with Mercury IVS2, Perseus IA, and Mercury VIS2 engines. Some 17 of the Mk IVA variant were built for Finland with the Mercury VIS2, and delivered in January 1935. These aircraft were flown into combat in the Winter War of 1939–40, and were often fitted with ski-landing gear.

Country of origin:	United Kingdom
Type:	single-seat biplane fighter
Powerplant:	one 490hp (365kW) Bristol Mercury VIS2 radial piston engine
Performance:	maximum speed 280km/h (174mph); service ceiling 8940m (29,300ft); range 482km (300 miles)
Weights:	empty 1008kg (2222lb); maximum take-off weight 1583kg (3490lb)
Dimensions:	span 10.3m (33ft 10in); length 7.7m (25ft 2in); height 2.7m (8ft 9in); wing area 28.47 sq m (307 sq ft)
Armament:	four fixed forward-firing .303in Vickers machine guns; underwing racks with provision for up to four 9kg (20lb) bombs

Bristol Type 105D Bulldog Mk IIa

Demonstrations by Bristol pilots nurtured considerable interest in the Bulldog. Denmark placed an order in 1931 for four Mk IIA aircraft powered by an unsupercharged high-compression Jupiter VIFH engine, and equipped with Viet gas starter equipment and armed with Madsen machine guns. The four aircraft were delivered to No 1 Squadron from Bristol's Filton factory in March 1931, and three were still being used in the training role at the time of the German invasion in April 1940. A number of Bulldog Mk II/IIAs were exported, most of them with a Gnome-Rhône Jupiter VI engine, to Estonia (12), Denmark (4), Latvia (12), Siam (2), Sweden (11) and the US Navy (2). Pictured is a Mk IIA of 1.Eskadrille, Haerens Flvertropper (Danish Army aviation troops), based at Kastrup in 1933. Note the short-wave wireless aerial.

Country of origin:	United Kingdom
Type:	single-seat biplane fighter
Powerplant:	one 490hp (365kW) Bristol Jupiter VIIF radial piston engine
Performance:	maximum speed 280km/h (174mph); service ceiling 8940m (29,300ft); range 482km (300 miles)
Weights:	empty 1008kg (2222lb); maximum take-off weight 1583kg (3490lb)
Dimensions:	span 10.3m (33ft 10in); length 7.7m (25ft 2in); height 2.7m (8ft 9in); wing area 28.47 sq m (307 sq ft)
Armament:	two fixed forward-firing .303in Vickers machine guns; underwing racks with provision for up to four 9kg (20lb) bombs

British Army Aeroplane No. 1

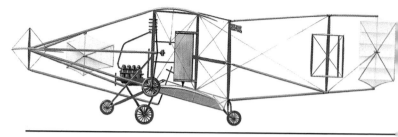

On 14 May 1909, at Laffan's Plain in Hampshire, Samuel Franklin Cody achieved the first aeroplane flight in Europe of more than 1.6km (1 mile) in his British Army Aeroplane No. 1 (named with typical military brevity). The aircraft was built in great secrecy in 1907 at the Army Balloon Factory at Farnborough, where Cody was engaged as the chief kiting instructor to the Royal Engineers' Balloon Corps. In October 1908 he made the first officially recognised aeroplane flight in the No.1, which borrowed many of the design features of the Wright Brothers' aircraft. For the British military aeroplane trials of 1912, Cody built a monoplane, but when this was wrecked in a landing collision with a cow, he reinstalled the 120hp (89kW) Austro-Daimler engine in a biplane. Despite its obsolescent design, this demonstrated sufficiently impressive performance to win the trials and the £5000 prize. No production orders were forthcoming.

Country of origin:	United Kingdom
Type:	single-seat biplane
Powerplant:	50hp (37kW) Antoinette inline piston engine
Performance:	maximum speed (based on similar Cody Michelin Cup biplane) 105km/h (65mph)
Weights:	maximum take-off weight 1338kg (2950lb)
Dimensions:	span 15.85m (52ft 4in); length 11.73m (38ft 6in); height 3.96m (13ft); wing area 59.46 sq m (640 sq ft)

CAMS 55/2

The Chantiers Aéro-Maritimes de la Seine (CAMS) was founded in 1920 to manufacture seaplanes and speedboats. Its first products were license-built Savio-Marchetti S.9 and S.13 types, but after CAMS engaged the designer of these boats, Rafaele Confleti, it embarked on a series of successful flying-boats. In 1923 Confleti was replaced by Maurice Hurel, who designed the twin-engine biplane CAMS 51 flying-boat in 1926, from which the CAMS 45 GR (Grand Raid), CAMS 53 and CAMS 55 were developed. The CAMS 53 was the most successful French commercial flying-boat of its era, operating in a mail- and passenger-carrying role on Mediterranean and North African routes until 1936. The military CAMS 55 made its maiden flight in 1928 with Hurel at the controls. Production orders followed for 34 55/1s, 29 55/2s and 32 55/10s with greater fuel capacity and Gnome-Rhône Mistral 9Kbr engines.

Country of origin:	France
Type:	long-range maritime reconnaissance flying-boat
Powerplant:	two 480hp (358kW) Gnome-Rhône Jupiter 9Akx radial piston engines
Performance:	maximum speed 195km/h (121mph); service ceiling 3400m (11,155ft); maximum range 1875km (1165 miles)
Weights:	empty 4590kg (10,119lb); maximum take-off weight 6900kg (15,212lb)
Dimensions:	span 20.4m (66ft 11in); length 15.03m (49ft 3in); height 5.41m (17ft 9in); wing area 113.45 sq m (1221 sq ft)
Armament:	two .303in Lewis machine guns in bow cockpit; two .303in Lewis machine guns in midships cockpit; underwing racks with provision for two 75kg (165lb) bombs

CANT Z.501

Cantiere Navale Triestino (CANT) was established in 1923 as a subsidiary of the Cantiere Navali di Monfalcone shipbuilding company. After securing the services of ex-CAMS employee Rafaele Confleti it began production of flying-boats. In 1931 CANT was reorganised as Cantieri Riuniti dell'Adriatico (CRDA), and Fillipo Zappata took over the mantle of chief designer. The Regia Aeronautica required a long-range reconnaissance flying-boat and Zappata designed the CANT Z.501 in response. This had a wooden lower hull, with fabric-covered upper hull, biplane wing and flying surfaces, and was powered by a single tractor engine mounted directly onto the top wing. The prototype first flew in February 1934, and soon established several distance records. The first production aircraft entered service in 1937 and was used in support of Nationalist forces in Spain. By June 1940 more than 200 were in service with 17 squadrons, wartime production adding another 154.

Country of origin:	Italy
Type:	four/five-man long-range reconnaissance flying-boat
Powerplant:	one 900hp (671kW) Isotta-Fraschini Asso XI RC radial piston engine
Performance:	maximum speed 275km/h (171mph); service ceiling 3962m (13,000ft); range 2397km (1490 miles)
Weights:	empty 3840kg (8466lb); maximum take-off weight 7305kg(15510lb)
Dimensions:	span 22.5m (73ft 10in); length 14.3m (46ft 11in); height 4.42m (14ft 6in); wing area 62 sq m (667 sq ft)
Armament:	one 7.7mm machine gun on flexible mount in front cockpit (later replaced by an enclosed observation position); one 7.7mm machine gun on flexible mount in midships cockpit; one 7.7mm machine gun on flexible mount in engine nacelle position; underwing racks with provision for 640kg (1411lb) of bombs

CRDA (CANT) Z.506B Airone

The Z.506 was derived from the Z.505 prototype that was planned as a mailplane to connect Italy with its East Africa colonies. The aircraft was subsequently placed in production as a 15-passenger civil transport (20 aircraft) before production switched to the CRDA (CANT) Z.506B Airone (heron) military derivative. This aircraft entered service in 1938 with a ventral gondola for the bomb bay, the glazed bomb aimers position and a gunners position. Production of the Z.506B totalled some 324 aircraft, of which 95 were in service at the time of Italy's entry into World War II. The type was initially operated in the bomber role, but then revised with stronger defensive armament and reassigned to the maritime reconnaissance, convoy escort, and anti-submarine roles. A number of aircraft were also converted to the Z.506S standard for the air-sea-rescue task, and a number were retained in service until 1959.

Country of origin:	Italy
Type:	five-seat maritime reconnaissance and bomber floatplane
Powerplant:	three 750hp (559kW) Alfa Romeo 126 RC.34 9-cylinder single-row radial engines
Performance:	maximum speed 350km/h (217mph); service ceiling 8000m (26,245ft); range 1705 miles (2745 km)
Weights:	empty 8300kg (18,298lb); maximum take-off 12,705kg (28,008lb)
Dimensions:	span 26.50m (86ft 11in); length 19.24mn (63ft 1in); height 7.45m (24ft 5in)
Armament:	one 12.7mm trainable machine gun in the dorsal turret; one 7.7mm trainable rearward-firing machine gun in the rear of the ventral gondola; one 7.7mm trainable lateral-firing machine gun in each of the two lateral positions; internal bomb load of 1200kg (2646lb)

Caproni Ca.1

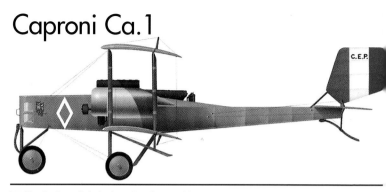

The Societa di Aviazione Ing Caproni in Italy and Igor Sikorsky in Russia showed remarkable foresight in producing the first heavy bombers. Caproni flew the Ca.30 bomber in 1913, at a time when the British had no explicit military aircraft and little compulsion to use them. The Ca.30 had a short central nacelle with three 80hp (60kW) Gnome rotary engines, one driving a pusher screw, the others geared to tractor propellers on the tail booms. The later Ca.31 first flew in late 1914 with three 100hp (75kW) Fiat A.10 engines mounted on the front of the tail booms; it was put into production as the Ca.1. Some 162 aircraft were produced before production switched to the Ca.2, with the central engine replaced by a 150hp (112kW) Isotta-Fraschini V.4B, and the main production variant, the Ca.3, with three Isotta-Fraschini V.4Bs. The latter gave rise to a post-war development, the 36M. Pictured is a Ca.1 of the Aéronautique Militaire, on the Plateau de Malzéville during 1916.

Country of origin:	Italy
Type:	four-seat heavy day bomber
Powerplant:	three 100hp (75kW) Fiat A.10 6-cylinder piston engines
Performance:	maximum speed 116km/h (72mph); range 550km (340 miles)
Weights:	empty 2500kg (5512lb); maximum take-off weight 3302kg (7280lb)
Dimensions:	span 22.2m (72ft 10in); length 10.9m (35ft 9in); height 3.7m (12ft 2in)
Armament:	one or two 7.7mm Revelli machine guns on flexible mount in front cockpit; plus a maximum bomb load of 850kg (1874lb)

Caproni Ca.3

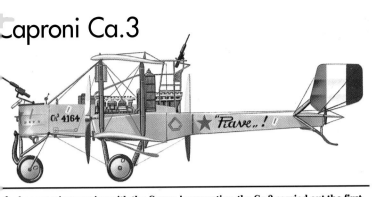

After entering service with the Corpo Aeronautica, the Ca.2 carried out the first Italian bombing raids of the war on 25 August 1915, and soon established a proud tradition of arduous missions on the Austro–Hungarian front over difficult mountainous terrain for what were essentially extremely flimsy aircraft. They were followed into service in 1917 by the Ca.3. This aircraft had more powerful engines and greater bomb-load, and was undoubtedly the most successful Allied bomber of the war. Some 83 Ca.3s were built under licence in France by Robert Esnault-Pelterie, and equipped two units of the Aéronautique Militaire. At the beginning of 1918 the Ca.5 was introduced, although this designation in fact encompassed three different aircraft – the Ca.44, Ca.45, and Ca.46. Pictured is a Ca.3 of Squadriglia VII, Gruppo XI of the Corpo Aeronautica.

Country of origin:	Italy
Type:	four-seat heavy day bomber
Powerplant:	150hp (112kW) Isotta-Fraschini V.4B inline piston engines
Performance:	maximum speed 140km/h (87mph); service ceiling 4100m (13,450ft); range 450km (280 miles)
Weights:	empty 2300kg (5071lb); maximum take-off weight 3312kg (7302lb)
Dimensions:	span 22.2m (72ft 10in); length 10.9m (35ft 9in); height 3.7m (12ft 2in)
Armament:	two or four 7.7mm Revelli machine guns on flexible mounts in cockpit positions; plus a maximum bomb load of 450kg (992lb)

Caudron R.11

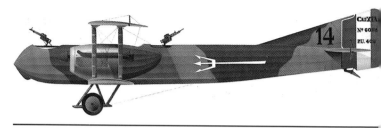

The Caudron brothers, René and Gaston, began design and manufacture of aircraft in 1909 and during the war built a very successful series of artillery observation aircraft under designation G.3. Former Aviation Militaire pilot Paul Delville took over the job of chief designer when Gaston was killed testing the R.4 twin-engine reconnaissance/bomber aircraft. Delville improved on the R.4 design with the R.5 and R.10 prototypes, but it was the R.11 that proved most successful. This owed much to the R.4 having a full length fuselage, single fin and rudder, unequal-span wings and twin tractor engines, but the R.11 differed by having a more streamlined nose, no nose wheel, and engines mounted in nacelles. Production began in 1917, though the first aircraft were not delivered until February 1918. The R.11 was not used for reconnaissance, but as an escort fighter for bomber formations. Pictured is an R.11 of Escadrille C.46, Aviation Militaire, flown by the bombers of the 13e Escadre in 1918.

Country of origin:	France
Type:	three-seat escort fighter
Powerplant:	two 215hp (160kW) Hispano-Suiza 8Bba inline piston engines
Performance:	maximum speed 183km/h (114mph); service ceiling 5950m (19,520ft); endurance 3hrs
Weights:	empty 1422kg (3135lb); maximum take-off weight 2167kg (4777lb)
Dimensions:	span 17.92m (58ft 9in); length 11.22m (36ft 9in); height 2.8m (9ft 2in); wing area 54.25 sq m (584 sq ft)
Armament:	two .303in Lewis machine guns on flexible mount in front cockpit; two .303in Lewis machine guns on flexible mount in rear cockpit; one .303in Lewis machine gun on fixed mount in the front cockpit firing downwards and to the rear

Consolidated Catalina IIA

In 1993 Douglas and Consolidated entered the battle to supply the US Navy with its first cantilever monoplane flying-boat to replace the P2Y-2s and Y-3s. Douglas' entry was good but could not beat Isaac M. Landon's design, which evolved into one of the greatest aircraft in history. The XP3Y-1 prototype followed the same general configuration of its predecessor, with a parasol-mounted wing, but the introduction of internal bracing and retractable wingtip stabilising floats significantly reduced drag. First flown in March 1935, the XP3Y-1 was transferred to the Navy for trials, and after minor modifications to improve the performance an order for 60 PBY-1s was awarded in June 1935. The second production batch, designated PBY-2, had minor equipment changes, while the PBY-3 and PBY-4 introduced the Wright R-1830-66 and R-1830-72 engines. Pictured is a Catalina Mk GR Mk IIA, the British service designation for ex-RCAF aircraft fitted with ASV.II radar.

Country of origin:	USA
Type:	seven/nine-seat patrol flying-boat
Powerplant:	two 1200hp (895kW) Pratt & Whitney R-1830-92 Wasp radial piston engines
Performance:	maximum speed 288km/h (179mph); service ceiling 4480m (14,700ft); range 4096km (2545 miles)
Weights:	empty 9485kg (20,910lb); maximum take-off weight 16,066kg (35,420lb)
Dimensions:	span 30.48m (100ft); length 18.82m (61ft 9in); height 5.82m (19ft 1in); wing area 140.65 sq m (1514 sq ft)
Armament:	one .303in Vickers K machine gun on flexible mount in nose position; one .303in Vickers K machine gun on flexible mount in tunnel; two .303in Browning machine guns on flexible mount in each of the two dorsal blisters; plus a bomb load of 907kg (2000lb)

Consolidated Catalina IVA

In 1939 the British tested a Consolidated PBY-4 and were so impressed with its performance that an open-ended order was immediately placed and the rights for licensed production were acquired for the Canadian Vickers works at Montreal. The first Royal Air Force variant had the service designation Catalina Mk I; this was similar to the PBY-5, a strengthened version of the PBY-4 with 1200hp (895kW) Pratt & Whitney R-1830-92 radial engines and modified vertical tail. After the Lend-Lease Act had been passed the RAF received 225 PBY-5Bs (a non-amphibious version of the PBY-5A of 1940), followed by 97 Catalina IVAs with ASV Mk II radar. Pictured is Catalina IVA of No 210 Squadron, RAF, wearing the standard colour scheme adopted by maritime patrol aircraft in 1942. Some 650 Catalinas were delivered to the RAF Coastal Command during World War II and these proved instrumental in operations against U-boats in the North Atlantic.

Country of origin:	USA
Type:	nine-seat maritime reconnaissance and bomber flying-boat
Powerplant:	two 1200hp (895kW) Pratt & Whitney R-1830-92 Twin Wasp, 14-cylinder, two-row radial engines
Performance:	maximum speed 288km/h (179mph); service ceiling 4480m (14,700ft); range 5713 km (3550 miles)
Weights:	empty 9485kg (20,910lb); maximum take-off 16,067kg (35,420lb)
Dimensions:	span 31.70m (104ft); length 19.45m (63ft 10in); height 5.76m (18ft 11in); wing area 130 sq m (1400 sq ft)
Armament:	one .303in Vickers K machine gun on flexible mount in nose position; one .303in Vickers K machine gun on flexible mount in tunnel; two .303in Browning machine guns on flexible mount in each of the two dorsal blisters; plus a bomb load of 907kg (2000lb)

Consolidated Model 16 Commodore

The Model 16 Commodore was a passenger-carrying development of the Consolidated P2Y, with 22-seater accommodation and twin 575hp (429kW) Pratt & Whitney Hornet radial engines. Fourteen aircraft were sold to the New York, Rio and Buenos Aires Line, which was set up to operate services from Miami through the West Indies to South America. The type was used to inaugurate a direct Miami–Santiago route on 18 February 1930, at the height of a bitter struggle between Pan American and NYRBA for control of the eastern coastal routes. However, Pan American had the lucrative US mail contract from Miami to Paramaribo and influential friends in South America, and by the time Pan American had been handed the through-mail contract to Buenos Aires on 24 September 1930, it had already taken over NYBRA company and inherited the entire fleet of Commodores.

Country of origin:	USA
Type:	commercial transport flying-boat
Powerplant:	two 575hp (429kW) Pratt & Whitney Hornet radial piston engines
Performance:	maximum speed 224km/h (139mph); service ceiling 4905m (16,100ft); range 1899km (1180 miles)
Weights:	empty 5792kg (12,769lb); maximum take-off weight 11,460kg (25,266lb)
Dimensions:	span 30.48m (100ft); length 18.82m (61ft 9in); height 5.82m (19ft 1in); wing area 140.65 sq m (1514 sq ft)

Consolidated N4Y-1 (Model 21-A)

The Consolidated PT-1 was essentially a revised and re-engined version of the Dayton-Wright TW-3, one of the assets inherited by the Consolidated company when it was formed from Gallaudet and Dayton Wright in 1923. A production contract for 221 PT-1s was fulfilled. The US Navy adapted a version of the PT-1 which it designated the NY-1. This had structural changes to allow float gear to be fitted and a Wright Whirlwind J-4 or J-5 engine. The most prolific of the many versions were the NY-2, which had larger wing span (211 built), the NY-3 which incorporated the changes made to the NY-2 and was powered by a Wright R-760-94 (20 built), the Army Air Corps PT-3 with Wright J-5 and revised tail surfaces (250), and the O-17 with increased fuel capacity and improved streamlining (29). Pictured is the single example of the N4Y-1, a US Coast Guard PT-11 converted by installing an Avco Lycoming R-680.

Country of origin:	USA
Type:	two-seat primary trainer
Powerplant:	one 220hp (164kW) Avoc Lycoming R-680 radial piston engine
Performance:	maximum speed 190km/h (118mph); service ceiling 4175m (13,700ft); endurance 3hrs
Weights:	empty 870kg (1918lb); maximum take-off weight 1173kg (2585lb)
Dimensions:	span 9.63m (31ft 7in); length 8.2m (26ft 11in); height 2.95m (9ft 8in); wing area 26.01 sq m (280 sq ft)

Consolidated PB2Y Coronado

The XPB2Y-1 prototype was ordered by the US Navy in 1936. The Navy had perceived a need for a patrol flying-boat offering increased performance and weapons-carrying capability over the PBY-1 then entering service. The aircraft was delivered to the Navy in early 1938 following a first flight in December 1937, and after assessment against the Sikorsky XPBS-1 was adjudged to be the most suitable of the two for production. A number of problems were highlighted during flight testing, including serious lateral instability, but the delayed procurement enabled Consolidated to rectify these before the US Navy ordered six in March 1939 under the designation PB2Y-2 Coronado for use as service trials aircraft. Deliveries to VP-13 began in December 1940. The main production variant (210 built) was the PBY2-3 Coronado, which had increased armament and self-sealing tanks. Late production aircraft had ASV radar, and various engines were retrofitted.

Country of origin:	USA
Type:	nine-seat maritime patrol flying-boat
Powerplant:	four 1200hp (895kW) Pratt & Whitney R-1830-88 Twin Wasp, 14-cylinder, two-row radial engines
Performance:	maximum speed 359km/h (223mph); service ceiling 6250m (20,500ft); range 3814km (2370 miles)
Weights:	empty 18,568kg (40,935lb); maximum take-off weight 30,844kg (68,000lb)
Dimensions:	span 35.05m (115ft); length 24.16m (79ft 3in); height 8.38m (27ft 6in); wing area 165.36 sq m (1780 sq ft)
Armament:	two 0.5 in machine guns in bow turret; two 0.5 in machine guns in ventral turret; two 0.5 in machine guns in tail turret; one 0.5in trainable lateral-firing machine gun in each of two 'beam' positions; provision for up to 5443kg (12,000lb) of bombs in an internal bay

Consolidated P2Y-2

Captain Dick Richardson designed a monoplane flying-boat in 1927 to specifications laid down by a US Navy requirement. This had a fabric-covered parasol wing and aluminium skinned hull and, after winning a contract, first flew in prototype form (XPY-1) in January 1929. Much to Consolidated's chagrin a production contract for nine aircraft was awarded to the rival Glenn L. Martin company of Baltimore, and these were built under the designation P3M-1 and P3M-2. In May 1931 Consolidated received another US Navy contract for development of an improved XP2Y-1. This had an enclosed cockpit, a small lower wing, and three Wright R-1820E Cyclone radials, and first flew in March 1932. After testing the third engine was removed and in this form the aircraft was produced as the P2Y-1 (23 built). The last production P2Y-1 was fitted with twin R-1820-88 engines in wing fairings, and in 1936 all P2Y-1s in service were converted to this P2Y-2 standard.

Country of origin:	USA
Type:	five-seat patrol flying-boat
Powerplant:	two 750hp (559kW) Wright R-1820-88 Cyclone radial piston engines
Performance:	maximum speed 224km/h (139mph); service ceiling 4905m (16,100ft); range 1899km (1180 miles)
Weights:	empty 5792kg (12,769lb); maximum take-off weight 11,460kg (25,266lb)
Dimensions:	span 30.48m (100ft); length 18.82m (61ft 9in); height 5.82m (19ft 1in); wing area 140.65 sq m (1514 sq ft)
Armament:	one .3in Browning machine gun on flexible mount in bow position; one .3in Browning machine gun on flexible mount in each of the two dorsal hatches; plus a bomb load of 907kg (2000lb)

Consolidated PBY-5A

The XPBY-5A prototype first flew in November 1939, improving the versatility of the PBY series with the introduction of retractable tricycle landing gear at only a minor cost to performance. Some 33 PBY-5s were converted to PBY-5A standard on the line, and there followed a further 761 for the US Navy, Royal Canadian Air Force (as the Canso) and the Royal Air Force (Catalina Mk III). In 1942 the USAAF received the first of 56 PBY-5As for use in the search-and-rescue role, and in this service the aircraft were designated OA-10. The PBY-5A was also built in Canada as the Canadian Vickers PVB-1A, and the USAAF received another 230 Canadian Vickers-built amphibians that in service became OA-10As. Pictured is one of the unarmed OA-10As amphibians that passed from the USAAF's Air Rescue Service to the newly formed USAF in October 1947. The type remained in service with the USAF until 1954.

Country of origin:	USA
Type:	nine-seat maritime reconnaissance/bomber amphibian flying-boat
Powerplant:	two 1200hp (895kW) Pratt & Whitney R-1830-92 Twin Wasp, 14-cylinder, two-row radial engines
Performance:	maximum speed 288km/h (179mph); service ceiling 3960m (13,000ft); range with full load 3782km (2350 miles)
Weights:	empty 9485kg (20,910lb); maximum take-off 16,067kg (35,420lb)
Dimensions:	span 31.70m (104ft); length 19.45m (63ft 10in); height 6.15m (20ft 2in); wing area 130sq m (1400 sq ft)
Armament:	two 0.3 in trainable forward-firing machine guns in bow turret; one 0.3in trainable rearward-firing machine gun in ventral tunnel; one 0.5in trainable lateral-firing machine gun in each 'blister' position; external load of 2041kg (4500lb)

Consolidated PBY-6A

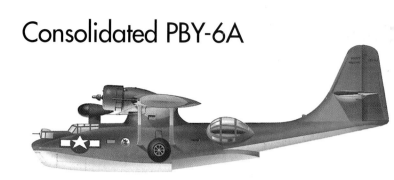

Further development of the amphibian resulted in the PBY-6A (235 machines) with revised armament and an enlarged tail, and the Naval Aircraft Factory PBN-1 Nomad (156 machines) to a PBY-5A standard improved with a larger tail unit, greater fuel capacity and revised armament. Boeing adopted the PBY-5 and -6A under the designation PB2B-1 and -2 respectively. These were supplied under the Lend-Lease Act to the Royal New Zealand Air Force, Royal Australian Air Force and RAF as the Catalina Mk IVB and VI. The aircraft pictured was one of the last Catalinas built, and one of the few delivered from the Consolidated-Vultee (after March 1943) plant at New Orleans. Note the pylon-mounted radar and nose turret containing twin 0.5in guns. The PBY-6A was finally retired from US military service in 1957, and the last in service with Latin American air forces were retired in 1966. Many ex-military machines were converted as transport and water bombers.

Country of origin:	USA
Type:	nine-seat maritime reconnaissance/bomber amphibian flying-boat
Powerplant:	two 1200hp (895kW) Pratt & Whitney R-1830-92 Twin Wasp, 14-cylinder, two-row radial engines
Performance:	maximum speed 288km/h (179mph); service ceiling 4480m (14,700ft); range 5713km (3550 miles)
Weights:	empty 9485kg (20,910lb); maximum take-off weight 16,067kg (35,420lb)
Dimensions:	span 31.70m (104ft); length 19.45m (63ft 10in); height 5.76m (18ft 11in)
Armament:	two 0.5 in trainable forward-firing machine guns in bow turret; one 0.3in trainable rearward-firing machine gun in ventral tunnel; one 0.5in trainable lateral-firing machine gun in each 'blister' position; external load of 2041kg (4500lb)

Curtiss BF2C-1

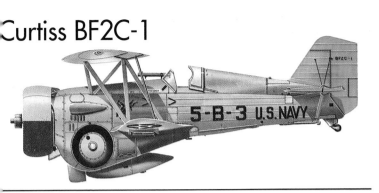

The US Navy attached great importance to dive-bombing and in the 1930s the Curtiss Goshawk family became well known in this role. The BF2C-1 was developed from the Model 35 Hawk II fighter, which was basically a P-6E with a radial engine and partially faired mainwheels. Two of these, designated XF11C-1 and XF11C-2, were purchased by the US Navy, powered by a 700hp (522kW) Curtiss V-1570-23 Conqueror and 600hp (447kW) Wright R-1510 Whirlwind engine respectively. The Navy ordered 28 F11C-2 production aircraft in October 1932, equipped with a special crutch for launching a 227kg (500lb) bomb in a dive. One of the F11C-2 production aircraft was modified with manually retracting landing gear (XFB2C-1), resulting in a US Navy order for 27 BF2C-1s that were delivered from October 1934. However, serious problems with the landing gear were encountered, prompting the swift withdrawal of this type. F11C-2s served until 1938.

Country of origin:	USA
Type:	single-seat dive-bomber
Powerplant:	one 600hp (448kW) Wright SR-1820F2 Cyclone radial piston engine
Performance:	maximum speed 325km/h (202mph); service ceiling 7650m (25,100ft); range 840km (522 miles)
Weights:	empty equipped 1378kg (3037lb); maximum take-off weight 1874kg (4132lb)
Dimensions:	span 9.6m (31ft 6in); length 6.88m (22ft 7in); height 2.96m (9ft 8in); wing area 24.34 sq m (262 sq ft)
Armament:	two fixed forward-firing .3in machine guns; underfuselage crutch for one 227kg (500lb) bomb, or four 51kg (112lb) bombs on underwing racks

Curtiss JN-4

The famous Curtiss 'Jenny' was one of the most important American aircraft of the inter-war period. The JN-4 has its origins in the Curtiss J, designed in 1914 by B. Douglas Thomas and used in operations against Pancho Villa's Mexican revolutionaries in 1916. The J evolved into the JN-2, and then the JN-3. This last aircraft was built in numbers totalling 100 aircraft for the US Army and the UK. The JN-4 in its original form closely resembled the JN-3, with the same unequal-span two-bay biplane wing and cross-axle main gear, and first appeared in 1916. The British took 105 and 21 went to the US Army, before the improved JN-4A and JN-4B appeared with larger tailplanes. Some 857 of these two types were built. The JN-4 Can (pictured here in the colours of the School of Aerial Fighting in 1918) was one of many civil and military versions. It was developed by Canadian Aeroplanes Ltd, which built 1260 of this aircraft.

Country of origin:	USA
Type:	two-seat primary trainer
Powerplant:	one 90hp (67kW) Curtiss OX-5 inline piston engine
Performance:	maximum speed 121km/h (75mph); service ceiling 1980m (6500ft)
Weights:	empty 630kg (1390lb); maximum take-off weight 871kg (1920lb)
Dimensions:	span 13.3m (43ft 8in); length 8.33m (27ft 4in); height 3.01m (9ft 10in); wing area 32.7 sq m (352 sq ft)

Curtiss Model 33/34 (PW-8)

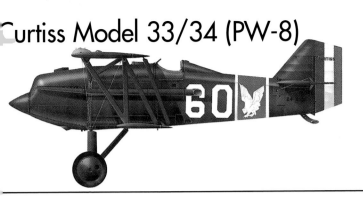

The inspiration that Curtiss gained from the company's racing activities is clearly visible in the designs of its fighter aircraft. In early 1922 Curtiss began development of a new fighter design, the L-18-1, which clearly owed much to the R-6. By the end of the year this had become the prototype PW-8, which flew in January 1923. It was a two-bay biplane with considerable wing stagger, a streamlined fuselage of metal construction, powered by a Curtiss D-12 engine. Following service trials of three prototypes with the US Army during the spring, an order for 25 production aircraft was received. Deliveries began in June 1924. The second prototype was modified with tapered wings for the 1924 Pulitzer Trophy, and took third place at this competition. This XPW-8B formed the basis for the new Curtiss Hawk P-1.

Country of origin:	USA
Type:	single-seat fighter biplane
Powerplant:	one 440hp (328kW) Curtiss D-12 12-cylinder Vee piston engine
Performance:	maximum speed 275km/h (171mph); service ceiling 6205m (20,350ft); range 875km (544 miles)
Weights:	empty 991kg (2185lb); maximum take-off weight 1431kg (3155lb)
Dimensions:	span 9.75m (32ft); length 7.03m (23ft 1in); height 2.76m (9ft 1in); wing area 25.94 sq m (279 sq ft)
Armament:	two fixed forward-firing .3in Browning machine guns

Curtiss Model 77 (SBC-3 Helldiver)

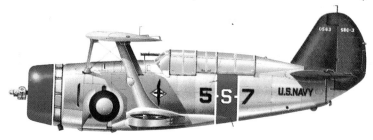

In its original form, as ordered by the US Navy in prototype form in 1932 under the designation XF12C-1, the Model 73 was a two-seat monoplane fighter. It was subsequently decided to use the aircraft in a scouting capacity and its designation was changed to XS4C-1. Flight testing during late 1934 proved the unsuitability of a parasol wing to dive bombing, and a new prototype was ordered as the XSBC-2 (Model 77), which had staggered biplane wings and a Wright R-1510-12 engine. In 1936 this was changed to the Pratt & Whitney R-1535-82 and the new designation XSBC-3 was adopted. In this form the aircraft was ordered by the US Navy as the SBC-3 Helldiver. Deliveries began in July 1936, to VS-5. A late production SBC-3 was used as a prototype for the SBC-4, of which 174 examples were ordered for the US Navy, the first arriving in March 1939. Fifty examples were acquired by France in 1940, but they were received too late to see combat.

Country of origin:	USA
Type:	two-seat carrier-based scout bomber
Powerplant:	one 700hp (522kW) Pratt & Whitney R-1535-82 Twin Wasp radial piston engine
Performance:	maximum speed 377km/h (234mph); service ceiling 7315m (24,000ft); range with 227kg (500lb) bomb 652km (405 miles)
Weights:	empty 2065kg (4552lb); maximum take-off weight 3211kg (7080lb)
Dimensions:	span 10.36m (34ft); length 8.57m (28ft 1in); height 3.17m (10ft 5in); wing area 29.45 sq m (317 sq ft)
Armament:	one fixed forward-firing .3in machine gun; one .3in machine gun on flexible mount, underfuselage rack for one 227kg (500lb) bomb

Curtiss Model O-1G

The winner of the US Army's 1925 competition for a light observation aircraft to be powered by a Packard engine was the Curtiss XO-1, which had lost out to the Liberty-engined Douglas XO-2 in the previous year's competition. The Packard engine was not a success and the ten production O-1s were powered by the Curtiss V-1150. This was standard to the O-1 aircraft, including the O-1B, which incorporated refinements such as wheel brakes and an underbelly jettisonable fuel tank (45 built for the USAAC); the O-1C VIP transport with larger rear cockpit and a baggage compartment (4 converted from O-1B standard); O-1E with refinements to control surfaces and engine cowling (41). The O-1G had redesigned tail surfaces and a steerable tail wheel. Thirty were delivered to the USAAC, bringing production of the O-1 to 127.

Country of origin:	USA
Type:	two-seat observation biplane
Powerplant:	one 435hp (324kW) Curtiss V-1150E inline piston engine
Performance:	maximum speed 227km/h (141mph); service ceiling 4665m (15,300ft); range 1014km (630 miles)
Weights:	empty equipped 1325kg (2922lb); maximum take-off weight 1972kg (4347lb)
Dimensions:	span 11.58m (38ft); length 8.28m (27ft 2in); height 3.2m (10ft 6in); wing area 32.79 sq m (353 sq ft)
Armament:	one fixed forward-firing .3in Browning machine gun; twin .3in Lewis machine guns on Scarff ring mounting in rear cockpit

Curtiss Model O-39 Falcon

Two variants of the Curtiss V-1150-engined O-1 Falcon were produced. The A-3 was a light bomber version of the O-1E for the US Army with twin .3in machine guns mounted on the lower wing and underwing racks, with provision for 91kg (200lb) of bombs. Production of the A-3 totalled 66 aircraft; six of these were converted as A-3A dual control trainers, followed by 78 A-3Bs which incorporated the improvements applied to the O-1E. The O-11 was the first of the Liberty-engined Falcons, some 66 of which were built from 1927. Several more one-off variants with different powerplants were evolved (XO-11 to XO-18). The final production version for the Army was the O-39, a Curtiss V-1570-engined variant similar to the O-1G, with smaller rudder, spatted wheels, radiator sourced from the P-6E Hawk, and on some, a glazed canopy.

Country of origin:	USA
Type:	two-seat observation biplane
Powerplant:	one 700hp (522kW) Curtiss V-1570-25 Conqueror inline piston engine
Performance:	maximum speed 227km/h (141mph); service ceiling 4665m (15,300ft); range 1014km (630 miles)
Weights:	empty equipped 1325kg (2922lb); maximum take-off weight 1972kg (4347lb)
Dimensions:	span 11.58m (38ft); length 8.28m (27ft 2in); height 3.2m (10ft 6in); wing area 32.79 sq m (353 sq ft)
Armament:	one fixed forward-firing .3in Browning machine gun

Curtiss NC

In 1909, having gained experience of aeronautics with Alexander Graham Bell's Aerial Experimental Association, Glenn Curtiss produced his first aircraft, the Curtiss No. 1 Golden Flyer. Curtiss also devoted much energy to the development of seaplanes and was perhaps the leading authority in this field at the outbreak of the war. His Model F was ordered into scale production for the US Navy and sold to a number of foreign navies. In 1917 he worked with the US Navy Board of Construction and Repair to produce an aircraft capable of routine transatlantic flights. The finalised design was for a wide-span biplane with three tractor engines and twin-boom mounted biplane tail, powered by three engines. The production order was for ten, but only NC-1 had been delivered when the war ended, and the order was cut to four. Another Liberty engine was later added to the central nacelle driving a pusher crew. Pictured is the sole NC-4, which is preserved in the US Naval Air Museum.

Country of origin:	USA
Type:	long-range flying-boat
Powerplant:	four 400hp (298kW) Liberty 12A inline piston engines
Performance:	maximum speed 137km/h (85mph); service ceiling 7600m (24,928ft); endurance 14hrs 45mins
Weights:	empty 7257kg (16,000lb); maximum take-off weight 12,701kg (28,000lb)
Dimensions:	span 38.4m (126ft); length 20.8m (68ft 3in); height 7.44m (24ft 5in); wing area 226.77 sq m (2441 sq ft)

Curtiss P-1B

The second XPW-8 prototype was modified at the behest of the US Army Air Corps to feature redesigned wings, and became the XPW-8B. However, during testing, problems associated with wing flutter prompted Curtiss to revert to the single-bay wing of the R-6 for the production P-1 Hawk. Ten were ordered in March 1925, and these differed from the prototype only in having extra centre-section bracing and a modified rudder. Service trials at McCook Field began in mid-August prior to delivery to the 27th and 94th Pursuit Squadrons at Selfridge Field, Michigan. The initial contract also covered production of five additional aircraft with the 505hp (377kW) Curtiss V-1400 engine, designated P-2. Continuing development of the P-1 resulted in the P-1A, with a lengthened fuselage, modified cowling and Curtiss D-12C engine. Twenty-five were ordered in September 1925, followed by 23 P-1Bs (pictured), and 33 P-1Cs with a V-1150 engine.

Country of origin:	USA
Type:	single-seat pursuit aircraft
Powerplant:	one 435hp (324kW) Curtiss V-1150-3 piston engine
Performance:	maximum speed 248km/h (154mph); service ceiling 6344m (20,800ft); range 1046km (650 miles)
Weights:	empty 970kg (2136lb); all-up weight 1349kg (2973lb)
Dimensions:	span 9.6m (31ft 6in); length 7.06m (23ft 2in); height 2.72m (8ft 11in); wing area 23.41 sq m (252 sq ft)
Armament:	two fixed forward-firing .3in machine guns

Curtiss P-6D Hawk

To produce the prototype XP-6 Hawk, Curtiss took the airframe of a P-1 and installed a Curtiss V-1570 Conqueror engine. This was flown into second place at the 1927 National Air Races at Skopane, Washington. A second (XP-A) conversion had the same Conqueror engine, untapered wings, and drag-reducing wing radiators, and took first place at the then remarkable speed of 201mph (323km/h). The US Army contracted Curtiss for 18 P-6s for evaluation, which had modified cowl and deeper fuselage. Nine had the 'Prestone' cooling system (including the aircraft pictured) and were designated P-6A. One of these was used as trials aircraft for the turbo-charged V-1570C Conqueror engine driving a three-blade screw. In the spring of 1932 all the P-6s were re-engined with this unit, becoming P-6Ds. The XP-6B, which flew from the eastern United States to Alaska, was a P-1C fitted with the same V-1570 engine.

Country of origin:	USA
Type:	single-seat pursuit aircraft
Powerplant:	one 700hp (522kW) Curtiss V-1570C Conqueror inline piston engine
Performance:	maximum speed 319km/h (198mph); service ceiling 7530m (24,700ft); range 459km (285 miles)
Weights:	empty equipped 1224kg (2669lb); maximum take-off weight 1559kg (3436lb)
Dimensions:	span 9.6m (31ft 6in); length 7.06m (23ft 2in); height 2.72m (8ft 11in); wing area 23.41 sq m (252 sq ft)
Armament:	two fixed forward-firing .3in machine guns

Curtiss P-6E Hawk

Most prolific and impressive of the P-6 Hawk family was the P-6E, which was the last biplane fighter to be delivered to the United States Army Air Corps. This was generally similar to the P-6D, but had a slimmer forward fuselage with the engine radiator mounted slightly forward of the landing gear, which comprised single-strut main legs with spat type wheel fairings. Forty-six were ordered in July 1931 at a unit cost of $12,211, and deliveries were completed by the end of the next year. The aircraft demonstrated exceptional manoeuvrability and useful top speed, serving with the 1st and 8th Pursuit Groups. One P-6E was powered by an unsupercharged V-1570F engine and designated XP-6G. The Arctic Owl paint scheme of this P-6E identifies it as belonging to the 17th Squadron of the 1st Pursuit Group, while based at Selfridge Field.

Country of origin:	USA
Type:	single-seat pursuit aircraft
Powerplant:	one 600hp (448kW) Curtiss V-1570-23 Conqueror inline piston engine
Performance:	maximum speed 319km/h (198mph); service ceiling 7530m (24,700ft); range 917km (570 miles)
Weights:	empty equipped 1224kg (2669lb); maximum take-off weight 1539kg (3392lb)
Dimensions:	span 9.6m (31ft 6in); length 7.06m (23ft 2in); height 2.72m (8ft 11in); wing area 23.41 sq m (252 sq ft)
Armament:	two fixed forward-firing .3in machine guns

Curtiss R-6

During the 1920s competition provided the greatest spur for aircraft development. The first Curtiss racing machines, the Texas Wildcat and Cactus Kitten, were developed for the James Gordon Bennett Trophy race at Etampes in September 1920 (postponed for seven years due to the war). The Pulitzer Trophy was started as an endurance test in May 1919 by the newspaper magnates, Ralph, Joseph Jr and Herbert Pulitzer, as part of the National Air Races. In 1920 it became a closed-circuit speed competition and was regarded by manufacturers as an ideal opportunity to showcase their talents and attract military orders. Curtiss built the CR-1 specifically to take part in the 1921 Pulitzer Trophy Race, at Omaha, Nebraska, and won. Over the next four years of competition Curtiss machines dominated, losing only once. Pictured is the R-6, one of two built for the US Army, which was flown into second place by Lester Maitland at Selfridge Field in 1922.

Country of origin:	USA
Type:	single-seat racing biplane
Powerplant:	one 465hp (347kW) Curtiss D-12 12-cylinder Vee piston engine
Performance:	maximum speed 380km/h (236mph); range 455km (283 miles)
Weights:	loaded 884kg (1950lb)
Dimensions:	span 5.79m (19ft); length 5.75m (18ft 11in); height 2.41m (7ft 11in)

Curtiss SBC-3 Helldiver

Eighty-three of the SBC-3 type were delivered, followed by 175 SBC-4 aircraft, which had a more powerful Wright R-1820-22 engine. The first SBC-4 was delivered in March 1939 and was subsequently operated by VB-8 and VS-8 on board the USS Hornet and by Marine Squadron VMO-151. In early 1940 the US Navy diverted 50 of its SBC-4s to France but these were received too late to be used in combat. Five were flown back to England and used as ground trainers, where they were known as Clevelands. Although obsolescent at the outbreak of war, at least 69 SBC-3 were still in service with US Navy scouting squadrons, but these were replaced by the Douglas SBD Dauntless before they could be tested in anger. The SBC-4s were in service with VB-8 and VS-8 on board the USS *Hornet* and VMO-151 when the USA entered the war.

Country of origin:	USA
Type:	two-seat carrier-based scout bomber
Powerplant:	one 900hp (671kW) Wright R-1820-34 R-1820-82 Twin Wasp radial piston engine
Performance:	maximum speed 377km/h (234mph); service ceiling 7315m (24,000ft); range with 227kg (500lb) bomb 652km (405 miles)
Weights:	empty 2065kg (4552lb); maximum take-off weight 3211kg (7080lb)
Dimensions:	span 10.36m (34ft); length 8.57m (28ft 1in); height 3.17m (10ft 5in); wing area 29.45 sq m (317 sq ft)
Armament:	one fixed forward-firing .3in machine gun; one .3in machine gun on flexible mount; underfuselage rack for one 227kg (500lb) bomb

Curtiss T-32 Condor II (YC-30)

Two separate versions of the Condor were built by Curtiss, the first being the Model 18, a passenger-carrying derivative of the XB-2 bomber of 1927. Six examples of this were built for service with Eastern Air Transport and Transcontinental Air Transport in the early 1930s. By 1932 Curtiss, along with the rest of the US aviation industry, was searching for a new, saleable product to lift the company out of the depression. In response, Chief Designer George Page produced the T-32, which first flew in January 1930 and was for a short time known as the Condor II. By the time it entered production in 1933 the Curtiss T-32 Condor was already obsolete. Twenty-one were built, nine each to Eastern Air Transport and Transcontinental Air Transport, two as YC-30s (pictured) for the USAAC, and one specially equipped for the 1933–5 Byrd Antarctic Expedition.

Country of origin:	USA
Type:	12-seat passenger transport biplane
Powerplant:	two 710hp (529kW) Wright SCR-1820-F3 Cyclone radial piston engines
Performance:	maximum speed 283km/h (176mph); service ceiling 6705m (22,000ft); range 1352km (840 miles)
Weights:	empty 5095kg (11,233lb); maximum take-off weight 7938kg (17,500lb)
Dimensions:	span 24.99m (82ft); length 15.09m (49ft 6in); height 4.98m (16ft 4in); wing area 118.54 sq m (1276 sq ft)

Curtiss-Wright CW-14R Osprey

In 1930 Curtiss and the Travel Air Company merged to form the Curtiss-Wright Aeroplane Company. The first truly commercially successful produce of the partnership was the CW-1 Junior, an ultralight parasol wing sportsplane. The CW-12 Sport Trainer of 1930 was aimed squarely at the trainer market and was developed in three variants, before introduction of the CW-14. This was developed from a Travel Air Company design, the 4000/4 Speedwing. Under Curtiss-Wright production it was known as the Sportsman and, for the military export market, the Osprey. The CW-14 was built in five variants – the CW-A14D was a three-seater (5 built), the CW-B14B Speedwing Deluxe and CE-B14R Special Speedwing Deluxe were 'GT' versions with powerful engines, and the CW-C14B and CW-C14R were armed military aircraft for the export market. Pictured is a CW-C14R Osprey of the Bolivian Cuerpo de Aviaciones in 1935.

Country of origin:	USA
Type:	two-seat reconnaissance and light attack biplane
Powerplant:	one 300hp (224kW) Wright R-975E Whirlwind nine-cylinder radial piston engine
Performance:	maximum speed 241 km/h (150mph); service ceiling 5000m (16,400ft); range386km (250 miles)
Weights:	empty 800kg (1764lb); maximum take-off weight 1700kg (3749lb)
Dimensions:	span 11.44m (37ft 6in); length 9m (29ft 6in); height 3.4m (11ft 2in)
Armament:	one .3in machine-gun on flexible mount in rear cockpit; underwing racks with provision for up to 500kg (1103lb) of stores

de Havilland D.H.16

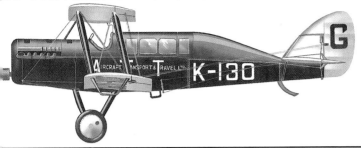

At the end of World War I there was an increased interest in civil aviation coupled with large numbers of ex-military aircraft available, and de Havilland therefore redesigned the airframe of the Airco D.H.9A to accommodate four passengers in a covered rear cockpit and designated it the D.H.16. The aircraft flew for the first time at Hendon in March 1919, and was subsequently sold to Aircraft Transport and Travel Ltd, which used it for pleasure before Major Cyril Patterson inaugurated the London–Le Bourget route on 25 August 1920. AT & T operated eight D.H.16s before it went out of business at the end of 1920. Three were powered by Rolls Royce Eagle VIII engines and the other three had Napier Lions. The only other D.H.16 built was sold to Compania Rioplatense de Aviacion in Argentina, which operated the aircraft on a service to Montevideo. The AT & T machines were all scrapped.

Country of origin:	UK
Type:	four-seat commercial biplane
Powerplant:	one 450hp (336kW) Napier Lion inline piston engine
Performance:	maximum speed 219km/h (136mph); service ceiling 6400m (21,000ft); range 684km (425 miles)
Weights:	empty 1431kg (3155lb); maximum take-off weight 2155kg (4750lb)
Dimensions:	span 14.17m (46ft 6in); length 9.68m (31ft 9in); height 3.45m (11ft 4in); wing area 45.5 sq m (490 sq ft)

de Havilland D.H.34

The de Havilland D.H.34 of 1921 succeeded the D.H.18 as de Havilland's next production airliner. The new aircraft utilised the reliable Napier Lion engine and had increased accommodation for nine passengers in the cabin. The cockpit was resituated to a position forward of the wings and provision was also made to carry a spare engine behind the rear seats. The first customer was Daimler Hire Ltd, owner and operator of The Daimler Airways, which placed an initial order for two. The first aircraft flew in March 1922, and was delivered to the airline only five days later. The aircraft pictured was used by Daimler to inaugurate its service to Paris on 2 April, coinciding with the launch of a duplicate service by the Instone Air Line, also flying D.H.34s. Soviet carrier Dobrolet took the last example of the 12 aircraft that were built.

Country of origin:	UK
Type:	nine-seat commercial biplane
Powerplant:	one 450hp (336kW) Napier Lion piston engine
Performance:	maximum speed 206km/h (128mph); service ceiling 4420m (14,500ft); range 587km (365 miles)
Weights:	empty 1431kg (3155lb); maximum take-off weight 3266kg (7200lb)
Dimensions:	span 15.65m (51ft 4in); length 11.89m (39ft); height 3.66m (12ft); wing area 54.81 sq m (590 sq ft)

de Havilland D.H.37

Bearing more than a passing resemblance to the earlier Airco D.H.4, the D.H.37 was virtually custom-built to the detailed requirements of Alan Butler, a de Havilland company director and well-known aviator of the period. Butler's specification was for an unequal-span touring biplane with unstaggered wings, accommodation for two passengers in tandem cockpits and a Rolls Royce Falcon engine. Butler took delivery of the aircraft in June 1922 and over the course of the next five years it was used extensively for business and pleasure, flying throughout Europe. In 1927 Butler returned the aircraft to de Havilland for refurbishment and had it converted as a single-seater racer with a 300hp (224kW) ADC Nimbus engine. One other D.H.37 was sold to the Controller of Civil Aviation in Australia in 1924, before passing to the Guinea Gold Company in 1927.

Country of origin:	United Kingdom
Type:	two-seat touring biplane
Powerplant:	one 275hp (205kW) Rolls-Royce Falcon III inline piston engine
Performance:	maximum speed 196km/h (122mph); service ceiling 6400m (21,000ft)
Weights:	empty 961kg (2118lb); maximum take-off weight 1505kg (3318lb)
Dimensions:	span 11.28m (37ft); length 8.53m (28ft); height 3.35m (11ft); wing area 36.97 sq m (398 sq ft)

de Havilland D.H.50

I gnoring the trend towards all-metal monoplanes, British manufacturers persisted with the fabric-covered, steel-framed biplane for the light transport market, exemplified by the de Havilland D.H.50 of 1922. This utilised the Siddeley Puma engine of the D.H.9C and carried four passengers in an enclosed cockpit between the wings, with the pilot to the rear in an open cockpit. Between late 1924 and early 1925 the first prototype D.H.50 was flown by Alan Cobham on a long-distance flight funded by Imperial Airways to survey Burma and India. A second aircraft, powered by an Armstrong Siddeley Jaguar radial and designated D.H.50J, accomplished the round trip from Croydon to Cape Town in 210 flying hours between 16 November 1925 and 13 March 1926. It was then fitted with floats to survey the route to Australia in the summer. Sixteen production aircraft were built, most serving overseas. Licensed manufacture was undertaken in Australia (11), Belgium (3), and Czechoslovakia (7).

Country of origin:	United Kingdom
Type:	four-seat passenger biplane
Powerplant:	one 385hp (287kW) Armstrong Siddeley Jaguar radial piston engine
Performance:	maximum speed 180km/h (112mph); service ceiling 4450m (14,600ft); range 612km (380 miles)
Weights:	empty 1022kg (2352lb); maximum take-off weight 1769kg (3900lb)
Dimensions:	span 13.03m (42ft 9in); length 9.07m (29ft 9in); height 3.35m (11ft); wing area 40.32 sq m (434 sq ft)

de Havilland D.H.60 Gipsy Moth

VH-ULM

mprovements in the D.H.60 added considerably to the aircraft's weight, and,
coupled with the knowledge that the Cirrus engine used many Renault parts
which by 1927 were becoming increasingly scarce, the company requested Major
Halford to design a new engine specifically to power a new version of the Moth. In
response Halford designed the 100hp (75kW) Gipsy, and the legendary D.H.60G
Gipsy Moth was born. The Gipsy Moth was used for countless long-distance flights in
the late 1920s, its success due in no small part to the reliability of Halford's engine.
Perhaps the most famous exponent of the aircraft was Amy Johnson, who piloted
her D.H.60G Jason on an epic 20-day solo flight from Croydon to Darwin. Later
versions were the D.H.60M, with metal-skinned fuselage, the D.H.60GIII Moth with
Gipsy III engine, and the final variant the D.H.60T Trainer Moth, which was
intended for military use and powered by the Gipsy II engine.

Country of origin:	United Kingdom
Type:	two-seat touring biplane
Powerplant:	one 100hp (475kW) de Havilland Gipsy inline piston engine
Performance:	maximum speed 164km/h (102mph); service ceiling 4420m (14,500ft); range 51km (320 miles)
Weights:	empty 417kg (920lb); maximum take-off weight 748kg (1650lb)
Dimensions:	span 9.14m (30ft); length 7.29m (23ft 11in); height 2.68m (8ft 9in); wing area 22.57 sq m (243 sq ft)

de Havilland D.H.60 Moth

De Havilland achieved worldwide success with the Moth family of two-seat touring biplanes built from 1925 to 1933. The family's roots can be traced back to 1924, when the company initiated design studies for an aircraft that would provide affordable flying for Britain's affluent middle classes. The prototype resembled a scaled-down version of the D.H.51, having a plywood-skinned fuselage, staggered biplane wings, and tandem cockpits with accommodation for two. The prototype D.H.60 was powered by an ADC Cirrus engine designed by Major F. B. Halford, and first flew in February 1925. The first aircraft were delivered to state-sponsored flying clubs and private owners. In 1926 a further 35 aircraft were built, 14 of which were exported. Pictured is a sixth production example. Engine power was increased progressively from 60hp (45kW) in early D.H.60s to 85hp (63kW) for later aircraft with the Cirrus II engine, and finally 90hp (67kW) for the Cirrus III-powered D.H.60X

Country of origin:	United Kingdom
Type:	two-seat touring biplane
Powerplant:	one 60hp (45kW) ADC Cirrus inline piston engine
Performance:	maximum speed 150km/h (93mph); service ceiling 4420m (14,500ft); range 51km (320 miles)
Weights:	empty 417kg (920lb); maximum take-off weight 748kg (1650lb)
Dimensions:	span 9.14m (30ft); length 7.29m (23ft 11in); height 2.68m (8ft 9in); wing area 22.57 sq m (243 sq ft)

de Havilland D.H.66 Hercules

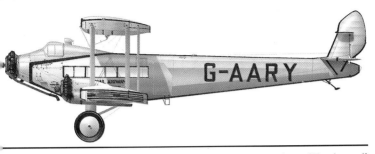

n 1925 the Air Ministry decided that responsibility for the carriage of Empire mail from Cairo to Baghdad should pass from the Royal Air Force to Imperial Airways, which in turn would be responsible for extending the service eastward to India. At that time Imperial Airways' fleet was devoid of any aircraft suitable for the arduous operations over such difficult terrain in tropical weather, and this requirement was met by the de Havilland D.H.66 Hercules. Imperial contracted for an initial fleet of five, and the first of these flew in September 1926. In January 1927 the first scheduled service was undertaken and by April 1929 the service was extended to Karachi. The problems of flying this difficult route took their toll on the fleet – three were lost in crashes, although only one was replaced. Pictured is a D.H.50 G-AARY City of Karachi, built to replace the first aircraft, G-EBMZ, which crashed in September 1929.

Country of origin:	United Kingdom
Type:	seven-seat commercial transport biplane
Powerplant:	three 420hp (313kW) Bristol Jupiter VI radial piston engines
Performance:	maximum speed 206km/h (128mph); service ceiling 3960m (13,000ft); range 845km (525 miles)
Weights:	empty 4110kg (9060lb); maximum take-off weight 7076kg (15,600lb)
Dimensions:	span 24.23m (79ft 6in); length 16.92m (55ft 6in); height 5.56m (18ft 3in); wing area 143.72 sq m (1547 sq ft)

de Havilland D.H.82a Tiger Moth

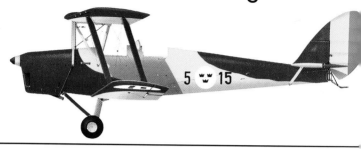

A replacement for the D.H.60 was sought through Air Ministry Specification 15/31. De Havilland retained the D.H.60 fuselage for the new aircraft but added a swept top wing, to create the D.H.82. Various other adaptations were made to improve egress from the cockpit. The first aircraft were delivered to the No. 3 Flyi_ School at Grantham in November 1931 with the designation Tiger Moth Mk I. Five Central Flying School instructors demonstrated the new trainer and its inverted flying capability at the 1932 Hendon Display. Examples were also supplied to the a_ forces of Brazil, Denmark, Persia, Portugal and Sweden. Two were fitted with floa_ supplied by Short Brothers and built to Specification T.6/33 for RAF evaluation at Rochester and Felixstowe. Pictured is a D.H.82a Tiger Moth produced in Sweden a_ the Sk11a for the Swedish Air Force.

Country of origin:	United Kingdom
Type:	two-seat elementary trainer biplane
Powerplant:	one 120hp (89kW) de Havilland Gipsy III inline piston engine
Performance:	maximum speed 164km/h (102mph); service ceiling 4420m (14,500ft); range 515km (320 miles)
Weights:	empty 506kg (1115lb); maximum take-off weight 828kg (1825lb)
Dimensions:	span 8.94m (29ft 4in); length 7.29m (23ft 11in); height 2.69m (8ft 10in); wing area 22.20 sq m (239 sq ft)

de Havilland D.H.82a Tiger Moth Mk II

The greatest number of Tiger Moths were built to Air Ministry Specification T.26/33 as Tiger Moth Mk IIs, with a rear fuselage decking in plywood rather than fabric and stringers, and provision for a blind flying hood (for instrument-only flying training) over the rear cockpit. Large scale production of this D.H.82a Tiger Moth II was undertaken at de Havilland's factory in Hatfield, and also at company facilities in Toronto, Canada, and Wellington, New Zealand, between 1934 and 1945. Most of Britain's wartime pilots were trained on the Moth and after the conflict many of the 7290 aircraft produced became available to civilian customers at a knockdown price, making them a common sight at airfields after the war. Pictured is a Tiger Moth Mk II of the University of London Air Squadron based at Fairoaks in 1950, where it was used to train RAF-sponsored students.

Country of origin:	United Kingdom
Type:	two-seat elementary trainer biplane
Powerplant:	one 130hp (89kW) de Havilland Gipsy Major I inline piston engine
Performance:	maximum speed 167km/h (104mph); service ceiling 4145m (13,600ft); range 483km (300 miles)
Weights:	empty 506kg (1115lb); maximum take-off weight 828kg (1825lb)
Dimensions:	span 8.94m (29ft 4in); length 7.29m (23ft 11in); height 2.69m (8ft 10in); wing area 22.20 sq m (239 sq ft)

de Havilland D.H.84

Development of the D.H.84 was at the behest of Mr Edward Hillman, proprietor of Hillman's Airways, who required ten-seat passenger aircraft to meet the expanding demand of his airline's services. The first Dragon actually had accommodation for only six in an extensively glazed plywood-and-spruce fuselage and first flew in November 1932. After a very short period of flight testing Hillman took delivery of the aircraft in December and four production aircraft followed soon after. Hillman subsequently ordered two more, and extended the passenger-carrying ability of the fleet by eliminating the rear baggage-carrying compartment. The D.H.84 was soon adopted by many other small airlines and production of this first version totalled 62 aircraft. A further 87 were built in Australia during World War II by the de Havilland Australian factory, and used as navigation trainers for the Royal Australian Air Force.

Country of origin:	United Kingdom
Type:	twin-engine eight-seat passenger biplane
Powerplant:	two 130hp (97kW) de Havilland Gipsy Major I inline piston engines
Performance:	maximum speed 216km/h (134mph); service ceiling 4420m (14,500ft); range 877km (545 miles)
Weights:	empty 1060kg (2336lb); maximum take-off weight 2041kg (4500lb)
Dimensions:	span 14.43m (47ft 4in); length 10.52m (34ft 6in); height 3.3m (10ft 1in); wing area 34.93 sq m (376 sq ft)

de Havilland D.H.84M

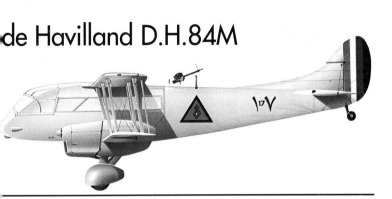

The Dragon 2 was introduced after 62 of the Dragon I aircraft had been completed. This had individually glazed cabin windows instead of the continuous glazing of the original, faired in landing gear legs and 9km/h (6mph) maximum speed improvement. A militarised version of this aircraft was ordered by Iraq as the D.H.84M, with extended fin (similar to that fitted to float-equipped D.H.84s in Canada), twin nose-mounted .303in Vickers Mk V machine guns and an open mid-upper turret with one .303in Lewis machine gun on a Scarff ring mounting. The Iraqi Air Force ordered eight and used them for air policing its desert frontier. Denmark took two – it is not clear if they were saw combat or indeed still extant by the outbreak of World War II – and Portugal three of these militarised versions. Both the Turkish and Irish military forces used the civil Dragon 2 for general duties.

Country of origin:	United Kingdom
Type:	twin-engine reconnaissance biplane
Powerplant:	two 130hp (97kW) de Havilland Gipsy Major I inline piston engines
Performance:	maximum speed 216km/h (134mph); service ceiling 4420m (14,500ft); range 877km (545 miles)
Weights:	empty 1060kg (2336lb); maximum take-off weight 2041kg (4500lb)
Dimensions:	span 14.43m (47ft 4in); length 10.52m (34ft 6in); height 3.3m (10ft 1in); wing area 34.93 sq m (376 sq ft)
Armament:	twin nose mounted .303in Vickers Mk V machine guns and an open mid-upper turret with one .303in Lewis machine gun on a Scarff ring mounting

de Havilland D.H.86a

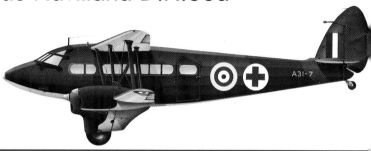

The D.H.86 was built to an Australian Government requirement for a four-engine passenger aircraft to operate on the Singapore–Australia leg of the proposed Croydon–Brisbane service. It shared much of the general layout of the earlier D.H.84 in a much scaled-up form, but had a completely new wing and was powered by four engines. The first flight was made in January 1934, and after successfully gaining its certificate of airworthiness the first two production D.H.86 aircraft, with the two crew members in tandem seating, was delivered to Railway Air Services in Australia in 1934. The prototype was reconfigured in accordance with Qantas' wishes that the two crew members should be sat side-by-side, and this modification required some widening of the nose. In this form 29 aircraft were delivered to civil operators. The D.H.86A (pictured) was a modified version for the RAF; the D.H.86B had further revisions to the control surfaces.

Country of origin:	United Kingdom
Type:	four-engine transport/air ambulance biplane
Powerplant:	two 200hp (149kW) de Havilland Gipsy Six inline piston engines
Performance:	maximum speed 267km/h (166mph); service ceiling 5305m (17,400ft); range 1287km (800 miles)
Weights:	empty 2943kg (6489lb); maximum take-off weight 4649kg (10,250lb)
Dimensions:	span 19.66m (64ft 6in); length 14.05m (46ft 1in); height 3.96m (13ft); wing area 59.55 sq m (641 sq ft)

de Havilland D.H.87B Hornet Moth

To provide prospective Moth customers with a greater degree of comfort, de Havilland constructed two versions with an enclosed cabin. The D.H.85 Leopard Moth of 1929, the successor to the D.H. 80 Puss Moth, was a shoulder wing three-seat cabin monoplane built in numbers totalling 284 aircraft. The D.H.87 Hornet Moth was introduced in 1934 as a two-seat cabin biplane with a Gipsy Major I engine. The first prototype flew at Hatfield, and deliveries began a year later after a testing programme, production totalling 164 aircraft. The D.H.87A had elliptical wings whereas the D.H.87B has squared-off wing tips. A number of D.H.87Bs were sold to Canada and, fitted with Fairchild floats, were operated from lakes in the northern territories. The Royal Air Force trialled two float-equipped versions of the Moth Mk I at Rochester and Felixstowe in 1933, but this version was never adopted.

Country of origin:	United Kingdom
Type:	two-seat floatplane
Powerplant:	one 130hp (89kW) de Havilland Gipsy Major I inline piston engine
Performance:	maximum speed 167km/h (104mph); service ceiling 4145m (13,600ft); range 483km (300 miles)
Weights:	empty 506kg (1115lb); maximum take-off weight 828kg (1825lb)
Dimensions:	span 8.94m (29ft 4in); length 7.29m (23ft 11in); height 2.69m (8ft 10in); wing area 22.20 sq m (239 sq ft)

de Havilland D.H.89A Dragon Rapide

Notwithstanding the success of the earlier D.H.84 Dragon, de Havilland bowed to commercial pressures to build a faster, more comfortable twin-engine aircraft that was to be its successor and the most successful of the Dragon family – the D.H.89a. This was essentially a scaled-down version of the D.H.86, and had fully faired landing gear and refined nose contours to reduce drag. Edward Hillman stayed faithful to the manufacturer and was the launch customer for the first Dragon Rapide, as it was named, and his Hillman Airways airline received three of the new aircraft between July and September 1934. The second version was the D.H.89A which featured split-trailing edge flaps fitted outboard of the engine nacelles on the lower wings. Pictured here is a D.H.89A Dragon Rapide of British European Airways. Note the Royal Mail emblem on the fuselage and tail.

Country of origin:	United Kingdom
Type:	twin-engine passenger biplane
Powerplant:	two 200hp (149kW) de Havilland Gipsy Six inline piston engines
Performance:	maximum speed 253km/h (157mph); service ceiling 5944m (19,500ft); range 930km (578 miles)
Weights:	empty 1486kg (3276lb); maximum take-off weight 2495kg (5500lb)
Dimensions:	span 14.63m (48ft); length 10.52m (34ft 6in); height 3.12m (10ft 3in); wing area 31.21 sq m (336 sq ft)

de Havilland D.H.90 Dragonfly

By the start of World War II, some 180 Dragons had been built, and these were supplemented in wartime by orders for D.H.89B Dominie Mk Is equipped for wireless and navigation training. The Dominie Mk II was equipped for general communications duties. Post-war production included five variants (Rapide Mk II to Mk VI) of the D.H.89A. The D.H.90 Dragonfly of 1935 was a luxury version of the D.H.89. Externally there were similarities, although the Dragonfly had a deeper, shorter fuselage of monocoque structure with less extensive glazing and a sharper nose. The added strength of the monocoque structure allowed de Havilland engineers to delete the nacelle/wing root bracing struts, providing easier access to the cabin. Production totalled 66 aircraft, the type proving particularly popular among wealthy private owners who could afford the £2650 asking price.

Country of origin:	United Kingdom
Type:	twin-engine passenger biplane
Powerplant:	two 130hp (97kW) de Havilland Gipsy Major inline piston engines
Performance:	maximum speed 232km/h (144mph); service ceiling 5515m (18,100ft); range 1006km (625 miles)
Weights:	empty 1134kg (2500lb); maximum take-off weight 1814kg (4000lb)
Dimensions:	span 13.11m (43ft); length 9.65m (31ft 8in); height 2.79m (9ft 2in); wing area 23.78 sq m (256 sq ft)

Dewoitine HD.730

Emile Dewoitine established his own company in October 1920 and produced a series of single-seat parasol wing fighter aircraft during the 1920s before the company was absorbed into the nationalised SNCAM concern in 1938. By that time Dewoitine was well advanced with the design of a catapult-launched light observation and scouting aircraft for the French Navy, designated the HD.730. This had twin-float landing gear, twin-fin tailplane and a low cantilever wing mounted on a fuselage providing accommodation for two seated in tandem. Two prototypes were flown with the Renault 6Q-03 engine in early 1940, but trials proved that much more power was required. Development was continued under the Vichy regime and a third prototype was produced with reduced wing span, but by the end of 1945 official interest in the aircraft had faded.

Country of origin:	France
Type:	two-seat reconnaissance floatplane
Powerplant:	one 220hp (164kW) Renault 6Q-03 inline piston engine
Performance:	maximum speed 230km/h (143mph); service ceiling 5120m (16,800ft); range 1350km (839 miles)
Weights:	empty 1173kg (2586lb); maximum take-off weight 4123kg (1870lb)
Dimensions:	span 12.6m (41ft 4in); length 9.75m (32ft); height 3.18m (10ft 5in); wing area 20 sq m (215 sq ft)
Armament:	one fixed forward firing 7.5mm Darne machine gun; one 7.5mm Darne machine gun on flexible mount for observer/gunner; underwing racks with provision for up to eight 10kg (22lb) bombs

Dorand Ar.1

n 1916 the French Government issued a specification to the aviation industry for a biplane with a tractor engine to replace the Farman F.20. Only Colonel Dorand, ommander of the French Army's Technical Section, showed any interest and bmitted an updated version of one of his (unsuccessful) 1914 biplanes, the D.O I. he new aircraft was generally similar to its predecessor, with back-staggered ings, but benefited from a much more powerful engine. Redesignated as the orand AR.I this aircraft completed trials in September 1916 and was produced in rge numbers for Aviation Militaire for service over the Western and Italian Fronts. he second production version had reduced span wings and a 190hp (142kW) enault 8Ge engine. The Air Service of the American Expeditionary Force acquired 2 AR.1s and 120 AR.2s respectively.

Country of origin:	France
Type:	two-seat observation biplane
Powerplant:	(AR.1) one 200hp (149kW) Renault 8Gdy inline piston engine
Performance:	maximum speed 148km/h (92mph); service ceiling 5500m (18,045ft); endurance 3hrs
Weights:	maximum take-off weight 1315kg (2900lb)
Dimensions:	span 13.29m (43ft 7in); length 9.14m (30ft); height 3.3m (10ft 10in); wing area 50.17 sq m (540 sq ft)
Armament:	one fixed forward-firing .303in Vickers machine gun; plus one or two .303 Lewis guns on flexible mount in rear cockpit

Dornier Do 18D-2

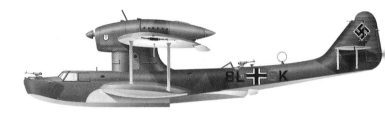

In 1934 Dornier responded to calls for an updated Militär-Wal and a more modern flying-boat for Lufthansa's South American routes by producing the prototype Do 18A. This was similar to the so-called '8-tonne Wal' in both size and weight, but had numerous aerodynamic refinements and a tapered wing with rounded tips and a central pylon to mount the radiators for the Junkers Jumo diesel engines. Its first flight was in March 1935, followed by production of small numbers of Do 18E aircraft for Lufthansa and a single Do 18F (redesignated Do 18L after installation of BMW 132N engines). The Do 18 was trialled and adopted by the Luftwaffe for coastal reconnaissance and entered service in 1938 as the Do 18D-1. The Dornier Do-1 was followed by the Do-2 (pictured) and Do-3, with minor equipment changes.

Country of origin:	Germany
Type:	four-engine coastal reconnaissance flying-boat
Powerplant:	two 600hp (447kW) Junkers Jumo 880hp (656kW) inline diesel engines
Performance:	maximum speed 260km/h (162mph); service ceiling 4200m (13,780ft); range 3500km (2175 miles)
Weights:	empty 5850kg (12,897lb); maximum take-off weight 10,000kg (22,046lb)
Dimensions	:span 23.7m (77ft 9in); length 19.25m (63ft 2in); height 5.35m (17ft 6in); wing area 98 sq m (1054 sq ft)
Armament:	one 13mm MG 131 machine gun in the bow position; one 20mm MG 151 cannon in the dorsal turret; provision for two 50kg (110lb) bombs under the starboard wing

ornier Do 18G-1

elays in the development of the Blohm und Voss Bv 138 led to continued
production of the Do 18 into World War II, with production totalling 160
craft of all types including 75 Do 18Ds. The major wartime production version of
e Do 18 was the G-1 with upgraded defensive armament (including a powered
rsal turret) and powerplant to improve performance. Small numbers of the Do
H dual-control trainer variant were also built. By the winter of 1939–40 the Do 18
uipped four Staffeln of the *Künstenfliegergruppen* (coastal flying groups).
tured is a Do 18G of 6.Seenotstafel, Luftwaffe, operating in the central
diterranean in 1941 in the air-sea-rescue role. Although this aircraft retains its
nament, a number of Do 18Gs converted for air-sea-rescue had their armament
noved, being reclassified as Do 18N-1s.

Country of origin:	Germany
Type:	four-engine coastal reconnaissance flying-boat
Powerplant:	two 600hp (447kW) Junkers Jumo 880hp (656kW) inline diesel engines
Performance:	maximum speed 260km/h (162mph); service ceiling 4200m (13,780ft); range 3500km (2175 miles)
Weights:	empty 5850kg (12,897lb) maximum take-off weight 10,000kg (22,046lb)
Dimensions:	span 23.7m (77ft 9in); length 19.25m (63ft 2in); height 5.35m (17ft 6in); wing area 98 sq m (1054 sq ft)
Armament:	one 13mm MG 131 machine gun in the bow position; one 20mm MG 151 cannon in the dorsal turret; provision for two 50kg (110lb) bombs under the starboard wing

Dornier Do 24K-1

The Dornier Do 24 originated from a requirement issued in 1935 by the Dutch Navy for a flying-boat to replace the Dornier Wals then being used in the Dutch East Indies. The Do 24 was an all-metal monoplane with a hull of typical Dornier design and a strut-braced parasol wing carrying the three engines. The first two prototypes were evaluated for German use powered by Junkers Jumo 205C Diesel engines. The third prototype, which was actually the first to make its maiden flight on 3 July 1937, and the fourth prototypes, were each powered by 875hp (652kW) Wright R-1820-F52 Cyclone radial engines, in order to meet the Netherlands' desire to use the same type of engine as that of the Martin Model 139 bombers used in the East Indies. The prototypes for the Netherlands were successful and were flown to the Indies. In February 1942 the K-1 pictured was flown to Australia and used by the RAAF. Another ten K-1s were completed by the Dornier subsidiary in Switzerland.

Type:	air-sea-rescue and transport flying-boat
Powerplant:	three 875hp (652kW) Wright R-1820-G102 Cyclone radial piston engines
Performance:	maximum speed 332km/h (206mph); service ceiling 8050m (26,405ft); range 4700km (2920 miles)
Weights:	empty 10,600kg (23,369lb); maximum take-off weight 18,400kg (40,565lb)
Dimensions:	span 27m (88ft 7in); length 22.05m (72ft 4in); height 5.75m (18ft 10in); wing area 108 sq m (1163 sq ft)
Armament:	one 20mm Hispano-Suiza HS-404 trainable cannon in dorsal turret; one 7.92mm MG 15 trainable forward-firing machine gun in bow turret; one 7.92mm MG 15 trainable rearward-firing machine gun in tail turret

Dornier Do 24T-1

In autumn 1937 licensed production of 48 Do 24K-2 aircraft, with Wright R-1820-G102 Cyclone engines, was started by Aviolanda in the Netherlands (de Schelde building the wings). Only 25 had been delivered before the German occupation of the Netherlands in May 1940. Three completed boats and a number of part-built airframes were sent to Germany for evaluation in air-sea-rescue and the Dutch line was re-established under the control of German company Weser Flugzeugbau for production of aircraft to Do 24K-2 standard. Deliveries continued until supplies of the Wright engines were exhausted. There followed 159 examples of the Do 24T with the revised powerplant of three 1000hp (756kW) BMW-Bramo 323R-2 Fafnir radial engines. These comprised Do 24T-1s, T-2s and T-3s. Another 48 Do 24T-1 aircraft were built for the Luftwaffe at the Sartrouville factory of the SNCA du Nord in France between 1942 and August 1944; 40 more were delivered to the French Navy after the liberation.

Type:	air-sea-rescue and transport flying-boat
Powerplant:	three 1000hp (746kW) BMW-Bramo 323R-2 Fafnir radial piston engines
Performance:	maximum speed 340km/h (211mph); service ceiling 5900m (19,355ft); range 2900km (1802 miles)
Weights:	empty 9200kg (20,286lb); maximum take-off weight 18,400kg (40,565lb)
Dimensions:	span 27m (88ft 7in); length 22.05m (72ft 4in); height 5.75m (18ft 10in); wing area 108 sq m (1163 sq ft)
Armament:	one 20mm MG 151 trainable cannon in dorsal turret; one 7.92mm MG 15 trainable forward-firing machine gun in bow turret; one 7.92mm MG 15 trainable rearward-firing machine gun in tail turret

Dornier Do 24T-2

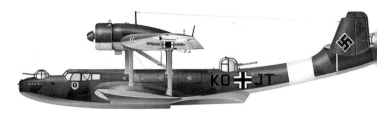

Some 49 Do 24T-2 machines with minor equipment changes were built by Weser Flugzeugbau for the use mainly of the 1., 2. and 3./Seenotgruppe based at Biscarosse near Bordeaux, and Berre near Marseilles. These were followed by 12 Do 24T-3 aircraft which were supplied to Spain under the designation HR.5, deliveries starting in June 1944, to provide search-and-rescue cover in the Mediterranean for aircrew of both sides. The final wartime variant was the Do 31, a single prototype built in 1944 with an Arado-designed boundary-layer control system which was successfully tested but never put into production. The type remained in Spanish service until well into the 1970s and was a common sight in and around the Balearic islands, operating from a base at Pollensa, Majorca. As late as 1983, development work on the aircraft was continuing with the Do 24TT prototype with an advanced technology wing for the Do 228 commuter airliner.

Type:	air-sea-rescue and transport flying-boat
Powerplant:	three 1000hp (746kW) BMW-Bramo 323R-2 Fafnir radial piston engines
Performance:	maximum speed 340km/h (211mph); service ceiling 5900m (19,355ft); range 2900km (1802 miles)
Weights:	empty 9200kg (20,286lb); maximum take-off weight 18,400kg (40,565lb)
Dimensions:	span 27m (88ft 7in); length 22.05m (72ft 4in); height 5.75m (18ft 10in); wing area 108 sq m (1163 sq ft)
Armament:	one 20mm MG151 trainable cannon in dorsal turret; one 7.92mm MG 15 trainable forward-firing machine gun in bow turret; one 7.92mm MG 15 trainable rearward-firing machine gun in tail turret

Dornier Do 26

The last of the Dornier flying-boats was the Do 26. Like so many of its contemporaries, the aircraft was a civil design that was later adapted for military use, in this instance for the transatlantic mail route eagerly predicted before the war that required an aircraft capable of carrying a crew of four and half a ton of mail between Lisbon and New York. The aerodynamic profile was much improved by incorporating retracting floats, mounted at mid-point on a parasol wing. Lufthansa ordered three Do 26s in 1937, and the first of these flew in May 1938 with Junkers Jumo 205 diesels. Another aircraft to this standard was completed before the war (pictured), and saw limited service on the transatlantic route before production switched to the armed Do 26D for the Luftwaffe. Four aircraft were built and together with the two Lufthansa aircraft were used prominently in the Norwegian Campaign.

Type:	transatlantic mail flying-boat
Powerplant:	three 600hp (447kW) Junkers Jumo 205Ea diesel engines
Performance:	maximum speed 335km/h (208mph); service ceiling 4800m (15,750ft); range 9000km (5592 miles)
Weights:	empty 10,700kg (23,589lb); maximum take-off weight 20,000kg (44,092lb)
Dimensions:	span 30m (98ft 5in); length 24.6m (80ft 8in); height 6.85m (22ft 6in); wing area 120 sq m (1292 sq ft)

Dornier Do JIId Wal

As Head of Design and Construction at Zeppelin-Werke Lindau GmbH in Friedrichshafen, Dr Claudius Dornier made pioneering advances in the development of flying-boats. After the war the works were re-established at Manzell Dornier Metallbau, but the punitive terms of the Versailles agreement meant no construction could take place at the site. So Dornier established a subsidiary company in Pisa and built the Do J Wal (Whale), the most successful peacetime design that confirmed his status as the greatest flying-boat designer of his generation. It was first flown in 1922 and introduced the classic Dornier flying-boat configuration with a two step hull incorporating aerodynamic sponsons to give stability on the water, and carrying a strut-braced untapered parasol wing. The Wal was operated by the Spanish and Italian navies in large numbers; pictured is a Dornier-built JIId, serving with I-G 70 Gruppo at Puerto de Pollensa in Majorca during the Spanish Civil War.

Country of origin:	Germany
Type:	twin-engine patrol flying-boat
Powerplant:	two 690hp (515kW) BMW VI inline piston engines
Performance:	cruising speed 140km/h (87mph); service ceiling 3500m (11,480ft); range 2200km (1350 miles)
Weights:	loaded 5700kg (12,566lb)
Dimensions:	span 22.5m (73ft 10in); length 17.25m (56ft 7in); height 5.2m (17ft)
Armament:	optional machine gun in nose and dorsal positions

Dornier Super Wal

The Wal was built in many different guises in numbers totalling 320 aircraft, by Dornier and four licensed manufacturers – SCMP and its successor CMASA in Italy, CASA in Spain, Aviolanda in the Netherlands and Kawasaki in Japan. After introduction to service in 1922, Dornier steadily improved the design to incorporate more powerful engines, larger wings and increased structural strengthening. By 1933 the gross weight had increased to nearly 10 tonnes, the wing span two 2m (6.5ft), and the length by nearly 7m (23ft). Developed versions included the Do R Super Wal of 1926, with two cabins to accommodate a total of 19 passengers and a crew of four, and 650hp (485kW) Rolls Royce Condor engines. Three were built followed by 16 of the Do R4 Super Wal aircraft with four Siemens-produced Bristol Jupiter engines in two tandem pairs. Pictured is the sole Napier Lion engined Do R4 Super Wal, operated by Lufthansa.

Country of origin:	Germany
Type:	four-engine commercial flying-boat
Powerplant:	four 485hp (362kW) Napier Lion VIII W-12 inline piston engines
Performance:	maximum speed 210km/h (130mph); service ceiling 2000m (6500ft); range 2000km (1243 miles)
Weights:	empty 9850kg (21,716lb) maximum take-off 14,000kg (30,864lb)
Dimensions:	span 28.60m (93ft 10in); length 24.60m (80ft 8in); height 6.0m (19ft 8in); wing area 137 sq m (1474 sq ft)

Douglas DF-151

In the 1930s the burgeoning market for long-range flying-boats encouraged Douglas to finance the development of a twin-engine aircraft in this class. Designated the DF, it had a deep, two-step hull with a shoulder mounted cantilever wing incorporating retracting stabilising floats outboard of the nacelles, which enclosed Wright SGR-1820G-2 engines. For shorter flights 32 passengers could be accommodated, whereas on longer night-flights the cabin could sleep 16. There was space also for two galleys, sanitary facilities and a useful cargo load. Despite the undoubted attributes of the aircraft, Douglas failed to secure a buyer in the USA. The prototype and first production aircraft (DF-195) were sold to the Soviet Union and the second pair was bought (surreptitiously) by Greater Japan Air Lines. One aircraft was evaluated by Kawanishi as HXD-1, the other by the Japanese Navy as HXD-2, until it crashed in August 1938.

Country of origin:	USA
Type:	commercial long-range flying-boat
Powerplant:	two 1000hp (746kW) Wright SGR-1820G-2 radial piston engines
Performance:	maximum speed 286km/h (178mph); service ceiling 4235m (13,900ft); range with 12 passengers 5311km (3300 miles)
Weights:	empty 7854kg (17,315lb); maximum take-off weight 12,927kg (28,500lb)
Dimensions:	span 28.86m (95ft); length 21.3m (69ft 10in); height 7.47m (24ft 6in); wing area 120.31 sq m (1295 sq ft)

Douglas DWC

Davis-Douglas was established in 1920 for the express purpose of building the aircraft with which to make the first non-stop Pan American flight. The failure of this venture prompted Mr Davis to withdraw and the company subsequently became Douglas. A key building block for the new company was the award by the US Navy of a contract for the Douglas DT torpedo bomber. At this time interest in a transglobal long-distance flight was high in the US Army and Douglas produced a version of the DT-2 designated the DWC for this express purpose. The prototype was completed in late summer 1923, and once official approval had been gained, four more were delivered by March 1924. On 4 April 1924 these four aircraft departed on their round-the-world flights. Two aircraft were lost en route, but the survivors (including 'Chicago', pictured above) completed the 46,582km (28,945 miles) journey on 28 September the same year.

Country of origin:	USA
Type:	two-seat long-range biplane
Powerplant:	one 420hp (313kW) Liberty V-12 piston engine
Performance:	maximum speed 166km/h (103mph); service ceiling 3050m (10,000ft); range 3541km (2200 miles)
Weights:	empty 1950kg (4300lb); maximum take-off weight 3137kg (6915lb)
Dimensions:	span 13.56m (44ft 6in); length 8.81m (28ft 11in); height 3.07m (10ft 1in); wing area 38.18 sq m (411 sq ft)

Douglas DWC

The Douglas World Cruisers were substantially modified from the DT-2 torpedo-bomber for their 1924 round-the-world trip under the auspices of the US Army. Replacing military equipment with fuel tanks resulted in a vastly-increased fuel load, six times greater than the original capacity. The cooling system for the engine was also adapted to allow for local conditions. The four aircraft were individually numbered and named Seattle, Chicago, Boston and New Orleans. Their route was from east to west, via Canada and Alaska (where Seattle was lost in an accident), overflying remote and inaccessible territories. The Boston (pictured above) was forced down after suffering problems with its engine off the Faroe Islands, but Chicago and New Orleans returned safely from their epic voyage of 46,582km (28,945 miles). It is often forgotten that the first successful flight over the Pacific was accomplished during the circumnavigation.

Country of origin:	USA
Type:	two-seat long-range biplane
Powerplant:	one 420hp (313kW) Liberty V-12 piston engine
Performance:	maximum speed 166km/h (103mph); service ceiling 3050m (10,000ft); range 3541km (2200 miles)
Weights:	empty 1950kg (4300lb); maximum take-off weight 3137kg (6915lb)
Dimensions:	span 15.24m (50ft); length 10.82m (35ft 6in); height 4.14m (13ft 7in); wing area 65.68 sq m (707 sq ft)

Douglas M-2

In 1918 the US Post Office inaugurated its internal air-mail service with surplus Airco D.H.4s, but by 1925 these were rapidly approaching the end of their service lives and a replacement was sought. Douglas converted one of the O-2 biplanes on order for the US Army on the production line as the M-1, with the forward cockpit covered in sheet metal to form a reinforced mail compartment with the pilot's controls relocated to the rear (observer's station). After the air-mail service had been put out to private tender Douglas received an order for six M-2 aircraft (with revised frontal radiator) from the Western Air Express Company. Western inaugurated its Los Angeles–Salt Lake City service in April 1926. The US Post Office ordered 50 of the M-3 version, 40 of which were revised to M-4 standard on the production line with a 1.47m (4ft 10in) wing extension. Fifty-seven were built; one privately owned aircraft was even used to smuggle liquor during Prohibition!

Country of origin:	USA
Type:	single-seat mailplane
Powerplant:	one 420hp (313kW) Liberty V-1650-1 V-12 piston engine
Performance:	maximum speed 225km/h (140mph); service ceiling 5030m (16,500ft); range 1127km (700 miles)
Weights:	empty 1544kg (3405lb); maximum take-off weight 2223kg (4900lb)
Dimensions:	span 13.56m (44ft 6in); length 8.81m (28ft 11in); height 3.07m (10ft 1in); wing area 38.18 sq m (411 sq ft)

Douglas O-2H

Although unremarkable in design and construction, the Douglas O-2 family gave sterling service and proved suitably flexible to allow a large number of variants to be developed for different roles. The two prototype XO-2s had the Liberty V-1650 engine and Packard 1A-1500 engine respectively, but the latter unit proved unreliable and was rejected. A production order for 45 O-2 aircraft for the USAAC, was followed by another 25 O-2s, 18 O-2As equipped for night flying, six O-2B s with dual controls, and 46 O-2Cs with modified radiators and landing gear. The major production versions were the O-2H (96 built) with completely redesigned fuselage, new tailplane rigid interplane struts and improved landing gear, and the O-2J transport and liaison aircraft with armament deleted. Numerous other variants were built in small number with float equipment and different engines, before introduction of the O-25. Pictured is an O-2H of the 91st Observation Squadron, USAAC, in 1928.

Country of origin:	USA
Type:	two-seat observation biplane
Powerplant:	one 420hp (313kW) Liberty V-1650-1 V-12 piston engine
Performance:	maximum speed 206km/h (128mph); service ceiling 4960m (16,270ft); range 579km (360 miles)
Weights:	empty 1375kg (3032lb); maximum take-off weight 2170kg (4785lb)
Dimensions:	span 12.09m (39ft 8in); length 8.76m (28ft 9in); height 3.2m (10ft 6in); wing area 38.18 sq m (411 sq ft)
Armament:	one fixed forward-firing .3in machine gun; one .3in machine gun on flexible mount in rear cockpit; underwing racks with provision for up to four 45kg (100lb) bombs

English Electric P.5 Cork

In 1917 the Admiralty contracted the Phoenix Dynamo Manufacturing Company to construct a new flying-boat around a new monocoque hull designed by Lieutenant Commander Linton Hope and built by Southampton chandler May, Harden and May. Phoenix Dynamo had experience in the field of flying-boat construction with the earlier Porte series, and after delivery of the first hull from trough completed final assembly of the first aircraft in August 1918, by which time Phoenix had become a part of English Electric. Flight trials began in September, but problems with the dope on the fabric-covered wings forced English Electric to substitute the second set of wings. The second aircraft had an enlarged rudder and pylon-mounted lower wing. The Armistice relegated the P.5 to a research role, although it emerged in 1925 in slightly different form as the P.5 Kingston.

Country of origin:	United Kingdom
Type:	reconnaissance flying-boat
Powerplant:	two 350hp (261kW) Rolls-Royce Eagle VIII inline piston engines
Performance:	maximum speed 169km/h (105mph); service ceiling 4600m (15,100ft); range 1287km (800 miles)
Weights:	empty 3373kg (7437lb); maximum take-off weight 3813kg (7437lb)
Dimensions:	span 26.06m (85ft 6in); length 14.99m (49ft 2in); height 6.45m (21ft 2in); wing area 118.26 sq m (1273 sq ft)
Armament:	one .303in Lewis machine gun on flexible mount in bow cockpit; one .303in Lewis machine gun on flexible mount in each of two waist positions (second prototype had provision for four further .303in Lewis machine guns in two nacelles above the top wing); plus bomb load of 472kg (1040lb)

Fairey Albacore TB.Mk I

Although planned as a replacement for the Fairey Swordfish, the Albacore never achieved the same fame as its illustrious predecessor and in many respects was a less useful aircraft. The Albacore was designed to Specification S.41/36 and ordered straight off the drawing board in May 1937. The two prototypes underwent a hasty programme of evaluation at the AAEE which revealed a few vices, but with the pressing needs of war, these proved insufficiently serious to hold up the production lines. The first of 98 production TB.Mk I aircraft was delivered in March 1940, and until it was superseded in 1943 by the Fairey Barracuda the aircraft was involved in many of the sea actions and a number of land operations in the Arctic, the Western Desert, the Mediterranean and the Indian Ocean. Pictured is a TB.Mk I of No 826 Squadron, Fleet Air Arm.

Country of origin:	United Kingdom
Type:	three-seat torpedo bomber
Powerplant:	one 1130hp (843kW) Bristol Taurus XII 14-cylinder radial piston engine
Performance:	maximum speed 259km/h (161mph); service ceiling 6310m (20,700ft); range with 726kg (1600lb) weapons load 1497km (930 miles)
Weights:	empty 3289kg (7250lb); maximum take-off weight 4745kg (10,460lb)
Dimensions:	span 15.24m (50ft); length 12.14m (39ft 10in); height 4.32m (14ft 2in); wing area 57.88 sq m (623 sq ft)
Armament:	one fixed forward-firing .303in Vickers machine gun in starboard wing; twin .303in Vickers 'K' machine guns on flexible mount in rear cockpit; plus one 730kg (1610lb) torpedo under fuselage, or six 113kg (250lb) or four 227kg (500lb) bombs on underwing racks

Fairey Fox Mk I

Fairey Aviation Company was formed in 1915 in the corner of a factory in Hayes, Middlesex, for the licensed manufacture of Short 827 seaplanes, but became one of the greatest of British aircraft manufacturers and by 1915 was producing its own aircraft. The Fox stemmed from a visit by Richard Fairey to the USA in 1923, when he was struck by the Curtiss V-12 engine and the fine streamlined nose cowling it permitted. He acquired manufacturing rights and Marcel Lobelle and P. A. Ralli designed the Fairey Fox light bomber around it, although in the event production aircraft were fitted with imported engines. The prototype demonstrated a top speed a full 48km/h (30mph) faster than any contemporary RAF fighter. RAF Commander Lord Trenchard ordered a 'complete squadron' and 28 were delivered. Although beaten by the Hawker Hart for RAF orders it gained widespread foreign acceptance; Avions Fairey in Belgium built 178, of which 94 were the all-metal Fox VI.

Country of origin:	United Kingdom
Type:	two-seat day bomber
Powerplant:	one 480hp (358kW) Fairey Felix Vee piston engine
Performance:	maximum speed 251km/h (156mph); service ceiling 5180m (17,000ft); range 1046km (650 miles)
Weights:	empty 1183kg (2609lb); maximum take-off weight 1867kg (4117lb)
Dimensions:	span 11.58m (38ft); length 9.5m (31ft 2in); height 3.25m (10ft 8in); wing area 30.1 sq m (324 sq ft)
Armament:	one fixed forward-firing .303in machine gun; one .303in machine gun on flexible mount in rear cockpit; plus up to 209kg (460lb) of bombs

Fairey Swordfish Mk I

Despite its archaic appearance and modest performance, when tested in combat some ten years after it first appeared on the Fairey drawing board, the Swordfish proved to be a superbly effective aircraft. In September 1930 the Air Ministry issued a specification calling for a torpedo-carrying fleet spotter. In response Fairey built the TSR 1, powered by a 635hp (474kW) Bristol Pegasus radial engine, and flew it for the first time in March 1933. The aircraft was shown to be both underpowered and directionally unstable, and was lost in a crash some six months later. The second prototype (TSR II) was built to a revised specification, with lengthened fuselage, uprated Pegasus engine and revised tail unit. This first flew in April 1934 and after minor revisions was ordered into production as the Swordfish Mk I in 1935. Pictured is one of the first production batch, delivered to No 823 Squadron embarked on HMS *Glorious* in 1936.

Country of origin:	United Kingdom
Type:	three-seat torpedo bomber biplane
Powerplant:	one 690hp (515kW) Bristol Pegasus IIIM3 9-cylinder radial engine
Performance:	maximum speed 222km/h (138mph); service ceiling 3260m (10,700ft); range with torpedo 885km (550 miles)
Weights:	empty 2359kg (5200lb); maximum take-off weight 4196kg (9250lb)
Dimensions:	span 13.92m (45ft 6in); length 11.12m (36ft 4in); height 3.93m (12ft 10in); wing area 56.39 sq m (607 sq ft)
Armament:	one fixed forward-firing .303in Vickers machine gun; one .303in Vickers 'K' gun or Browning machine gun on flexible mount in rear cockpit; underfuselage crutch for one 18in (457mm) 731kg (1610lb) torpedo, or 681kg (1500lb) bomb or mine

Fairey Swordfish Mk II

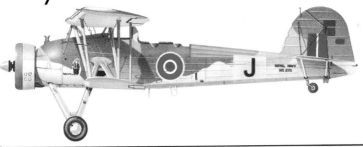

The main wartime version of the Swordfish was the Mk I, which served in some of the most famous actions of World War II, two of the most notable being the attack on the Italian fleet at Taranto in November 1940 which ended the threat of the Italian fleet in the Mediterranean, and the attack on the German pocket battleship *Bismarck* in May 1941. Some 689 Swordfish Mk Is were produced by the outbreak of the war. From 1940 all production was handled by Blackburn Aircraft, which built 300 Mk Is, and then 1080 of the Mk II version with metal-skinned lower wings to facilitate rocket firing by eliminating the risk of the wings catching fire. Early Mk IIs had a 690hp (515kW) Pegasus engine while later aircraft had a 750hp (560kW) Pegasus 30. Pictured is a Swordfish Mk II of No I Naval Gunnery School, Yarmouth, Nova Scotia, in 1943.

Country of origin:	United Kingdom
Type:	three-seat torpedo bomber biplane
Powerplant:	one 750hp (560kW) Bristol Pegasus 30 9-cylinder radial engine
Performance:	maximum speed 222km/h (138mph); service ceiling 3260m (10,700ft); range with torpedo 885km (550 miles)
Weights:	empty 2359kg (5200lb); maximum take-off weight 4196kg (9250lb)
Dimensions:	span 13.92m (45ft 6in); length 11.12m (36ft 4in); height 3.93m (12ft 10in); wing area 56.39 sq m (607 sq ft)
Armament:	one fixed forward-firing .303in Vickers machine gun; one .303in Vickers 'K' gun or Browning machine gun on flexible mount in rear cockpit; underfuselage crutch for one 18in (457mm) 731kg (1610lb) torpedo, or 681kg (1500lb) bomb or mine, or up to eight 3in 27kg (60lb) rockets or four 113kg (250lb) bombs on rails under the wings

Fairey Swordfish Mk III

Production of the Swordfish Mk II continued until February of 1944. The Fleet Air Arm had made strident efforts to find its replacement, but the Fairey Albacore failed to live up to expectations and development of the Fairey Barracuda was seriously delayed. In the event, the 'Stringbag' soldiered on and production switched to the Mk III, which was fitted with a large ASV scanner between the landing gear legs. This prevented the carriage of underfuselage stores, although the wing pylons were retained, and it became normal practice for Swordfish units to operate in packs, one Mk III in the search role accompanied by Mk IIs carrying bombs and torpedoes. Some 327 Mk IIIs were built. The aircraft shown here was operated by No 119 Squadron. In early 1945 the squadron was based at Knocke in Belgium, operating against enemy 'E' and 'R' boats off the Dutch coast.

Country of origin:	United Kingdom
Type:	three-seat anti-submarine biplane
Powerplant:	one 750hp (560kW) Bristol Pegasus 30 9-cylinder radial engine
Performance:	maximum speed 222km/h (138mph); service ceiling 3260m (10,700ft); range with torpedo 885km (550 miles)
Weights:	empty 2359kg (5200lb); maximum take-off weight 4196kg (9250lb)
Dimensions:	span 13.92m (45ft 6in); length 11.12m (36ft 4in); height 3.93m (12ft 10in); wing area 56.39 sq m (607 sq ft)
Armament:	one fixed forward-firing .303in Vickers machine gun; one .303in Vickers 'K' gun or Browning machine gun on flexible mount in rear cockpit; up to eight 3in 27kg (60lb) rockets or four 113kg (250lb) bombs on rails under wings

Fairey Swordfish Mk IV

The final version of the Swordfish was the Mk IV, converted from Mk IIs and Mk IIIs by adding a rudimentary enclosure over the cockpit. This modification was no doubt welcomed by the Swordfish crews, who were often called upon to mount long patrols over the North Atlantic, exposing them to the extremes of weather. The aircraft pictured here is one of the aircraft serving with the No I Naval Air Gunnery School in Nova Scotia. The last Swordfish Mk III was completed in August 1944. Appropriately, it was a Swordfish that flew the Fleet Air Arm's last operational sortie by a biplane on 28 June 1945. By then the Swordfish had served with distinction as a torpedo-bomber, shore-based minelayer, convoy protector, flare-dropper, rocket-armed anti-shipping and anti-submarine aircraft, as well as a suitable platform for training and general duties. The last surviving airworthy Swordfish is still operated by the FAA for air displays.

Country of origin:	United Kingdom
Type:	three-seat anti-submarine biplane
Powerplant:	one 750hp (560kW) Bristol Pegasus 30 9-cylinder radial engine
Performance:	maximum speed 222km/h (138mph); service ceiling 3260m (10,700ft); range with torpedo 885km (550 miles)
Weights:	empty 2359kg (5200lb); maximum take-off weight 4196kg (9250lb)
Dimensions:	span 13.92m (45ft 6in); length 11.12m (36ft 4in); height 3.93m (12ft 10in); wing area 56.39 sq m (607 sq ft)
Armament:	one fixed forward-firing .303in Vickers machine gun; one .303in Vickers 'K' gun or Browning machine gun on flexible mount in rear cockpit; up to eight 3in 27kg (60lb) rockets or four 113kg (250lb) bombs on rails under wings

Farman F.40

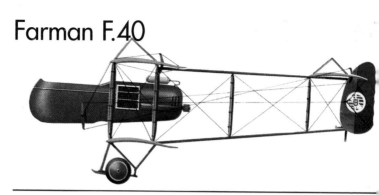

Henry and Maurice Farman began their careers in aviation in the Edwardian era and by the outbreak of World War I were at the forefront of the trailblazing French aeronautical industry. Their F.40 pusher biplane was a joint design and incorporated features of their earlier independent designs. It appeared at the end of 1915 and entered largescale production in early 1916. More than 40 French escadrilles were equipped with the type, popularly known as the 'Horace' Farman, and it was produced in a mind-boggling array of variants, including the F.40P with Le Prieur rockets; F.41 with shorter wings and less streamlined crew nacelle, F.56 with 170hp (127kW) Renault engine, and F.60 with 190hp (142kW) Renault engine. was also operated by the RNAS and with French units in Macedonia and Serbia. Pictured is an F.40 of the Esquadrilha Expedicionara a Mocambique (a unit of the Portuguese Air Force) based at Mocimboca de Praia, Mozambique, in 1917.

Country of origin:	France
Type:	two-seat observation biplane
Powerplant:	one 135hp (101kW) Renault 12-cylinder Vee piston engine
Performance:	maximum speed 135km/h (84mph); service ceiling 4000m (13,125ft); endurance 2hrs 20mins
Weights:	empty 748kg (1649lb); maximum take-off weight 1120kg (2469lb)
Dimensions:	span 17.6m (57ft 9in); length 9.25m (30ft 4in); height 3.9m (12ft 9in); wing area 52 sq m (560 sq ft)
Armament:	one or two .303 Lewis guns on flexible mount in nose position; light bombs and (F.40P) Le Prieur rockets

arman Goliath

The Armistice in November 1918 curtailed development of the Farman FF.60 as a heavy bomber and the two prototypes were completed to civil configuration ith cabins in the nose and midships accommodating four and eight passengers espectively. The first flight was undertaken in January 1919, and as the civil rcraft was entering production as the F.60, so a military version began flight sting. The first civil F.60 entered service in March 1920 on the Le Bourget–roydon route. The first bomber F.60s were delivered to the Aéronautique Militaire 1922. Despite its seemingly ungainly design the Farman Goliath was the most idely produced twin-engined aircraft of the 1920s, and was built in numerous ariants for civil and military customers with different nose and engine onfigurations. Some 360 aircraft were built, a remarkable achievement in a decade hen any aircraft built in double figures is notable.

Country of origin:	France
Type:	(civil F.60) passenger transport biplane
Powerplant:	two 260hp (194kW) Salmson CM.9 9-cylinder radial piston engines
Performance:	maximum speed 160km/h (99mph); service ceiling 4000m (13,125ft); range 400km (248 miles)
Weights:	empty equipped 2500kg (5512lb); maximum take-off weight 4770kg (10,516lb)
Dimensions:	span 26.50m (86ft 11in); length 14.33m (47ft); height 4.91m (16ft 1in); wing area 161 sq m (1733 sq ft)

Felixstowe F.5

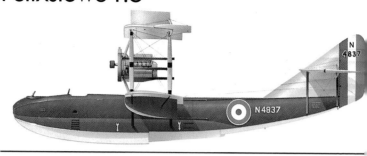

Commander John C. Porte of the RNAS joined the Curtiss company in 1913 and designed the early 'H' series flying-boats for the company. He returned to Britain for war service and was appointed commander of the RN Air Station at Felixstowe, where he operated H.4 series boats over the North Sea. Porte's attempt to improve upon the hull of this design resulted in the F.2A, the standard RNAS flying-boat of the war. About 100 were built by S. E. Saunders of Cowes, and ten by Aircraft Manufacturing Co of Hendon. The long-span F.3 carried a much heavier bomb load, while the completely redesigned F.5 was the standard RAF flying-boat from 1918 until it was replaced by the Supermarine Southampton in August 1925. In 1918 the US Navy adopted a variant powered by the Liberty engine which was built by Curtiss (60 aircraft), Canadian Aeroplanes of Toronto (30) and the US Naval Aircraft Factory (138).

Country of origin:	United Kingdom
Type:	reconnaissance flying-boat
Powerplant:	two 350hp (261kW) Rolls-Royce Eagle VIII 12-cylinder Vee piston engines
Performance:	maximum speed 142km/h (88mph); service ceiling 2075m (6800ft); endurance 7hrs
Weights:	empty 4128kg (9100lb); maximum take-off weight 5752kg (12,682lb)
Dimensions:	span 31.6m (103ft 8in); length 15.01m (49ft 3in); height 5.72m (18ft 9in); wing area 130.9 sq m (1409 sq ft)
Armament:	one .303in Lewis machine gun on flexible mount in nose position; one .303in Lewis machine gun on flexible mount in each of three midships positions; underwing racks with provision for four 104kg (230lb) bombs

iat CR.1

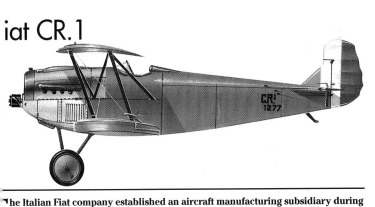

The Italian Fiat company established an aircraft manufacturing subsidiary during
World War I, and in 1918 it engaged the services of designer Celestino Rosatelli.
 the first Rosatelli design was the BR single-engine bomber biplane, followed in
23 by the CR single-seat fighter. The two prototypes were built and tested in 1923
d after proving its superiority to the SIAI S.52, the aircraft was selected for
rgescale production for the newly formed Regia Aeronautica. Production aircraft
re designated CR.1 and the first deliveries of an eventual 240 aircraft began in
25. During the 1930s many Italian CR.1s were modified to take the 44hp (328kW)
otta Fraschini Asso Caccia engine, and these served until 1937. The aircraft was
ported to Latvia (9 machines) and was tested with different engines as the CR.2,
R.10 and CR.5.

Country of origin:	Italy
Type:	single-seat fighter biplane
Powerplant:	one 300hp (224kW) Hispano-Suiza 42 8-cylinder radial engine
Performance:	maximum speed 272km/h (169mph); service ceiling 7450m (24,440ft); endurance 2hrs 35mins
Weights:	empty equipped 839kg (1850lb); maximum take-off weight 1154kg (2544lb)
Dimensions:	span 8.95m (29ft 4in); length 6.16m (20ft 2in); height 2.4m (7ft 10in); wing area 23 sq m (248 sq ft)
Armament:	two fixed forward-firing .303in Vickers machine guns

Fiat CR.20

The CR.1 was the first in a line of classic Rosatelli- designed single-seat Fiat fighter biplanes, and reached its climax in the 1930s. The CR.20 of 1926 was a unequal-span biplane of steel tube and fabric construction, and in prototype form was powered by the Fiat AR.20 engine. The first flight was made in June 1926 and the autumn of the same year it took centre stage at the influential Paris Salon de l'Aéronautique. Production for the Regia Aeronautica began in 1927, and the CR. swiftly became its standard fighter aircraft. The CR.20 took part in the Italian conquest of Libya and Abyssinia as a ground attack aircraft. By the late 1930s the type had been relegated to training units. Forty-six examples of a twin-float seapl variant was built by Macchi and CMASA as the CR.20 Idro. Pictured is a CR.20 of Magyar Királyi Légierö (Royal Hungarian Air Force) in 1936.

Country of origin:	Italy
Type:	single-seat fighter biplane
Powerplant:	one 410hp (306kW0 Fiat A.20 12-cylinder Vee piston engine
Performance:	maximum speed 260km/h (161mph); service ceiling 8500m (27,885ft); endurance 2hrs 30mins
Weights:	empty 970kg (2138lb); maximum take-off weight 1390kg (3064lb)
Dimensions:	span 9.8m (32ft 1in); length 6.71m (22ft); height 2.79m (9ft 1in); wing area 25.5 sq m (274 sq ft)
Armament:	two fixed forward-firing .303in Vickers machine guns

Fiat CR.20bis

In service, the fragile cross-axle rubber-sprung landing gear of the CR.20 proved to be something of an achilles heel and Fiat set about improving the arrangement. The CR.20bis of 1930 had oleo-pneumatic shock absorbers and wheel brakes and was built in numbers totalling 232 aircraft. The CR.20bis AQ had a Fiat A.20 AQ engine for improved high-altitude performance, while the CR.20 Asso had an Issota Fraschini powerplant in a special cowling and larger horizontal stabilizer. Numbers were bought by Austria, Hungary, Lithuania, Paraguay, Poland and the Soviet Union. After the *Anschluss* with Austria in 1938 a number of aircraft were repainted in Luftwaffe colours and briefly saw service as trainers. Pictured here is a CR.20bis of the Escuadron de Caza 'Los Indios' ('The Indians' Fighter Squadron), Fuerza Aereas del Ejercito Nacional Paraguayo (Paraguayan National Army Air Force) in the 1930s.

Country of origin:	Italy
Type:	single-seat fighter biplane
Powerplant:	one 410hp (306kW) Fiat A.20 12-cylinder Vee piston engine
Performance:	maximum speed 260km/h (161mph); service ceiling 8500m (27,885ft); endurance 2hrs 30mins
Weights:	empty 970kg (2138lb); maximum take-off weight 1390kg (3064lb)
Dimensions:	span 9.8m (32ft 1in); length 6.71m (22ft); height 2.79m (9ft 1in); wing area 25.5 sq m (274 sq ft)
Armament:	two fixed forward-firing .303in Vickers machine guns

Fiat CR.32quater

The CR.32 was the most important biplane fighter of the 1930s, certainly in terms of the number built (1712) and arguably because of its influence on the Spanish Civil War. The CR.32 stemmed from the CR.30, designed by Chief Engineer Rosatelli 1931 as a single-seat fighter and bearing many of his hallmarks, such as W-form interplane bracing. Fitted with a Fiat A.30 Vee-12 engine, the CR.30 offered a considerable leap in performance over the CR.1 and was ordered for the Regia Aeronautica. Rosatelli was not content to rest in his laurels and refined the Cr.30 to produce the CR.32, which was built in larger numbers and formed the backbone of the Regia Aeronautica fighter force in 1935–40. The CR.32 was used extensively in Spain, and its performance in this theatre lulled the Italian Air Ministry into the false belief that the fighter biplane was a viable weapon of war. In June 1940, 324 were still in front-line service, despite being hopelessly outclassed by the new monoplanes.

Country of origin:	Italy
Type:	single-seat fighter biplane
Powerplant:	one 600hp (447kW) Fiat A.30 RA bis 12-cylinder Vee piston engine
Performance:	maximum speed 375km/h (233mph); service ceiling 8800m (28,870ft); range 680km (422 miles)
Weights:	empty 1325kg (2921lb); maximum take-off weight 1850kg (4079lb)
Dimensions:	span 9.5m (31ft 2in); length 7.45m (24ft 5in); height 2.63m (8ft 7in); wing area 22.10 sq m (238 sq ft)
Armament:	two fixed forward-firing .303in Breda-SAFAT machine guns

Fiat CR.42 Falco

By the mid-1930s most of Celestino Rosatelli's contemporaries had switched their attentions to designing stressed-skin monoplanes, but the Fiat Chief Engineer persisted with the open-cockpit, fabric-covered CR family and developed the Cr.41 (a variant of the CR.32 with 900hp (671kW) Gnome-Rhône radial engine and modified tail surfaces). From this stemmed the CR.42. Although this was a robust, clean and attractive aircraft, it was obsolete by the time of its first flight in 1936. Despite this fact, the CR.42 found a ready market and went into largescale production for the Regia Aeronautica and for Belgium, Hungary and Sweden. Pictured is one of the Cr.42s that served in North Africa with 97a Squadriglia. The unit was based at Benina in Libya during 1940. Until the Hawker Hurricane arrived the Falco was the best fighter available to either side, but as it became further outdated it was used in a ground-attack role.

Country of origin:	Italy
Type:	(CR.42) single-seat fighter
Powerplant:	one 840hp (626kW) Fiat A.74 R1C.38 14-cylinder, two-row radial engine
Performance:	maximum speed 472km/h (293mph); climb to 6000m (16,405ft) in 7mins 30secs; service ceiling 9835m (32,265ft); range 670km (416 miles)
Weights:	empty 1975kg (4354lb); maximum take-off 2415kg (5324lb)
Dimensions:	span 10.96m (35ft 11.5in); length 7.79m (25ft 6.75in); height 2.96m (9ft 8in)
Armament:	two 12.7mm Breda-SAFAT fixed forward-firing machine guns in upper part of forward fuselage

Fiat CR.42 Falco

When Italy declared war in June 1940 the Regia Aeronautica had 242 CR.42s which were active during its campaign in southern France and used sporadically in the Battle of Britain. The CR.42 was used for operations over the Mediterranean and in Northern and East Africa, and in the desert proved effective against ground targets. In July 1941 the first CR.42 AS (Africa Settentrionale) with tropical dust filters and racks for two 91kg (200lb) bombs were delivered, but losses mounted from September 1942 and they were withdrawn from this role. The CR.42 CN was a night-fighter variant with exhaust flame-dampers, radio and underwing searchlights; the CR.42 DB a one-off prototype with a 1160hp (865kW) Daimler-Benz 601E engine; the ICR.42 a float-equipped CR.42 built by CMASA; the CR.42 LW a night-harassment and antipartisan version built for the Luftwaffe. The CR.42 two-seaters were Swedish single-seat aircraft converted after the war as liaison aircraft.

Country of origin:	Italy
Type:	(CR.42) single-seat fighter
Powerplant:	one 840hp (626kW) Fiat A.74 R1C.38 14-cylinder, two-row radial engine
Performance:	maximum speed 472km/h (293mph); climb to 6000m (16,405ft) in 7mins 30secs; service ceiling 9835m (32,265ft); range 670km (416 miles)
Weights:	empty 1975kg (4354lb); maximum take-off 2415kg (5324lb)
Dimensions:	span 10.96m (35ft 11in); length 7.79m (25ft 7in); height 2.96m (9ft 8in)
Armament:	two 12.7mm Breda-SAFAT fixed forward-firing machine guns in upper part of forward fuselage

iat CR.42bis Falco

A group of 50 CR.42bis aircraft were stationed in Belgium from October 1942 to January 1941 under the command of Luftflotte II, but these suffered such ɔrrendous losses at the hands of RAF pilots that they were redeployed to North ʀica, and when the situation became untenable the survivors were flown to Italy ʀ readiness for the invasion of June 1943. During the autumn and early winter ㅔied forces advanced steadily forward to the Gothic line supported by a vast air ㅔmada. With their own stocks running low, the Germans took a leaf out of the ㅆssian's book and pressed any available aircraft into service for night nuisance ㅛacks. This CR.42bis Falco was requisitioned and served with 2.Staffel of ㅊchtschlachtgruppe (9 NSGr.9), formed at Casella Torino in February 1944 under ㅔe command of Luftflotte II. Note the cut-down spats.

Country of origin:	Italy
Type:	(CR.42) single-seat fighter
Powerplant:	one 840hp (626kW) Fiat A.74 R1C.38 14-cylinder, two-row radial engine
Performance:	maximum speed 472km/h (293mph); climb to 6000m (16,405ft) in 7mins 30 seconds; service ceiling 9835m (32,265ft); range 670km (416 miles)
Weights:	empty 1975kg (4354lb); maximum take-off weight 2415kg (5324lb)
Dimensions:	span 10.96m (35ft 11in); length 7.79m (25ft 7in); height 2.96m (9ft 8in)
Armament:	two 12.7mm Breda-SAFAT fixed forward-firing machine guns in upper part of forward fuselage

Fiesler Fi 167

In 1936 the German Navy laid down the keel of its first aircraft carrier, which was launched in 1938 but never completed. Shortly after, the *Luftfahrministerum* (German Air Ministry) issued to selected companies a requirement for a multi-role carrierborne warplane with excellent short take-off and landing (STOL) capability, folding biplane wing cellule, carrier arrestor gear, and the strength to make dive-bombing attacks at high speeds. Only Arado and Fieseler responded, and the two Fi 167 prototypes revealed good handling (including the ability to land at very low speeds), performance and payload. Fieseler received an order for 12 Fi 167A-0 pre-production aircraft with jettisonable main landing gear units but the abandonment of the carrier programme obviated the need for the Fi 167 and nine aircraft were passed to Romania for coastal operations over the Black Sea. Shown here is an Fi 167A-0 of Erprobungstaffel 167, based in the Netherlands during 1940–2.

Country of origin:	Germany
Type:	two-seat torpedo bomber and reconnaissance aircraft
Powerplant:	one 1100hp (820kW) Daimler-Benz DB 601B 12-cylinder inverted-Vee engine
Performance:	maximum speed 325km/h (202mph); service ceiling 8200m (26,905ft); range 1500km (932 miles)
Weights:	empty 2800kg (6173lb); maximum take-off weight 4850kg (10,692lb)
Dimensions:	span 13.50m (44ft 3in); length 11.40m (37ft 5in); height 4.80m (15ft 9in)
Armament:	one 7.92mm fixed forward-firing machine gun; one 7.92mm machine gun on flexible mount in rear cockpit; plus external torpedo and bomb load of 1000kg (2205lb)

Fokker C.I

The C.I was in effect an enlarged version of the earlier D.VII. The prototype was tested as the V 38 at Schwerin in 1918 and was placed in to production immediately , but none had been completed by the time of the Armistice. Fokker smuggled the uncompleted C.I airframes out of Germany under the eyes of the French and into the Netherlands, where production continued. In total some 250 aircraft were produced, with engines of between 185 and 260hp. The Dutch military was the largest customer, taking 62 C.Is for use in the reconnaissance role. The USSR purchased 42, many of which were fitted with skis and Denmark bought two and built three others. The C.Ia of 1929 was a version for the Dutch army air corps with 200hp (149kW) Armstrong Siddeley Lynx radial engine and redesigned tail, the C.I-W was an experimental floatplane, the C.II a three-seat passenger carrying aircraft with enclosed passenger cockpit and the C.III was an advanced trainer sold to Spain.

Country of origin:	Germany
Type:	two-seat reconaissance aircraft
Powerplant:	one 185hp (138kW) B.M.W IIIa 6-cylinder inline piston engine
Performance:	maximum speed 175km/h (109mph); service ceiling 4000m (13,125ft); range 620km (385 miles)
Weights:	empty equipped 855kg (1,885lb); maximum take-off weight 1255kg (2,767lb)
Dimensions:	span 10.5m (34ft 5 1/2in); length 7.23m (23ft 8 1/4in); height 2.87m (9ft 5in); wing area 26.25sq m (282.56sq ft)
Armament:	one fixed forward firing .303in machine gun, one .303in machine gun on ring mount over rear cockpit, underwing racks with provision for four 12.5kg (27.5lb) bombs

Fokker C.V

Fokker survived the slump in the post-war military aircraft market thanks to the outstanding sales success of the Fokker C.IV. A remarkable 159 of this sturdy, reliable aircraft were produced from 1923, and these were followed in 1924 by the excellent C.V. The prototype for this aircraft flew in May of that year, followed by production aircraft offered in five configurations with different wings. The C.V-A, C.V-B and C.V-C had parallel chord wings of 37.5 sq m (404 sq ft), 40.8 sq m (439 sq ft) and 46.10 sq m (496 sq ft) respectively, and the C.V-D and C.V-E had sesquiplane wings of 28.8 sq m 310 sq ft) and 39.30 sq m (423 sq ft). The flexibility of the design won many customers, most of them for the C.V-D and C.V-E models. Bolivia and Holland were the first customers; after purchasing small batches of aircraft, production licences were granted to Denmark, Norway, Sweden, Italy, Hungary (as the WM Budapest 9, 11 or 14), and Switzerland.

Country of origin:	Denmark (Netherlands)
Type:	two-seat reconnaissance/bomber aircraft
Powerplant:	one 750hp (544kW) Bristol Pegasus radial piston engine
Performance:	maximum speed 225km/h (140mph); service ceiling 5500m (18,045ft); range 770km (478 miles)
Weights:	empty 1250kg (2756lb); maximum take-off weight 1850kg (4079lb)
Dimensions:	span 12.5m (41ft); length 9.5m (31ft 2in); height 3.5m (11ft 5in); wing area 28.8 sq m (310 sq ft)
Armament:	one or two .7.9mm fixed forward-firing machine guns, one or two .7.9mm machine guns on flexible mount in rear cockpit; plus up to 200kg (441lb) of bombs or mines

okker C.X

The success of the C.V series prompted Fokker to develop the C.X, which bore some resemblance to the C.V-E but had considerably better performance in production m due to the Rolls Royce Kestrel engine. However, worldwide competition in the hter market was very severe in the mid-1930s and Fokker could not achieve nificant export success. The first order was for ten for the Royal Netherlands East dies Navy, followed by 20 for the *Luchtvaartafdeling* (Royal Netherlands Air rce), the last 15 having enclosed cockpits and tailwheels. Fokker also developed a re capable C.X for Finland, with a Bristol Pegasus XXI radial engine. Four were ported (C.X Srs II, pictured) followed by licensed production of 35 more by the State rcraft Factory (CX.Srs III and Srs IV). All the available Dutch and Finnish aircraft rticipated in World War II. All the Dutch machines were destroyed between 10 and May 1940. The Finnish machines were active against German forces in 1944–5.

Country of origin:	Netherlands
Type:	two-seat bomber and reconnaissance biplane
Powerplant:	one 835hp (623kW) Bristol Pegasus radial piston engine
Performance:	maximum speed 280km/h (174mph); service ceiling 6400m (20,995ft); range 730km (454 miles)
Weights:	empty 1715kg (3781lb); maximum take-off weight 2545kg (5611lb)
Dimensions:	span 13m (42ft 8in); length 10.4m (34ft 1in); height 4.5m (14ft 9in); wing area 40 sq m (430 sq ft)
Armament:	one fixed forward-firing .31in machine gun; one .31in machine gun on flexible mount in rear cockpit

Fokker D.VII

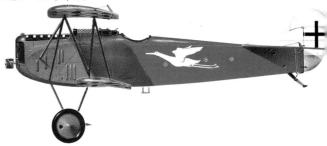

The early 'D' series scouts (D.I to D.VI) were unremarkable aircraft produced by Fokker between August 1915 and late 1917, with undistinguished service careers and unsparkling performance. They were eclipsed by the D.VII designed in late 1917 by a team led by Fokker's Chief Engineer Rheinhold Platz, in time for the German standard fighter competition of January 1918. The D.VII proved vastly superior to any of the other submissions and after modification with a longer fuselage and fixed fin it was put into production. The first unit to receive the type was Manfred von Richtofen's unit JG I, which was commanded by Hermann Göring after the death of the Red Baron in April 1918. Approximately one thousand of this extremely capable aircraft had been completed by the time of the Armistice. Pictured above is a D.VII of Jasta 13, based on the Western Front in 1918.

Country of origin:	Germany
Type:	single-seat fighting scout
Powerplant:	one 185hp (138kW) B.M.W III 6-cylinder inline piston engine
Performance:	maximum speed 200km/h (124mph); service ceiling 7000m (22,965ft); endurance 1hr 30mins
Weights:	empty 735kg (1620lb); maximum take-off weight 880kg (1940lb)
Dimensions:	span 8.9m (29ft 2in); length 6.95m (22ft 9in); height 2.75m (9ft); wing area 20.5 sq m (221 sq ft)
Armament:	two fixed forward-firing 7.92mm LMG 08/15 machine guns

Fokker Dr.I

When the Sopwith Triplane first appeared over the Western Front in late 1916 its performance far outshone any of the current German scouts, and the authorities immediately issued a request for triplane fighters. No fewer than 14 submissions were received, although they were all beaten to the mark by the Fokker Flugzeugwerke Dr.I (Dreidecker), because Fokker had seen the aircraft in action in April 1917 and did not have to wait for the captured example in July. Reinhold Platz, his chief engineer, was no advocate of the triplane layout but nevertheless quickly produced the V.3 prototype. This had stubby, unbraced wings, the only struts being those carrying the top wing. Flight trials revealed some unpleasant handling characteristics and the aircraft was extensively modified before a production order for 350 aircraft was granted.

Country of origin:	Germany
Type:	single-seat fighting scout
Powerplant:	one 110hp (82kW) Oberusel Ur.II 9-cylinder rotary piston engine
Performance:	maximum speed 185km/h (115mph); service ceiling 6100m (20,015ft); endurance 1hr 30mins
Weights:	empty 406kg (894lb); maximum take-off weight 586kg (1291lb)
Dimensions:	span 7.19m (23ft 7in); length 5.77m (18ft 11in); height 2.95m (9ft 8in); wing area 18.66 sq m (201 sq ft)
Armament:	two fixed forward-firing 7.92mm LMG 08/15 machine guns

Fokker Dr.I

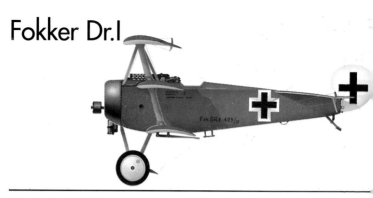

Fokker Dr.I 425/17 was the final mount of Manfred, Baron von Richtofen (the Re
Baron), the top-scoring German ace of World War I with 81 kills, and probably
the most famous fighter pilot of all time. In fact, Richtofen scored the majority of h
kills in other aircraft such as the Albatros D.III. By the time the rotary-engined Dr.
was introduced into service in October 1917, although undoubtedly a supremely
manoeuvrable fighter it was being outclassed by a new generation of fighting scou
and offered only mediocre performance due to the high drag of its triplane wing
structure. Its construction was relatively simple, and when coupled with a skilled
pilot it had the measure of many more powerful machines in a dogfight. However,
speed and range were poor by 1917 standards, and Fokker expressed some surpri
that the Dreidecker received such accolades.

Country of origin:	Germany
Type:	single-seat fighting scout
Powerplant:	one 110hp (82kW) Oberusel Ur.II 9-cylinder rotary piston engine
Performance:	maximum speed 185km/h (115mph); service ceiling 6100m (20,015ft); endurance 1hr 30mins
Weights:	empty 406kg (894lb); maximum take-off weight 586kg (1291lb)
Dimensions:	span 7.19m (23ft 7in); length 5.77m (18ft 11in); height 2.95m (9ft 8in); wing area 18.66 sq m (201 sq ft)
Armament:	two fixed forward-firing 7.92mm LMG 08/15 machine guns

Fokker Dr.I

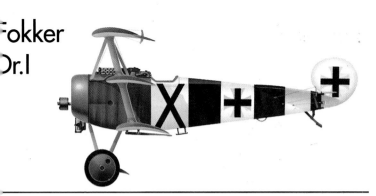

Much of the Dr.I's exaggerated claim to fame can be attributed to the skilled group of fliers who went to war in it. Many of these flew with JG 1, the legendary 'Flying Circus' of Manfred von Richtofen. JG 1 was formed in June 1917 from Jasta 4, 6, 10 and 11, and became known as 'Richtofen's Flying Circus' because of the large number of aircraft under his command, because of their meticulously planned and organised air combat techniques and, not least, because of the flamboyant paint schemes applied to many JG I aircraft. The colour schemes were not only decorative, but helped pilots to identify each other and perhaps strike fear into their opponents. Pictured here is a Dr.I of Jasta 26, with the old-style *Croix pattée* (Maltese Cross) clearly visible despite being overpainted with the new simplified cross for 1918.

Country of origin:	Germany
Type:	single-seat fighting scout
Powerplant:	one 110hp (82kW) Oberusel Ur.II 9-cylinder rotary piston engine
Performance:	maximum speed 185km/h (115mph); service ceiling 6100m (20,015ft); endurance 1hr 30mins
Weights:	empty 406kg (894lb); maximum take-off weight 586kg (1 291lb)
Dimensions:	span 7.19m (23ft 7in); length 5.77m (18ft 11in); height 2.95m (9ft 8in); wing area 18.66 sq m (201 sq ft)
Armament:	two fixed forward-firing 7.92mm LMG 08/15 machine guns

Fokker Dr.I

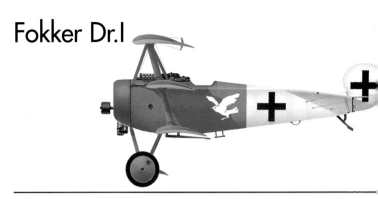

The early service career of the Dr. I was marked by a spate of crashes that were traced back to shoddy workmanship at the Schwerin factory, where its wings were manufactured. All Dr. Is were grounded and their wings stripped of fabric and inspected, and in many cases the spars had to be replaced. Thus it was not until late November 1917 that the aircraft became available in large numbers. Five variants were developed: the V5 had a 160hp (119kW) Goebel Goe.III rotary engine for trial purposes in the January 1918 fighter competition; the V6 had increased span wings and a 120hp (90kW) Mercedes engine, and later formed the basis of the V8 with five sets of wings; the V7 had a 160hp (119kW) Siemens-Halske engine and four blade screw; the V9 had modified wing struts; and the V10 had a 145hp (108kW) Oberusel Ur.II I engine and a ceiling of 9500m (31,170ft).

Country of origin:	Germany
Type:	single-seat fighting scout
Powerplant:	one 110hp (82kW) Oberusel Ur.II 9-cylinder rotary piston engine
Performance:	maximum speed 185km/h (115mph); service ceiling 6100m (20,015ft); endurance 1hr 30mins
Weights:	empty 406kg (894lb); maximum take-off weight 586kg (1291lb)
Dimensions:	span 7.19m (23ft 7in); length 5.77m (18ft 11in); height 2.95m (9ft 8in); wing area 18.66 sq m (201 sq ft)
Armament:	two fixed forward-firing 7.92mm LMG 08/15 machine guns

Fokker E.III

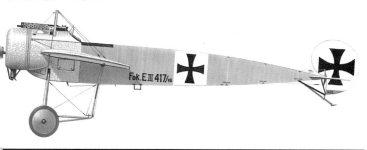

Anthony Fokker designed and built his first aircraft in 1912. The Fokker Spin was a tandem-seat monoplane, with considerable dihedral but no lateral control. It was rejected by the British, who considered it 'badly built', although this probably stemmed from the general dislike of monoplanes among British officialdom rather than any scientific examination. Fokker thereupon offered his services to Germany, which built his M.5 monoplane in large numbers. In April 1915 Roland Garros' aircraft, with his self-designed bullet deflector gear, fell into German hands, prompting them to develop a more effective interrupter gear. This was fitted to a short-span M.5k scout to produce the E.I, and from April until the end of December 1915 the Fokker monoplane was the scourge of Allied pilots on the Western Front. The E.III (pictured) was the definitive model, with some 300 aircraft produced, and was the chosen mount of the German aces Böelcke and Immelmann.

Country of origin:	Germany
Type:	single-seat fighting scout
Powerplant:	one 100hp (75hp) Oberusel U.I 9-cylinder rotary engine
Performance:	maximum speed 134km/h (83mph); service ceiling 3500m (11,500ft); endurance 2hrs 45mins
Weights:	empty 500kg (1100lb); loaded 635kg (1400lb)
Dimensions:	span 9.52m (31ft 3in); length 7.3m (23ft 11in); height 3.12m (9ft 6in); wing area sq m (sq ft)
Armament:	one fixed forward-firing 7.92mm LMG 08/15 machine gun

Fokker T.VIII-Wg

Fokker's T-series floatplanes were specifically designed for service in the East Indies, the major Dutch colonial possession of the interwar period. The T.IV was one of Fokker's most ungainly designs, but was a tough, seaworthy combat aircraft which operated with some distinction against the Japanese invaders. The T.VIII-W was built in three versions: the T.VIII-Wg was of mixed wood-and-metal construction; the T-VIII-Wm was all metal; and the T.VIII-Wc was a scaled-up version in wood-and-metal with more powerful engines. Five were in service by June 1939, when the Fokker factory was overrun. A total of 36 were built, 25 of which were requisitioned by the Luftwaffe (including five T.VIII-Wc aircraft on order for Finland). Eight survivors were flown to England on 14 May 1940, and were operated by their crews as No 320 (Dutch) Squadron of RAF Coastal Command until they ran out of spares in late 1940.

Country of origin:	Netherlands
Type:	three-seat torpedo-bomber/reconnaissance floatplane
Powerplant:	two 450hp (336kW) Wright Whirlwind R-975-E3 9-cylinder radial engines
Performance:	maximum speed 285km/h (177mph); service ceiling 6800m (22,310ft); range 2750km (1709 miles)
Weights:	empty 3100kg (6834lb); maximum take-off weight 5000kg (11,023lb)
Dimensions:	span 18m (59ft); length 13m (42ft 8in); height 5m (16ft 5in); wing area 44 sq m (474 sq ft)
Armament:	one fixed forward-firing .31in machine gun; one .31in machine gun on flexible mount in rear cockpit; plus up to 605kg (1334lb) of stores carried externally

Gloster Gamecock Mk I

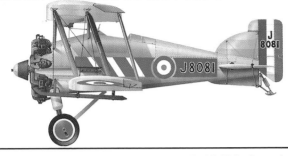

The Gloster Gamecock was a development of the Mk III Grebe, and was built to Air Ministry Specification 27/23. It differed from the Grebe primarily by way of Bristol Jupiter engine, which replaced the unreliable Armstrong Siddeley Jaguar. Other changes included improved ailerons, refined fuselage contours and internally mounted machine guns. It was first flown in February 1925, and 100 were required by the RAF, remaining in service until 1931. Although its wood-and-fabric construction was unremarkable, the Gamecock was a tough and reliable aircraft, able to survive almost anything thrown at it. The Gamecock Mk II (three aircraft were built) had a revised centre wing section. Gloster (as the company became known in 1926) supplied three Gamecock Mk IIs to Finland, which license-built another 15 under the name Kukko. Pictured is a Gamecock Mk I of No 32 Squadron, based at RAF Kenley.

Country of origin:	United Kingdom
Type:	single-seat biplane fighter
Powerplant:	one 425hp (317kW) Bristol Jupiter VI 9-cylinder radial engine
Performance:	maximum speed 249km/h (155mph); service ceiling 6705m (22,000ft); endurance 2hrs
Weights:	empty 875kg (1930lb); maximum take-off weight 1299kg (2863lb)
Dimensions:	span 9.08m (29ft 9in); length 5.99m (19ft 8in); height 2.95m (9ft 8in); wing area 24.53 sq m (264 sq ft)
Armament:	two fixed forward-firing .303in Vickers Mk I machine guns

Gloster Gauntlet Mk I

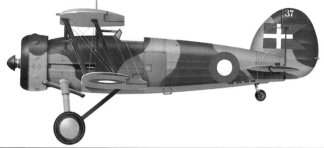

The Gauntlet was one of the most prolific RAF fighters of the 1930s, and in 1937 equipped no fewer than 14 squadrons. It had a rather convoluted development process due to the unsuccessful Goldfinch design, which was an all-metal version of the Gamecock built to an Air Ministry order and evaluated in prototype form but never ordered. Gloster then offered the aircraft as a single-seat fighter under Specification F.9/26 but again failed to win a production contract. The company had almost completed a new aircraft to meet F.9/26 when the Air Ministry issued a new Specification F.20/27 for a high-altitude single-seat fighter. Gloster's submission was the S.S.18 prototype, which was developed over a four-year period to its production form as the Gauntlet Mk I, which had a 640hp (477kW) Bristol Mercury VIS2 engine. The first aircraft of an order for 24 was delivered to the RAF in May 1935, by which time Gloster was under the control of Hawker.

Country of origin:	United Kingdom
Type:	single-seat fighter biplane
Powerplant:	one 640hp (477kW) Bristol Mercury VIS2 9-cylinder radial engine
Performance:	maximum speed 370km/h (230mph); service ceiling 10,120m (33,500ft); range 740km (460 miles)
Weights:	empty 1256kg (2770lb); maximum take-off weight 1801kg (3970lb)
Dimensions:	span 9.99m (32ft 9in); length 8.05m (26ft 5in); height 3.12m (10ft 3in); wing area 29.26 sq m (315 sq ft)
Armament:	two fixed forward-firing .303in Vickers Mk I machine guns

Gloster Gauntlet Mk II

The major production version of the Gauntlet was the Mk II, which embodied many Hawker construction techniques in the fuselage following the rationalisation of techniques within the newly formed Hawker Siddeley Group. Two orders for a total of 204 aircraft were completed, the last of them delivered in 1937. The last batches had a Fairey Reed three-blade metal propeller in place of the two-blade Watts of laminated wood. The Gauntlet was the last open-cockpit fighter to be produced for the RAF and served until June 1940 in the Middle East. Seventeen Gauntlets were produced under licence in Denmark. Ex-RAF Gauntlets were supplied to the Royal Australian Air Force (6), Finland (25), Rhodesia (3) and South Africa (6). Pictured is a Mk II of No 3 Squadron, Royal Australian Air Force, based at Helwan in Egypt in November 1940.

Country of origin:	United Kingdom
Type:	single-seat fighter biplane
Powerplant:	one 640hp (477kW) Bristol Mercury VIS2 9-cylinder radial engine
Performance:	maximum speed 370km/h (230mph); service ceiling 10,120m (33,500ft); range 740km (460 miles)
Weights:	empty 1256kg (2770lb); maximum take-off weight 1801kg (3970lb)
Dimensions:	span 9.99m (32ft 9in); length 8.05m (26ft 5in); height 3.12m (10ft 3in); wing area 29.26 sq m (315 sq ft)
Armament:	two fixed forward-firing .303in Vickers Mk I machine guns

Gloster Gladiator Mk I

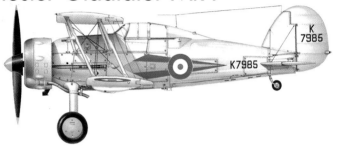

By late 1934 the competition to select a new fighter as a replacement for the Bristol Bulldog to Air Ministry Specification F.7/30 had still not been settled, war clouds were distantly gathering and the fabric-covered biplane was swiftly to be judged obsolete. Harry Folland designed the Gloster S.S.37 as a very late entrant to the competition. However, the Folland aircraft won and was ordered into production in July 1935 as the Gladiator Mk I. Features included four neat, single-bay wings, each having hydraulically depressed drag flaps; cantilever landing gear with Dowty internally sprung wheels; four guns; and in the production aircraft, a sliding canopy. Underwing points were also added for external stores to be carried. The first batch of 23 aircraft was delivered in February and March 1937, followed by a second order for 100 aircraft and a third for 28.

Country of origin:	United Kingdom
Type:	single-seat fighter biplane
Powerplant:	one 840hp (626kW) Bristol Mercury IX 9-cylinder radial piston engine
Performance:	maximum speed 414km/h (257mph); service ceiling 10,120m (33,500ft); range 708km (440 miles)
Weights:	empty 1562kg (3444lb); maximum take-off weight 2206kg (4864lb)
Dimensions:	span 9.83m (32ft 3in); length 8.36m (27ft 5in); height 3.53m (11ft 7in); wing area 30.01 sq m (323 sq ft)
Armament:	two fixed forward-firing .303in Vickers machine guns

Gloster Gladiator Mk II

Completion of the RAF order for Gladiator Mk Is in 1938 was followed by 147 Gladiator Mk Is against foreign contracts. Experience in RAF squadrons had disclosed some problems with the the Watts two-blade wooden propeller leading Fairey to trial one aircraft with a Fairey-Reed three-blade metal propeller. This became the standard fit on the Gladiator Mk II, which introduced a number of other modifications, namely an automatic mixture control, electric starter, and a Vokes desert air filter in the carburettor. A number of RAF Mk Is were converted to this standard, and this service was also received by 252 newbuild aircraft. Home-based RAF Gladiator units were re-equipped with the Mk II and the earlier version was shipped out to Egypt. Pictured is one of the 21 export Mk IIs sold to Portugal, in the markings of Esquadrilha de Caça Expedicionaria No 2 of the Arma de Aéronautica de Achada (Terceira Isle) in the Azores, during August 1941.

Country of origin:	United Kingdom
Type:	single-seat fighter biplane
Powerplant:	one 830hp (619kW) Bristol Mercury VIIIA 9-cylinder radial piston engine
Performance:	maximum speed 414km/h (257mph); service ceiling 10,120m (33,500ft); range 708km (440 miles)
Weights:	empty 1562kg (3444lb); maximum take-off weight 2206kg (4864lb)
Dimensions:	span 9.83m (32ft 3in); length 8.36m (27ft 5in); height 3.53m (11ft 7in); wing area 30.01 sq m (323 sq ft)
Armament:	four fixed forward-firing .303in Colt-Browning machine guns

Gloster Grebe Mk II

After learning his craft at Nieuport during World War I, Harry Folland took his talents to the Gloucester (later Gloster) Aircraft Company and from his drawing board emerged a long line of very successful biplane fighters. The family began with the Gloster Grouse of 1923, used exclusively for research, which was the airframe of the Gloster Sparrowhawk II company demonstrator married to a new biplane wing designed by Folland. This was followed by the Grebe, which together with the Armstrong Whitworth Siskin and Hawker Woodcock was the first new fighter to be selected for the RAF in the interwar years. The prototype completed a highly successful series of flight trials in 1923 and was subsequently redesignated Grebe Mk I. Production aircraft received some minor modifications and were designated Grebe Mk IIs, of which 129 were supplied to the RAF.

Country of origin:	United Kingdom
Type:	single-seat biplane fighter
Powerplant:	one 400hp (298kW) Armstrong Siddeley Jaguar IV 14-cylinder radial piston engine
Performance:	maximum speed 243km/h (151mph); service ceiling 7010m (23,000ft); endurance 2hrs 45mins
Weights:	empty 780kg (1720lb); maximum take-off weight 1189kg (2622lb)
Dimensions:	span 8.94m (29ft 4in); length 6.17m (20ft 3in); height 2.82m (9ft 3in); wing area 23.6 sq m (254 sq ft)
Armament:	two fixed forward-firing .303in Vickers machine guns

Gloster Sea Gladiator

The introduction of the Hawker Hurricane monoplane fighter spelled the end for the Gladiator in Royal Air Force front line service. Although it was involved in the defence of Norway and Malta, it achieved fame out of all proportion to its achievements during this action. An important adaptation of the Mk II took place at the end of 1938 with the appearance of the Sea Gladiator. Ten Gladiator Mk Is were fitted with arrestor gear, resulting in the conversion of the first Mk IIs to interim Sea Gladiator standard, followed by 60 as full-standard Sea Gladiators with catapult spools, arrestor hook, dinghy stowage (between the landing gear legs) and two additional Browning guns in the upper wing. Sea Gladiators were first embarked on HMS *Courageous* with No 801 Squadron in May 1939, and eventually equipped six other Fleet Air Arm squadrons.

Country of origin:	United Kingdom
Type:	single-seat fighter biplane
Powerplant:	one 830hp (619kW) Bristol Mercury VIIIA 9-cylinder radial piston engine
Performance:	maximum speed 414km/h (257mph); service ceiling 10,120m (33,500ft); range 708km (440 miles)
Weights:	empty 1562kg (3444lb); maximum take-off weight 2206kg (4864lb)
Dimensions:	span 9.83m (32ft 3in); length 8.36m (27ft 5in); height 3.53m (11ft 7in); wing area 30.01 sq m (323 sq ft)
Armament:	four fixed forward-firing .303in Colt-Browning machine guns

Gotha G.V

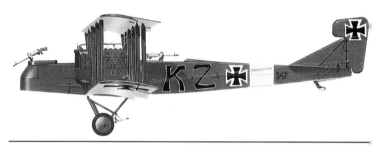

Alongside the airships and 'R' series from the Zeppelin works, the series of 'G' (*Grossflugzeug*, large aeroplane) designs from Gothaer Wagonfabrik played a major role in German strategic bombing in World War I. The G.I stemmed from a prototype built under the direction of Oskar Ursinus, a German Army major. Gotha built a small number under licence for tactical bombing over the Western and Eastern Fronts. The G.II was designed by with the fuselage mounted on the lower rather than upper wing, and with nosewheels to prevent nosing over. The G.II had a direct-drive Mercedes D.IVa, and a few had a tunnel extending to a rear gunners cockpit that covered the previous defensive 'blind spot'. This was standard fitment on the G.IV, the major production version, which first flew in December 1916 and was followed by a limited number of G.V and G.Va aircraft, used for a short time before night-bombing was abandoned by the German Air Service in April 1918.

Country of origin:	Germany
Type:	three-seat long-range biplane bomber
Powerplant:	two 260hp (194kW) Mercedes D.IVa 6-cylinder inline piston engines
Performance:	maximum speed 140km/h (87mph); service ceiling 6500m (21,325ft); range 500km (500 km)
Weights:	empty 2740kg (6041lb); maximum take-off weight 3975kg (8763lb)
Dimensions:	span 23.7m (77ft 9in); length 11.86m (38ft 11in); height 4.3m (14ft 1in); wing area 89.5 sq m (963 sq ft)
Armament:	two 7.92mm Parabellum machine guns on flexible mount in nose position; two 7.92mm Parabellum machine guns on flexible mount in dorsal position; plus maximum bomb load of 500kg (1102lb)

Grumman F2F-1

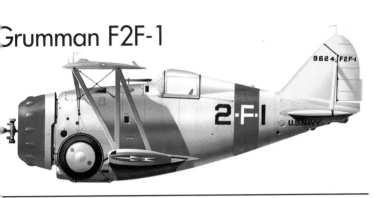

Encouraged by the success of the FF/SF-1 aircraft, Grumman design staff drew up a proposal for a single-seat version and in June 1932 offered it to the US Navy, which ordered a prototype in November. This was slightly smaller than its predecessor, and had ailerons on the upper wing only. Power was provided by a 625hp (466kW) XR-1535-44 Twin Wasp Junior engine. The aircraft had twin forward-firing Brownings and underwing racks for two small bombs. This XF2F-1 first flew in October 1933 and after a six-month evaluation at Anacostia was returned to Grumman for minor modifications to resolve problems with directional instability. The Navy placed an order for 54 F2F-1 fighters in May 1934 and the first was delivered the following January. The aircraft served with VF-2B on USS *Lexington* until September 1940.

Country of origin:	USA
Type:	single-seat carrierborne biplane fighter
Powerplant:	one 650hp (522kW) Pratt & Whitney R-1535-72 Twin Wasp Junior radial piston engine
Performance:	maximum speed 383km/h (238mph); service ceiling 8380m (27,500ft); range 1585km (985 miles)
Weights:	empty 1221kg (2691lb); maximum take-off weight 1745kg (3847lb)
Dimensions:	span 8.69m (28ft 6in); length 6.53m (21ft 5in); height 2.77m (9ft 1in); wing area 21.37 sq m (230 sq ft)
Armament:	two fixed forward-firing .3in Browning machine guns; underwing racks for two 53kg (116lb) bombs

Grumman F3F-1

The F3F stemmed from the G-11 design evolved by Grumman as a slightly enlarged version of the F2F-1 fighter with changes to correct the earlier warplane's lack of directional stability and tendency to spin. The US Navy ordered a single XF3F-1 prototype, and this made its maiden flight in March 1935 with the Pratt & Whitney R-1535-72 Twin Wasp Junior engine. Two other prototypes followed before the US Navy contracted for 54 examples of the F3F-1 production version that differed from the third XF3F-1 only in a slight increase in fuselage length. The aircraft were delivered between January and September 1936, and were initially flown by three squadrons, namely VF-5B and VF-6B (later VF-4 and VF-3) on the aircraft carriers *USS Ranger* and *USS Saratoga*, and VF-4M (later VMF-2) of the US Marine Corps which was shore-based at San Diego.

Country of origin:	USA
Type:	single-seat carrierborne and land-based fighter and fighter-bomber
Powerplant:	one 700hp (522kW) Pratt & Whitney R-1535-84 Twin Wasp Junior 14-cylinder radial engine
Performance:	maximum speed 372km/h (231mph); service ceiling 8685m (28,500ft); range 1609km (1000 miles)
Weight:	empty 1339kg (2952lb); maximum take-off weight 1997kg (4403lb)
Dimensions:	span 9.75m (32ft); length 7.09m (23ft 3in); height 2.77m (9ft 1in); wing area 24.15 sq m (260 sq ft)
Armament:	one 0.5in fixed forward-firing machine gun; one 0.3in fixed forward-firing machine gun in upper part of forward fuselage; plus external bomb load of 232lb (105kg)

Grumman F3F-3

In June 1936 Grumman proposed an F3F-1 development with the Wright R-1820-22 engine. The US Navy ordered an XF3F-2 prototype that made its initial flight in [Ju]ly 1936. This prototype also featured an increase in the internal fuel capacity and [a] three-bladed propellor, and these modifications were retained for the 81 F3F-2 [pr]oduction aircraft that were delivered between July 1937 and May 1938 and [su]pplemented by the XF3F-2 upgraded to production standard. Delivered between [De]cember 1938 and May 1939, the 27 F3F-3 aircraft differed only in their low-drag [en]gine cowlings, revised cockpit enclosure, and modified wing leading edges. Some [of] F3F aircraft were in service with training units and another 101 were on the [ve]rge of transfer to other such units in December 1941. The last of these aircraft was [re]tired in November 1943.

Country of origin:	USA
Type:	single-seat carrierborne and land-based fighter and fighter-bomber
Powerplant:	one 950hp (708kW) Wright R-1820-22 Cyclone 9-cylinder radial engine
Performance:	maximum speed 418km/h (260mph); service ceiling 9845m (32,300ft); range 1819km (1130 miles)
Weight:	empty 1476kg (3254lb); normal take-off weight 2040kg (4498lb); maximum take-off weight 2155kg (4750lb)
Dimensions:	span 9.75m (32ft); length 7.01m (23ft); height 2.84m (9ft 4in); wing area 24.15 sq m (260 sq ft)
Armament:	one 0.5in fixed forward-firing machine gun; one 0.3in fixed forward-firing machine gun in upper part of forward fuselage; plus external bomb load of 232lb (105kg)

Grumman GE-23 Delfin

In 1934 the Canadian Car and Foundry company decided to enter aircraft manufacture and acquired the rights to license-build the FF-1 scout. Between 193 and 1937 it built a total of 57 aircraft; 15 went to the the Royal Canadian Air Force as Goblin Is and one each to Japan and Nicaragua. Forty aircraft were ordered by Turkey under the designation GE-23 Delfin, but they were clandestinely redirected to the Spanish Republican forces via a Turkish agent. Both sides in the Spanish Civ War had to obtain weapons and ammunition secretively, as there was a international agreement banning the open supply of arms. The Delfins played a significant role against Nationalist opponents that were superior in terms of both numbers and technology, thanks to their secret support by Germany and Italy. Pictured here is a GE-23 of 1a Escuadrilla, Grupo No 28 of the Republican Air Force before capture by the Nationalist forces.

Country of origin:	Canada (USA)
Type:	two-seat scouting biplane
Powerplant:	one 700hp (522kW) Wright R-1820-78 9-cylinder radial piston engine
Performance:	maximum speed 333km/h (207mph); service ceiling 6400m (21,000ft); range 1428km (921 miles)
Weights:	empty 1474kg (3250lb); maximum take-off weight 2190kg (4828lb)
Dimensions:	span 10.52m (34ft 6in); length 7.47m (24ft 6in); height 3.38m (11ft 1in); wing area 28.8 sq m (310 sq ft)
Armament:	one fixed forward-firing .3in Browning machine gun; two .3in Browning machine guns on a gimballed mounting attached to observer's seat

Grumman G73 Mallard

Shortly after the end of World War II Grumman developed the G73 Mallard, a twin-engined amphibian for commercial use, drawing on their considerable military experience in producing such a plane. Using a high-mounted cantilever wing with an all-metal stressed skin two-step hull, and powered by two Pratt & Whitney Wasp radial piston engines, the Mallard provided air-conditioned, heated and sound-proofed accomodation for up to ten passengers. Balancer floats gave stability on water, and these could be utilised as auxiliary fuel tanks. Fifty-nine examples were built in total, including one equipped specially for the personal use of King Farouk of Egypt, although the interior and furnishings of standard models were also of a high standard. Pictured above is an example used by Chalk's International, a major operator of the type who used it on the route between Miami and the Bahamas for many years.

Country of origin:	USA
Type:	twin-engined amphibious flying-boat
Powerplant:	two 600hp (447kW) Pratt & Whitney R-1340-S3H1 Wasp 9-cylinder radial piston engines
Performance:	maximum speed 346km/h (215mph); service ceiling 7010m (23,000ft); range 2221km (1380 miles)
Weights:	empty 4241kg (9350lb); maximum take-off weight 5783kg (12,750lb)
Dimensions:	span 20.32m (66ft 8in); length 14.73m (48ft 4in); height 5.72m (18ft 9in); wing area 41.25 sq m (444 sq ft)

Grumman SF-1

The Grumman Aircraft Engineering Corporation was incorporated in December 1929 and began operations at Berthpage, Long Island, where it is still located. The company began its long association with the US Navy in 1931 when it was contracted to build seaplane floats incorporating retracting land wheels. Out of this contract grew the XFF-1 project, a two-seat biplane fighter which was the US Navy's first with retractable gear. The prototype was powered by a 616hp (459kW) Wright R-1820E radial piston engine and first flew in December 1931. Following trials at the US Navy's test facility at Anacostia the type was ordered into production in December 1932 as the FF-1. The first of 27 FF-1s was delivered to VB 5B in June 1933, followed into service from February 1934 by 33 SF-1 aircraft with increased fuel capacity at the expense of one of the machine guns and a 700hp (522kW) R-1820-78 radial engine.

Country of origin:	USA
Type:	two-seat carrierborne scouting biplane
Powerplant:	one 700hp (522kW) Wright R-1820-78 9-cylinder radial piston engine
Performance:	maximum speed 333km/h (207mph); service ceiling 6400m (21,000ft); range 1428km (921 miles)
Weights:	empty 1474kg (3250lb); maximum take-off weight 2190kg (4828lb)
Dimensions:	span 10.52m (34ft 6in); length 7.47m (24ft 6in); height 3.38m (11ft 1in); wing area 28.8 sq m (310 sq ft)
Armament:	one fixed forward-firing .3in Browning machine gun; two .3in Browning machine guns on a gimballed mounting attached to observer's seat

Halberstadt D.IV

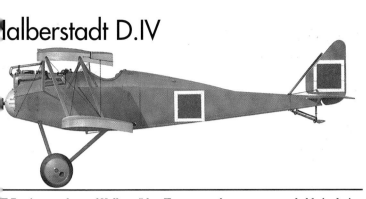

Wartime products of Halberstädter Flugzeugwerke were unremarkable in design and construction, but made a significant contribution to the strength of the Central Powers. The 'C' family of reconnaissance machines began with the C.I, which first flew in May 1916, and ended with the C.V of 1918. The CL light two-seat escorts were effectively employed for ground strafing and close support during the fighting at Somme and Cambrai in autumn 1917. The D.I, like the C.I, was developed from the first two-seat reconnaissance aircraft and appeared in late 1915 as a single-seat scout. Although it appeared frail, it had effective structural strengthening in comparison with the earlier two-seater and was ordered into production in March 1916 as the D.II after being re-engined with the Mercedes D.II; 132 aircraft were produced. Turkey received small numbers of the D.III with bigger ailerons and revised wing mounting, and the D.IV (pictured) with a 150hp (112kW) Benz Bz.III and twin machine guns.

Country of origin:	Germany
Type:	(D.II) single-seat biplane fighter
Powerplant:	one 120hp (89kW) Mercedes D.II inline piston engine
Performance:	maximum speed 150km/h (93mph); service ceiling 5000m (16,400ft); range 250km (155 miles)
Weights:	empty 520kg (1146lb); maximum take-off weight 730kg (1610lb)
Dimensions:	span 8.8m (29ft 10in); length 7.3m (23ft 11in); height 2.67m (8ft 9in); wing area 23.6 sq m (254 sq ft)
Armament:	one fixed forward-firing 7.92mm LMG 08/15 machine gun

Handley Page 0/10

Aa s well as its more famous bombing role, the Handley Page 0/400 also served a a navigation trainer during World War I with units based at Andover and Stonehenge. After the war these units expanded their field of operations to prepar crews for the planned imperial air-mail service. During 1919 Handley Page began modify some surplus aircraft that it bought back from the government with seated accommodation for 12 to 16 passengers as the 0/10. Some 25 of these were operate from the company facility at Cricklewood for joy-riding and on routes linking London to Paris, Brussels and Amsterdam. G-EATN was one of the last HP-built 0/400s, and was converted after the war to 0/10 standard with accommodation for 12 passengers for service with Handley Page Air Transport, which employed it on the Croydon–Paris route. It was also used to test the Aveline Stabilizer, an early tw axis automatic pilot.

Country of origin:	United Kingdom
Type:	12-seat passenger transport biplane
Powerplant:	two 360hp (268kW) Rolls Royce Eagle VIII Vee-12 piston engines
Performance:	maximum speed 122km/h (76mph); service ceiling 2590m (8500ft); range 724km (450 miles)
Weights:	empty 3629kg (8000lb); maximum takeoff weight 6350kg (14,000lb)
Dimensions:	span 30.48m (100ft); length 19.16m (62ft 10in); height 6.7m (22ft); wing area 153.1 sq m (1648 sq ft)

andley Page 0/100

1909 Frederick Handley Page opened at Barking in Essex the first factory
devoted solely to aircraft production. He took up the challenge presented by the
miralty's 0/100 Specification of December 1914 calling for a large bombing
craft, at a time when few people could conceive of such a machine. Handley Page
posed using two 120hp (90kW) Beardmore engines to power his machine. But the
namic Head of the Air Department, Commander Murray Sueter, displayed a
ntagious enthusiasm for the aircraft and the company scaled it up, choosing the
wer and more powerful Rolls Royce Eagle. The 0/100 first flew in December 1915,
sily exceeding the specification. Fifty-six were delivered to RNAS squadrons on the
stern Front, becoming operational in September 1916. Germany received a late
ristmas present on 1 January 1917 when, during its delivery flight from England,
crew of Aircraft No 1463 mistakenly landed the plane on a German field.

Country of origin:	United Kingdom
Type:	three-seat heavy bomber biplane
Powerplant:	two 250hp (186kW) Rolls Royce Eagle II Vee-12 piston engines
Performance:	maximum speed 122km/h (76mph); service ceiling 2590m (8500ft); range with bomb load 724km (450 miles)
Weights:	empty 3629kg (8000lb); loaded 6350kg (14,000lb)
Dimensions:	span 30.48m (100ft); length 19.16m (62ft 10in); height 6.7m (22ft); wing area 153.1 sq m (1648 sq ft)
Armament:	twin .303in Lewis guns on flexible mount in nose cockpit; one .303in Lewis gun on flexible mount in dorsal position; one .303in Lewis gun on flexible mount in ventral position; internal bomb bay with provision for eight 113kg (250lb) or 16 51kg (112lb) bombs

Handley Page 0/400

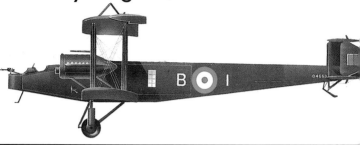

The US Air Service was eager to acquire the 0/400 and a production licence was negotiated for Standard Aircraft Corporation to build the aircraft with Packard Liberty 12 engines. A British aircraft was sent over to the USA as a pattern, along with sets of parts, but production got off to a slow start. The Air Ministry had placed an early order for 1500 0/400s for final assembly in England, but only 100 sets had been delivered to the UK by the Armistice, plus 7 assembled at Langley Field with Liberty 12 engines as US Army Aviation Service Nos 62445–62451. The remainder of the British order was cancelled. A total of 33 were built by Standard, although only 13 actually went into US Army Service. Pictured here is one of the first aircraft, No 62447, which was given the name Langley. No 62448 was used in Billy Mitchell's trials to demonstrate the potential of aircraft in the anti-shipping role, and later dropped a 1815kg (4000lb) bomb.

Country of origin:	United Kingdom
Type:	three-seat heavy bomber biplane
Powerplant:	two 350hp (261kW) Packard Liberty 12 inline piston engines
Performance:	maximum speed 122km/h (76mph); service ceiling 2590m (8500ft); range with bomb load 724km (450 miles)
Weights:	empty 3629kg (8000lb); loaded 6350kg (14,000lb)
Dimensions:	span 30.48m (100ft); length 19.16m (62ft 10in); height 6.7m (22ft); wing area 153.1 sq m (1648 sq ft)
Armament:	twin .303in Lewis guns on flexible mount in nose cockpit; one .303in Lewis gun on flexible mount in dorsal position; one .303in Lewis gun on flexible mount in ventral position; internal bomb bay with provision for up to 1814kg (4000lb) of bombs

Handley Page 0/400

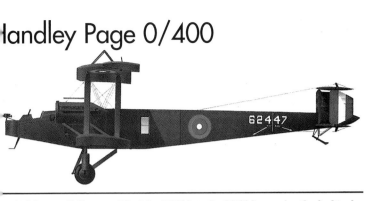

In 1916 George Volkert modified the 0/100 into the 0/400 by moving the fuel tanks from the nacelles into the fuselage and fitting Rolls Royce Eagle VIII engines. The other minor modification was the introduction of a compressed air engine starting system. Some 554 0/400s were built by British contractors with any one of four different engines fitted, namely the 284hp (212kW) Eagle IV, 360hp (268kW) Eagle VII, 275hp (205kW) Sunbeam Maori or 350hp (261kW) Liberty 12. In the summer of 1918 the 0/400 was the backbone of the newly formed Independent Bombing Force. Large formations of up to 40 aircraft mounted night-attacks on German industrial areas and communications centres, ranging as far as Mannheim. By the end of the conflict 0/400s were carrying 748kg (1650lb) bombs and also made a contribution to the campaign in Palestine. Shown above is an aircraft from No. 207 Sqn at Ligescourt, France, in 1918.

Country of origin:	United Kingdom
Type:	three-seat heavy bomber biplane
Powerplant:	two 360hp (268kW) Rolls Royce Eagle VIII Vee-12 piston engines
Performance:	maximum speed 122km/h (76mph); service ceiling 2590m (8500ft); range with bomb load 724km (450 miles)
Weights:	empty 3629kg (8000lb); loaded 6350kg (14,000lb)
Dimensions:	span 30.48m (100ft); length 19.16m (62ft 10in); height 6.7m (22ft); wing area 153.1sq m (1648 sq ft)
Armament:	twin .303in Lewis guns on flexible mount in nose cockpit; one .303in Lewis gun on flexible mount in dorsal position; one .303in Lewis gun on flexible mount in ventral position; internal bomb bay with provision for eight 113kg (250lb) or 16 51kg (112lb) bombs

Handley Page H.P.35 Clive

In the interwar years the RAF placed a great deal of faith and much of its resource into developing a strategic bombing force. Air Ministry Specification 31/22 prompted the development by Handley Page of a night-bomber version of the recently introduced W.8 passenger transport, which entered RAF service in 1925 a the Handley Page (H.P.24) Hyderabad. An improved version was developed to Specification 13/29 as the H.P.33, which differed primarily by way of its Bristol Jupiter VIII radial engines. Two prototypes were followed by six production Hinai Mk Is and 33 H.P.36 Hinaidi Mk IIs with an all-metal fuselage structure. The second prototype, with an all-wood structure, was later redesignated Clive Mk I and serve as a transport aircraft with accommodation for 23 troops. Two further production aircraft were built as the Clive Mk II, with an all-metal basic structure. During the early 1930s these served at Lahore, India, with the RAF Heavy Transport Flight.

Country of origin:	United Kingdom
Type:	heavy transport aircraft
Powerplant:	two 440hp (328kW) Bristol Jupiter VIII radial engines
Performance:	maximum speed 196km/h (122mph); service ceiling 4420m (14,500ft); range 1368km (850 miles)
Weights:	empty 3647kg (8040lb); maximum take-off weight 6577kg (14,500lb)
Dimensions:	span 22.86m (75ft); length 18.03m (59ft 2in); height 5.18m (17ft); wing area 136.66 sq m (1471 sq ft)

andley Page H.P.42W

n 1928 Imperial Airways ordered four Handley Page H.P.42E and H.P.42W airliners for use on its eastern and western routes. A cabin mock-up was xhibited at the Olympia Aero Show in July 1929 and on 17 November 1930 the rototype G-AAGX Hannibal made its first flight. The two models differed slightly in owerplant and cabin arrangement, the H.P.42Es having the Bristol Jupiter XLF ngine and seating for 18 (later 24), while the H.P.42W had the Jupiter X.FBM with a educed fuel load and baggage/mail compartment, allowing for a 38-seat onfiguration. Hannibal opened the Croydon–Paris route on 9 June 1931, and in ugust was despatched to Cairo for service on the eastern route. By the end of the ear it had been joined by three other H.P.42Es, and by January 1932 the last l.P.42W had been delivered. Only one of these excellent aircraft was lost during ight years of service, but war service soon consumed them.

Country of origin:	United Kingdom
Type:	civil transport aircraft
Powerplant:	four 555hp (414kW) Bristol Jupiter XFBM 9-cylinder radial engines
Performance:	maximum speed 204km/h (125mph); range 805km (500 miles)
Weights:	empty 8047kg (17,740lb); maximum take-off weight 12,701kg (28,000lb)
Dimensions:	span 39.62m (130ft); length 28.09m (92ft 2in); height 8.23m (27ft); wing area 277.68sq m (2,989sq ft)

Handley Page H.P.50 Heyford Mk IA

When it first appeared in 1930 the ungainly appearance of the H.P.50 was roundly derided, yet this aircraft formed the backbone of Britain's so-called strategic bombing fleet in the 1930s and soldiered on until more capable types were introduced. Its clumsy appearance was compounded by its unusual configuration, with shoulder-mounted biplane wing. Handley Page designers reasoned that incorporating a bomb bay into this lower wing would reduce the time required for rearming. Power was provided by two Rolls Royce Kestrels in nacelles mounted beneath the upper wing, and defensive armament took the form of three fuselage-mounted machine guns, one in a retractable dustbin turret. The RAF took delivery of 124 H.P.50s as Heyford Mks I, II and IIIs, which differed mainly in installed powerplant. Eleven squadrons were equipped with the type; by 1939 they had all re-equipped with Vickers Wellingtons, and the Heyford was relegated to training.

Country of origin:	United Kingdom
Type:	heavy night-bomber
Powerplant:	two 575hp (429kW) Rolls Royce Kestrel IIIS 12-cylinder Vee-piston engine
Performance:	maximum speed 229km/h (142mph); service ceiling 6400m (21,000ft); range with 726kg (1600lb) bomb load 1481kg (920 miles)
Weights:	empty 4173kg (9200lb); maximum take-off weight 7666kg (16,900lb)
Dimensions:	span 22.86m (75ft); length 17.68m (58ft); height 5.33m (17ft 6in); wing area 136.56 sq m (1470 sq ft)
Armament:	one .303in Lewis machine gun on flexible mount in nose position; one .303in Lewis machine gun on flexible mount in dorsal position; one .303in Lewis machine gun on flexible mount in ventral turret; internal bay with provision for up to 1588kg (3500lb) of bombs

Handley Page W.8b

The design of the 0/400 made it unsuitable for long-term use as a passenger transport and shortly after World War I Handley Page undertook development of a civil transport derivative identified as the W/400. This had a redesigned fuselage allowing for up to eight pairs of forward-facing seats with a central gangway. This was mated to the wings and undercarriage sourced from the V/1500 bomber, a scaled-up version of the 0/400 that arrived too late to see service in the World War I and was only built in small numbers. The prototype was first flown in August 1919 and subsequent flight-testing revealed the need for some refinements and greater power for the following W.8 prototype. Eight production W.8b aircraft were built, with Rolls Royce Eagle VIII engines and seating for 12 in a well-glazed cabin. Pictured is one of the aircraft operated by Imperial Airways.

Country of origin:	United Kingdom
Type:	12-seat passenger transport biplane
Powerplant:	two 360hp (268kW) Rolls Royce Eagle VIII Vee-12 piston engines
Performance:	maximum speed 122km/h (76mph); service ceiling 3050m (10,000ft); range 644km (400 miles)
Weights:	empty 3629kg (8000lb); loaded 6350kg (14,000lb)
Dimensions:	span 22.86m (75ft); length 18.31m (60ft 1in); height 6.7m (22ft); wing area 135.26 sq m (1456 sq ft)

Hansa-Brandenburg C.I

Ernst Heinkel cut his teeth as an aircraft designer whilst in the employment of the Hansa und Brandenburgische Flugzeugwerke Gmbh, which entered aircraft manufacture at the outbreak of World War I. As the chief designer for the company, Heinkel was responsible for the most important family of German floatplanes of the war. He also designed landplanes, a notable example being one of his earliest and mo successful designs the C.I two-seat armed reconnaissance aircraft. After entry into service in 1916 this was built in some numbers for the Austrian forces. The aircraft wa a conventional two-bay biplane of wood-and-fabric construction, with a tractor engine mounted in the nose of the fuselage that had a combined open cockpit for the pilot an observer/gunner. Production aircraft were seen with powerplants in the 160hp (119kW) to 230hp (172kW) range, and later examples had a single fixed forward-firing machine gun and light bomb racks on the lower wings.

Country of origin:	Germany
Type:	(Hiero engine) two-seat armed reconnaissance aircraft
Powerplant:	one 200hp (149kW) Hiero inline piston engine
Performance:	maximum speed 158km/h (98mph); service ceiling 6000m (19,685ft); endurance 3hrs
Weights:	empty 820kg (1808lb); maximum take-off weight 1320kg (2910lb)
Dimensions:	span 12.25m (40ft 2in); length 8.45m (27ft 9in); height 3.33m (10ft 11in)
Armament:	one 8mm Schwarzlöse machine gun on pivoted mount in rear of cockpit

Hansa-Brandenburg W.12

Ernst Heinkel's first floatplane design for Hansa-Brandenburg was the KDW (*Kampf Doppeldecker, Wasser* – or fighting biplane, water), a small single-seater developed from the D.1 landplane, for coastal patrol work on the Baltic, North Sea and Mediterranean shores. The KDW first flew in the summer of 1916, and production of 58 aircraft followed with Benz III, Maybach Mb III or Mercedes engines. The W.12 design was an attempt to rectify the inherent weakness of the KDW – its vulnerability to attack from the rear – and had a rear cockpit to accommodate an observer gunner. Constructed of wood and fabric, the W.12 had an unusual tail unit that provided an uninterrupted field of fire for the rear gun, and a wing that was sufficiently robust for Heinkel to dispense with bracing wires. The prototype flew in early 1917 and was followed by 146 production aircraft, one of which shot down the British airship C.27.

Country of origin:	Germany
Type:	two-seat fighter seaplane
Powerplant:	one 160hp (119kW) Mercedes D.III 6-cylinder inline piston engine
Performance:	maximum speed 160km/h (99mph); service ceiling 5000m (16,405ft); endurance 3hrs 30mins
Weights:	empty 997kg (2198lb); maximum take-off weight 1454kg (3206lb)
Dimensions:	span 11.2m (36ft 9in); length 9.6m (31ft 6in); height 3.3m (10ft 10in); wing area 35.3 sq m (380 sq ft)
Armament:	one or two fixed forward-firing 7.92mm LMG 08/15 machine guns; one 7.92mm Parabellum machine gun on flexible mount in rear cockpit

Hansa-Brandenburg W.33 (A.22)

The monoplane W.29 resulted from the need to improve the performance of Germany's fighter seaplanes, and was a classic design that set the pattern for the later Ernst Heinkel designs. Essentially a W.12 with a monoplane wing, the 78 aircraft that had been delivered by the Armistice did well in combat from April 1918. The majority had Benz Bz.III engines, but a few late-production examples had the more powerful 185hp (138kW) Benz Bz.IIIa. The W.33 was a scaled-up version that was produced in the summer and autumn of 1918. Wartime production totalled 26. After the war the W.33 was used by Denmark and was built by state factory IVL near Helsinki as the A.22 until the late 1920s. Pictured is a ski-equipped A.22 of No Detached Maritime Flying School, Finnish Air Force, based at Viipuri. The skis were used for winter operations from ice.

Country of origin:	Germany
Type:	two-seat fighter seaplane
Powerplant:	one 245hp (183kW) Maybach Mb.IV inline piston engine
Performance:	maximum speed 175km/h (109mph); service ceiling 5000m (16,404ft); endurance 5hrs
Weights:	empty 1500kg (3300lb); maximum take-off weight 2045kg (4510lb)
Dimensions:	span 15.85m (52ft); length 11.1m (36ft 4in); height 3.39m (11ft 1in);
Armament:	one or two fixed forward-firing 7.92mm Spandau machine guns; one 7.92mm Spandau machine gun on pivoted mount in rear cockpit

Hawker Audax

One of the great proliferation of Hart variants, the Hawker Audax was developed to Air Ministry Specification 7/31, which called for an army co-operation aircraft to replace the venerable Armstrong Whitworth Atlas of only three years vintage, primarily for service in the Middle East and on the North West Frontier of India. The prototype Audax was created by modifying the airframe of an early Hart (K1438) with a message pick-up hook, and first flew in December 1931. In this form the Audax was ordered into production and first entered service in February 1932 with No 4 Squadron. A distinguishing feature was the long exhaust pipe which extended to the fuselage mid-point. Production for the RAF totalled 624 in three main versions, most of them with the Kestrel X engine. The Audax (Export) was sold to Canada, Egypt, Iraq and Persia, the example shown here being the first of 24 Bristol Pegasus IIM2-engined aircraft delivered to Iraq in 1935.

Country of origin:	United Kingdom
Type:	two-seat army cooperation aircraft
Powerplant:	one 580hp (433kW) Bristol Pegasus II.M2 radial piston engine
Performance:	maximum speed 274km/h (170mph); service ceiling 6555m (21,500ft); endurance 3hrs 30mins
Weights:	empty 1333kg (2938lb); maximum take-off weight 1989kg (4386lb)
Dimensions:	span 11.35m (37ft 3in); length 9.02m (29ft 7in); height 3.17m (10ft 5in); wing area 32.33 sq m (348 sq ft)
Armament:	one fixed forward-firing .303in Vickers Mk II machine gun; one .303in Lewis machine gun on pivoted mount in rear cockpit; underwing racks with provision for four 9kg (20lb) or two 51kg (112lb) stores

Hawker Demon Mk I

The performance of the Hawker Hart caused great consternation among the Air Staff, hastening the development by Hawker of a two-seat fighter version to Specification 15/30 as an interim measure before the Hawker Fury became available. Six aircraft were built with two front guns and Rolls Royce Kestrel IIS engines, and were delivered for use by No 23 (Fighter Squadron) at Kenley in July 1931. These were followed by 237 Hawker Demons, which differed from the Hart by having a revised rear cockpit to improve the field of fire for the gun; radio communications equipment; and in some later models a tailwheel. Hawker also built 54 Demons for the RAAF, and 20 dual-control Demon Mk II trainers for the RAF and RAAF, which received 10 apiece. In late 1934 a Demon was flown with a Frazer Nash power-operated gun turret, and many aircraft were subsequently modified and known as the Turret Demon.

Country of origin	United Kingdom
Type:	two-seat fighter biplane
Powerplant:	one 584hp (392kW) Rolls Royce Kestrel IIS 12-cylinder Vee piston engine
Performance:	maximum speed 303km/h (188mph); service ceiling 6500m (21,320ft); range 756km (470 miles)
Weights:	empty 1148kg (2530lb); maximum take-off weight 2066kg (4554lb)
Dimensions:	span 11.35m (37ft 3in); length 8.94m (29ft 4in); height 3.17m (10ft 5in); wing area 32.33 sq m (348 sq ft)
Armament:	two fixed forward-firing .303in Vickers Mk II machine guns; one .303in Lewis Mk machine gun on pivoted mount in rear cockpit

Hawker Fury Mk I

The delightful Hawker Fury fighter has its roots in the radial-engined Hoopoe prototype, which was produced by Hawker as a private-venture to meet Naval ecification N.21/26 and was subsequently tailored to the new Rolls Royce Kestrel gine enclosed in a contoured nose. This design exceeded by a good margin the quirements of Air Ministry Specification F.20/27, and in prototype form as the wker Hornet it was displayed at the 1929 Olympia Aero Show. Before mmencing flight trials the Hornet was re-engined with a supercharged Kestrel d demonstrated such impressive performance that Specification 13/30 was itten around it, with Sidney Camm as a consultant. The preliminary order for ree development aircraft, designated the Fury in accordance with Air Ministry menclature, was followed by the first batch of 18 production aircraft.

Country of origin:	United Kingdom
Type:	single-seat fighter interceptor
Powerplant:	one 525hp (392kW) Rolls-Royce Kestrel IIS 12-cylinder Vee piston engine
Performance:	maximum speed 333km/h (207mph); service ceiling 8535m (28,000ft); range 491km (305 miles)
Weights:	empty 1190kg (2623lb); maximum take-off weight 1583kg (3490lb)
Dimensions:	span 9.14m (30ft); length 8.13m (26ft 8in); height 3.1m (10ft 2in); wing area 23.41 sq m (252 sq ft)
Armament:	two fixed forward-firing .303in Vickers Mk III machine guns

Hawker Fury Mk II

Despite achieving only modest sales success with the Fury, partly due to the depressed world fighter market stemming from the economic slump of 1930, Hawker persisted with development of the aircraft to produce a descendant that could be tendered to Specification F.7/30, one of the few forward-thinking documents drawn up by the prewar Air Staff. Sidney Camm designed a developmen aircraft with spatted wheels, Goshawk supercharger and steam-condenser evaporative cooling which was tested during the spring of 1932. Hawker then built the so-called High Speed Fury, which was trialled with various wing and strut configurations from May 1933, and later with armament and the new 730hp (545k Goshawk engine. Re-engined with the Kestrel VI engine this became the Fury Mk II which was accepted as the basis for an interim fighter needed to serve during the Hawker Hurricane's development period. Production for the RAF was 98 aircraft.

Country of origin:	United Kingdom
Type:	single-seat fighter interceptor
Powerplant:	one 700hp (447kW) Rolls-Royce Kestrel VI 12-cylinder Vee piston engine
Performance:	maximum speed 359km/h (223mph); service ceiling 8990m (29,500ft); range 435km (270 miles)
Weights:	empty 1240kg (2734lb); maximum take-off weight 1637kg (3609lb)
Dimensions:	span 9.14m (30ft); length 8.13m (26ft 8in); height 3.1m (10ft 2in); wing area 23.41 sq m (252 sq ft)
Armament:	two fixed forward-firing .303in Vickers Mk III machine guns

Hawker Hart Mk I

The Hawker Hart prototype was created by a Hawker design team led by Sidney Camm in 1926 to Air Ministry Specification 12/26, which called for a new light bomber employing the new Rolls Royce Kestrel engine, a maximum top speed of 7km/h (160mph), and a bomb load of 203kg (448lb). Hawker was contracted for a single prototype and flight-testing began in June 1927. In June 1929 a contract for 15 Hart Mk Is was raised and these were delivered in January 1930 to No 33 Squadron, Eastleigh. In the annual air defence exercises of that year the Hart demonstrated a higher top speed than any contemporary RAF fighter. One of the original production batch was sent for evaluation in the harsh climes of the North West Frontier and performed admirably, prompting the Air Staff to select it as standard equipment for the RAF. A further contract for 32 aircraft was issued in 1930, and another for 50 in 1931. Pictured is a Hart Mk I of No 33 Squadron, based at Upper Heyford in 1934.

Country of origin:	United Kingdom
Type:	two-seat light day bomber
Powerplant:	one 525hp (392kW) Rolls Royce Kestrel IB 12-cylinder Vee piston engine
Performance:	maximum speed 298km/h (184mph); service ceiling 6500m (21,320ft); range 756km (470 miles)
Weights:	empty 1148kg (2530lb); maximum take-off weight 2066kg (4554lb)
Dimensions:	span 11.35m (37ft 3in); length 8.94m (29ft 4in); height 3.17m (10ft 5in); wing area 32.33 sq m (348 sq ft)
Armament:	one fixed forward-firing .303in Vickers Mk II machine gun; one .303in Lewis machine gun on pivoted mount in rear cockpit; underwing racks with provision for up to 236kg (520lb) of bombs

Hawker Hart Trainer Series 2A

The Hart was built in a great number of variants, including 57 Hart (India) and Hart (Special) aircraft with tropical equipment and Kestrel IB, V or X (fitted to late 77 Specials only) engines, and the Hart Communications aircraft (three converted from Mk I bombers and four newly built) without bomb equipment and armament. The Hart (Export) sold well; eight were supplied to Estonia with Kestrel engines and interchangeable float/wheeled landing gear, and four Hawker-built examples were delivered to Sweden with the Pegasus IM2 radial engine and interchangeable float/wheeled landing gear. Sweden also license-built 42 others at Trollhätten between 1935 and 1936 with Nohab IU2 engines. The most prolific of the family were the dual-control trainers, 507 of which were built in four main batches between 1934 and 1936. Pictured is the restored Series 2A example in the collection of the RAF Museum at Hendon.

Country of origin:	United Kingdom
Type:	two-seat advanced trainer
Powerplant:	one 510hp (300kW) Rolls Royce Kestrel XDR 12-cylinder Vee piston engine
Performance:	maximum speed 298km/h (184mph); service ceiling 6500m (21,320ft); range 756km (470 miles)
Weights:	empty 1148kg (2530lb); maximum take-off weight 2066kg (4554lb)
Dimensions:	span 11.35m (37ft 3in); length 8.94m (29ft 4in); height 3.17m (10ft 5in); wing area 32.33 sq m (348 sq ft)

awker Hind

ir Ministry Specification G.7/34 called for a light bomber that could serve as an
interim replacement for the Hawker Hart until more modern types such as the
tol Blenheim and Fairey Battle began to enter service. Sidney Camm proposed
pdated version of the Hart, powered by a 640hp (477kW) Kestrel V engine.
er distinguishing features were a cut-down rear cockpit, which afforded a better
of fire for the observer, and a tailwheel in place of the skid. The prototype
was flown in September 1934 and was followed by 527 production aircraft
ch served in no less than 47 RAF bomber squadrons between 1935 and 1939.
Hind also served with the air forces of Afghanistan, Eire, India, Kenya, Latvia,
Zealand and Persia. Many RAF Hinds were converted for training by removing
armament, including the example pictured, which served with No 1 Flying
ning School in the early war years.

untry of origin:	United Kingdom
pe:	two-seat light day-bomber
werplant:	one 640hp (477kW) Rolls-Royce Kestrel V 12-cylinder Vee piston engine
rformance:	maximum speed 298km/h (184mph); service ceiling 8045m (26,400ft); range 692km (430 miles)
eights:	empty 1475kg (3251lb); maximum take-off weight 2403kg (5298lb)
mensions:	span 11.35m (37ft 3in); length 9.02m (29ft 7in); height 3.23m (10ft 7in); wing area 32.33 sq m (348 sq ft)
mament:	one fixed-forward firing .303in Vickers Mk II machine gun; one .303in Lewis machine gun on pivoted mount in rear cockpit; underwing racks with provision for up to 227kg (500lb) of bombs

Hawker Horsley Mk II

Pictured here in the colours of No 33 (Bomber) Squadron, based at Netheravon and Eastchurch in the early 1930s, the Hawker Horsley was a two-seat medium day-bomber developed by the company to Air Ministry Specification 26/23, which called for a replacement for the Airco D.H.9. Hawker began the construction of the prototype in 1924, this having unequal-span slightly swept biplane wings, a conventionally braced tail unit, tailskid landing gear and power provided by a Rolls-Royce Condor III inline piston engine. The prototype first flew in 1925, and was followed by an initial production aircraft of the Horsley Mk I aircraft. Early examples of the Horsley Mk II were of mixed wood-and fabric-construction, while the later aircraft had an all-metal basic structure. Total production for the RAF was 123 aircraft.

Country of origin:	United Kingdom
Type:	two-seat day-bomber
Powerplant:	one 665hp (496kW) Rolls-Royce Condor IIIA 12-cylinder Vee-piston engine
Performance:	maximum speed 201km/h (125mph); service ceiling 4265m (14,000ft); endurance 10hrs
Weights:	empty 2159kg (4760lb); maximum take-off weight 3538kg (7800lb)
Dimensions:	span 17.21m (56ft 6in); length 11.84m (38ft 10in); height 4.17m (13ft 8in); wing area 64.38 sq m (693 sq ft)
Armament:	one fixed-forward firing .303in Vickers Mk II machine gun; one .303in Lewis machine gun on pivoted mount in rear cockpit; external racks with provision for 680kg (1500lb) of bombs or one 46cm (18in) torpedo

awker Nimrod

he needs of naval aviation were poorly served by the Admiralty in the interwar years and even as late as 1932 the best fighter available to Fleet Air Arm (FAA) ter squadrons, the Fairey Flycatcher, had a top speed of only 214km/h 3mph). Some RAF wags opined that a sprightly fly might give the aircraft a run its money! A specification detailing the requirements for a replacement was ed in 1926 but none of the submissions, including Hawker's Hoopoe, was med to be acceptable. Undeterred, Hawker built the Norn, which later became Nimrod. The first production Nimrod Mk Is entered service in 1933 with Nos , 802, and 803 Squadrons, FAA, followed in September 1934 by 27 Nimrod Mk IIs h arrestor gear, more powerful engines, and tail surfaces of increased area. One raft was supplied to Japan and one to Portugal, and two went to Denmark.

ountry of origin:	United Kingdom
ype:	single-seat carrier-based fighter
owerplant:	one 608hp (453kW) Rolls-Royce VFP 12-cylinder Vee piston engine
erformance:	maximum speed 311km/h (193mph); service ceiling 8535m (28,000ft); endurance 1hr 40mins
Veights:	empty 1413kg (3115lb); maximum take-off weight 1841kg (4059lb)
imensions:	span 10.23m (33ft 7in); length 8.09m (26ft 6in); height 3m (9ft 10in); wing area 27.96 sq m (301 sq ft)
rmament:	two fixed forward-firing .303in machine guns; plus provision for four 20lb bombs on underwing racks

Hawker Spanish Fury

As RAF Fury squadrons wowed the crowds at the Hendon air displays of the e[...]1930s, foreign customers queued up to buy this aircraft, albeit in small numb[...] because of the relatively high unit cost and slow production of the Rolls Royce Kestrel engine. The largest overseas customer was Persia, whose air force had previously bought the Hart. It ordered 16 Furies with Pratt & Whitney Hornet ra[...] engines followed by six more with the Bristol Mercury VISP. Portugal took three 1935, and Spain received three aircraft as Hawker Spanish Furies in 1935 with single-leg cantilever landing gear and 700hp (522kW) Hispano-Suiza 12Xbrs engines. Pictured is a Hispano-engined Fury originally supplied to the Spanish Ai[...] Force; it was later captured and operated during the Civil War by the Nationalist Force, as can be seen by the tail marking.

Country of origin:	United Kingdom
Type:	single-seat fighter interceptor
Powerplant:	one 700hp (522kW) Hispano-Suiza 12Xbrs 12-cylinder piston engine[...]
Performance:	maximum speed 359km/h (223mph); service ceiling 8990m (29,500ft); range 435km (270 miles)
Weights:	empty 1240kg (2734lb); maximum take-off weight 1637kg (3609lb)
Dimensions:	span 9.14m (30ft); length 8.13m (26ft 8in); height 3.1m (10ft 2in); wing area 23.41 sq m (252 sq ft)
Armament:	two fixed forward-firing .303in Vickers machine guns

Hawker Tomtit Mk I

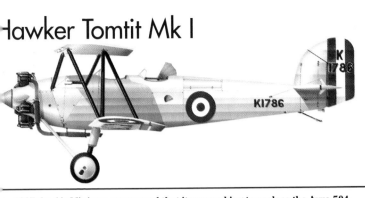

In 1927 the Air Ministry announced that it was seeking to replace the Avro 504. Designing an aircraft to replace the long-serving and much-loved 504 was not an unviable undertaking, but one that Sidney Camm set about with relish. The single-bay equal-span stagger-wing biplane that he produced was first flown in November 1928 as the Hawker Tomtit. The aircraft structure was of wood and fabric with the instructor and pupil accommodated in tandem cockpits in the fuselage. Over the rear cockpit was fitted a blind flying hood, to supplement the Reid and Sigrist instrumentation for blind-flying instruction. Three months after the first flight the first batch was ordered for the RAF for entry into service in 1930. Production total was 31 aircraft, including two for the Canadian Department of National Defence and four for the New Zealand Permanent Air Force. After a very brief RAF career, the Tomtit was replaced by the Avro Tudor.

Country of origin:	United Kingdom
Type:	two-seat military trainer
Powerplant:	one 150hp (112kW) Armstrong Siddeley Mongoose IIIC 5-cylinder radial piston engine
Performance:	maximum speed 200km/h (124mph); service ceiling 5945m (19,500ft)
Weights:	empty 499kg (1100lb); maximum take-off weight 794kg (1750lb)
Dimensions:	span 8.71m (28ft 7in); length 7.21m (23ft 8in); height 2.54m (8ft 4in); wing area 22.09 sq m (238 sq ft)

Hawker Yugoslav Fury Series II

Yugoslavia took delivery of six Hawker Yugoslav Fury Series Is in 1932, powered by the supercharged 525hp (392kW) Rolls Royce Kestrel IIS engine. One was subsequently returned to the Hawker works at Kingston to have a 720hp (537kW) Lorraine Petrel Hfrs engine fitted, and in trials this demonstrated an impressive top speed of 369km/h (229mph), but for the sake of commonality with the Hawker Hind aircraft currently in service the Yugoslavs opted for the Kestrel XVI engine for their next order for 10 aircraft. This Hawker Yugoslav Furt Series II had four-gun armament, low-drag radiator and single-leg landing gear. It was the fastest of the export Furies, with a top speed of 389km/h (242mph). Pictured is a Series II aircraft of the 35th Group, 5th Fighter Regiment, Royal Yugoslav Air Force, based at Kraljevo in April 1941 and in the front line when the Germans attacked.

Country of origin:	United Kingdom
Type:	single-seat fighter interceptor
Powerplant:	one 525hp (392kW) Rolls-Royce Kestrel IIS 12-cylinder Vee piston engine
Performance:	maximum speed 389km/h (242mph); service ceiling 8535m (28,000ft); range 491km (305 miles)
Weights:	empty 1240kg (2734lb); maximum take-off weight 1637kg (3609lb)
Dimensions:	span 9.14m (30ft); length 8.13m (26ft 8in); height 3.1m (10ft 2in); wing area 23.41 sq m (252 sq ft)
Armament:	two fixed forward-firing .303in Vickers machine guns

Heinkel He 51A-1

When Hansa Brandenburg went into liquidation in 1919 Dr Ernst Heinkel joined the Caspar Flugzeugwerke for a year but then took the bold step of setting up his own company, which was registered on 1 December 1922 at Warnemünde on the Baltic coast. The Treaty of Versailles forbade German manufacturers form building military aircraft and so Heinkel, like many other German designers, formed partnerships and subsidiaries in other countries. Heinkel's subsidiary in Sweden provided him with the necessary cover to allow him to carry on developing the 'W' family of seaplanes that had made his name in World War I. As the likelihood of Allied legal action receded, Heinkel dared to build the prototype of an aircraft that blatantly disregarded the Treaty – the He 37 – which first flew in 1928. This was followed by a succession of He 49 prototypes, which formed the basis for the He 51 delivered to the Luftwaffe from July 1934.

Country of origin:	Germany
Type:	single-seat fighter biplane
Powerplant:	one 750hp (559kW) BMW V1 7,3Z 12-cylinder Vee piston engine
Performance:	maximum speed 330km/h (205mph); service ceiling 7700m (25,260ft); range 570km (354 miles)
Weights:	empty 1460kg (3219lb); maximum take-off weight 1895kg (4178lb)
Dimensions:	span 11m (36ft 1in); length 8.4m (27ft 7in); height 3.2m (10ft 6in); wing area 27.2 sq m (293 sq ft)
Armament:	two fixed forward-firing 7.92mm MG 17 machine guns

Heinkel He 51B-1

The He 51 was the first fighter ordered by the *Reichsluftfahrtministerium* for the new Luftwaffe, but although the initial order for the He 51A was for only 75 aircraft ,this was beyond the construction capacity of Heinkel and many were built by Ago, Erla, Arado and Fiesler. In January 1936 the strengthened B-0 model replaced the He 51A-1 on the production line, followed by 38 of the float-equipped B-2 which had catapult spools and, on some, underwing racks for light bombs for service aboard German naval cruisers. In addition 79 C-1 and C-2 ground-attack fighters were built, and saw extensive action in the early Blitzkrieg campaigns. Prior to this, He 51A-1s and C-1s were in action in Spain with the Kondor Legion. Pictured is an B-1 of Flugzeugführerschule (A/B) 123, operating from Agram in Croatia during 1942.

Country of origin:	Germany
Type:	single-seat fighter biplane
Powerplant:	one750hp (559kW) BMW V1 7,3Z 12-cylinder Vee piston engine
Performance:	maximum speed 330km/h (205mph); service ceiling 7700m (25,260ft); range 570km (354 miles)
Weights:	empty 1460kg (3219lb); maximum take-off weight 1895kg (4178lb)
Dimensions:	span 11m (36ft 1in); length 8.4m (27ft 7in); height 3.2m (10ft 6in); wing area 27.2 sq m (293 sq ft)
Armament:	two fixed forward-firing 7.92mm MG 17 machine guns

Heinkel He 59D-1

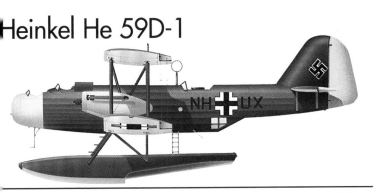

A successful Heinkel seaplane design was the He 59, with a twin-engine and biplane wing. It was actually intended as a reconnaissance bomber and first flew as the He 59b prototype in September 1931 with wheeled landing gear. Four months later the He 59a flew with twin-step floats, the configuration adopted for the production He 59B-1. The He 59B-2 had an all-metal nose, glazed panels for the bomb-aimer, and an extra MG 15 in a glazed ventral gun position. The B-3 had this armament deleted and auxiliary fuel tanks added; the C-1 was a stripped-down long-range reconnaissance version, the C-2 was equipped for air-sea-rescue, the He 59D-1 (pictured) was a crew trainer, the E-1 a torpedo trainer, the He 59E-2 a photo-reconnaissance version, and the N a navigation trainer. The 16 B-1 aircraft entered service in 1933, and in 1936 a number of B-2s went with the Legion Condor to Spain with a 20mm cannon in the nose for anti-shipping patrols. In 1939 they were in service with coastal reconnaissance units.

Country of origin:	Germany
Type:	five-seat reconaissance seaplane
Powerplant:	two 660hp (492kW) BMW VI 6,02ZU 12-cylinder Vee piston engines
Performance:	maximum speed 270km/h (168mph); service ceiling 7625m (25,000ft); range 3,000km (1863 miles)
Weights:	loaded 8,500kg (18,743lb)
Dimensions:	span 21.3m (69ft 11in); length 17m (55ft 9in); height 8.1m (26ft 5 3/4in)

Heinkel He 115C-1

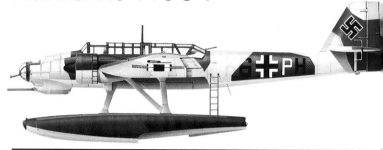

Early experience with the He 115A/B suggested that the variants' gun armament was too light, and early in 1940 one of the prototypes was tested with a 20mm fixed cannon in place of the trainable machine gun in the nose for improved offensive capability against light shipping. The trials were not notably successful, but clearly something needed to be achieved in the way of improving the He 115's firepower. This led to the He 115C-1 with a 15mm fixed forward-firing cannon as a supplement to the trainable machine gun in the nose, and a single 7.92mm fixed rearward-firing machine gun in the rear of each engine nacelle to deter pursuing fighters. Companion models were the He 115C-2 with strengthened floats, He 115C-3 minelayer, and He 115C-4 for arctic service. Many of the aircraft were later converted as convoy escorts. The He 115D was the designation of one aircraft with two 1600hp (1193kW) BMW 801C engines).

Country of origin:	Germany
Type:	coastal reconnaissance/torpedo bomber
Powerplant:	two 960hp (720kW) BMW 132K 6-cylinder radial piston engines
Performance:	maximum speed 365km/h (220mph); service ceiling 5500m (18,040ft); range 3350km (2080 miles)
Weights:	loaded 9100kg (20,065lb)
Dimensions:	span 22m (72ft 2in); length 17.3m (56ft 9in); height 6.6m (21ft 8in)
Armament::	one 13mm MG 131 machine gun on flexible mount in nose, one fixed forward firing 15mm MG 151 in nose, one 13mm MG 131 machine gun in rear of cockpit, provision for one 750kg (1,650lb) torpedo or 1,500kg (3,300lb) of bombs or mines

Henschel Hs 123A-1

Henschel Flugzeugwerke was established as a subsidiary of the Henschel & Son locomotive manufacturer in 1933, and under the direction of Chief Engineer Nicolaus began design and construction of aircraft. One of its first designs was the Hs 123, a sesquiplane dive-bomber built to the requirements of a 1933 *Reichsluftfahrtministerium* document. The first of four prototypes was tested at Rechlin in August 1935, two being destroyed in high-speed dives due to wing structural failure. The fourth was extensively modified to correct these problems, and the Luftwaffe ordered the aircraft into production as the Hs 123A-1, which entered service with 1.StG (Stukageschwader) 162 in the autumn of 1936. In December five Hs 123A-1s were sent to Spain with the Legion Condor, where many of the ground-support tactics employed in the later Blitzkrieg campaigns were pioneered. Pictured is an Hs 123A-1 of 7.StG 165 'Immelman', based at Fürstenfeldbruck in October 1937.

Country of origin:	Germany
Type:	single-seat dive bomber and close-support aircraft
Powerplant:	one 880hp (656kW) BMW 132Dc 9-cylinder radial engine
Performance:	maximum speed 340km/h (211mph); service ceiling 9000m (29,530ft); range 855km (531 miles)
Weights:	empty 1500kg (3307lb); maximum take-off weight 2215kg (4884lb)
Dimensions:	span 10.5m (34ft 5in); length 8.33m (27ft 4in); height 3.2m (10ft 6in); wing area 24.85 sq m (267 sq ft)
Armament:	two fixed forward-firing 7.92mm MG 17 machine guns; underwing racks with provision for up to 450kg (992lb) of bombs

Henschel Hs 123A-1

Despite some powerful advocates in the newly formed Luftwaffe, few of Hitler's tacticians placed any great faith in the role of the close support in the mid-1930s, until experiences in Spain taught them differently. All funds and efforts were directed into the Ju 87 programme, and the Hs 123 production line closed in October 1938. Although representative of a class of aircraft generally considered obsolete by the outbreak of World War II, the Henschel Hs 123 proved invaluable in the early stages of the Polish Campaign because of its ability to make pinpoint attacks with bombs and guns in front of advancing troops, and its capacity to absorb huge amounts of damage. Though the whole force was constantly threatened with disbandment, the sole surviving Hs 123 close-support unit II/LG2 was sent to the Balkans in April 1941 and fought round the clock until by the end of 1944 there were none left.

Country of origin:	Germany
Type:	single-seat dive bomber and close-support aircraft
Powerplant:	one 880hp (656kW) BMW 132Dc 9-cylinder radial engine
Performance:	maximum speed 340km/h (211mph); service ceiling 9000m (29,530ft); range 855km (531 miles)
Weights:	empty 1500kg (3307lb); maximum take-off weight 2215kg (4884lb)
Dimensions:	span 10.5m (34ft 5in); length 8.33m (27ft 4in); height 3.2m (10ft 6in); wing area 24.85 sq m (267 sq ft)
Armament:	two fixed forward-firing 7.92mm MG 17 machine guns; underwing racks with provision for up to 450kg (992lb) of bombs

Junkers W 34

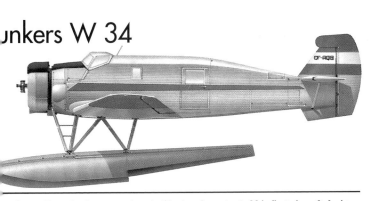

Professor Hugo Junkers was already 50 when he patented his first aircraft design in 1910, a biplane of such advanced design (a flying wing transport) that no-one took it seriously. In 1915 he pioneered the use of an all-metal aircraft structure with J.1, and in the 1920s applied his techniques to a hugely successful series of commercial transport aircraft, culminating in the legendary Ju 52. The W 33 and W 34 were inline- and radial-engined versions of the F 13 passenger transport first flown in 1919. The W 33 prototype flew in 1926 powered by a 310hp (231kW) Junkers L 5 engine, the standard powerplant for most production aircraft. The W 33 was used by the undercover Luftwaffe (pre-1933) for communications and as a patrol seaplane, and also by various airlines for cargo transport. Some 199 W 33s were built between 1927 and 1934; production of the W 34 and its military counterpart reached 1939. Pictured is one of four float-equipped W 34s operated by Canadian Airways.

Country of origin:	Germany
Type:	commercial transport floatplane
Powerplant:	one 600hp BMW Hornet C 6-cylinder radial piston engine
Performance:	maximum speed 265km/h (165mph); service ceiling 6300m (20,670ft); range 900km (560 miles)
Weights:	empty 1700kg (3748lb); maximum take-off weight 3200kg (7055lb)
Dimensions:	span 17.75m (58ft 3in); length 10.27m (33ft 8in); height 3.53m (11ft 7in); wing area 43 sq m (463 sq ft)

Kawanishi H6K5

The Kawanishi Kokuki Kabushiki Kaisha (Kawanishi Aircraft Company) was founded in November 1928 and took over the aircraft works and wind tunnel the Kawanishi Machine Works. Owing to the increased demand for seaplanes for the Japanese military, Kawanishi moved at the end of 1930 to a purpose-built factory Naruo. Here it built a number of seaplanes under licence from Shorts, and in the mid-1930s responded to the Imperial Japanese Navy's requirement for a high-performance long-range flying-boat with a design of its own, the Type S. The first four prototypes flew in July 1936 and after some modifications to the hull and installation of 1000hp (746kW) Mitsubishi 43 engines three entered service under the designation Navy Type 97 Flying-Boat Model I. A total of 217 aircraft were produced in four variants – the H6K2, -3, -4, and -5. They were used extensively in the Pacific Campaign, remaining in service until the end of World War II.

Country of origin:	Japan
Type:	long-range maritime reconnaissance flying-boat
Powerplant:	four 1300hp (969kW) Mitsubishi Kinsei 51 radial piston engines
Performance:	maximum speed 385km/h (239mph); service ceiling 9560m (31,365ft); range 6775km (4210 miles)
Weights:	empty 12,380kg (27,293lb); maximum take-off weight 23,000kg (50,706lb)
Dimensions:	span 40m (131ft 3in); length 25.63m (84ft 1in); height 6.27m (20ft 7in); wing area 170 sq m (1830 sq ft)
Armament:	two 7.7mm machine guns in forward turret; one 7.7mm machine gun in each of two beam blisters; one 7.7mm machine gun in dorsal position; one 20mm cannon in tail turret; provision for two 800kg (1764lb) torpedoes or up to 1000kg (2205lb) of bombs

atécoére 298

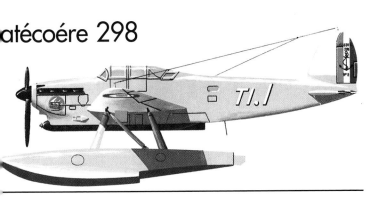

In 1917 Pierre Latécoére established Forges et Ateliers de Construction Latécoére at Toulouse-Montaudron. Drawing on experience gained producing seaplanes in the 20s, the Laté 298.01 prototype was designed to meet a 1933 requirement, and first flew in May 1936. Successful trials led to the Laté 298 production model. This entered service late 1938 with the French Naval Air Arm, which received 24 and 12 (eventually 27) examples of the Laté 298A and 298B with fixed and folding wings respectively. The Laté 298D was a 298B development with a fixed wing; 95 were ordered. In the event only about 60 machines were built before the German occupation. In 1942 the Germans allowed a resumption of Laté 298 production against a Vichy French requirement for 30 aircraft, but it is unclear how many of these Laté 298F machines (298D aircraft with simplified controls) were completed. Pictured is a 298 of Escadrille T1, Aéronavale, based at Berre, near Marseilles, in late 1939.

Country of origin:	France
Type:	(Laté 298D) three-seat coastal reconnaissance and torpedo bomber floatplane
Powerplant:	one 880hp (656kW) Hispano-Suiza 12Ycrs-1 12-cylinder Vee engine
Performance:	maximum speed 290km/h (180mph); service ceiling 6500m (21,325ft); range 2200 km (1367 miles)
Weights:	empty 3062kg (6750lb); maximum take-off weight 4800kg (10,582lb)
Dimensions:	span 15.50m (50ft 10in); length 12.56m (41ft 2in); height 5.23m (17ft 1in)
Armament:	two 7.5mm fixed forward-firing machine guns; one 7.5mm trainable machine gun in rear of cockpit; plus an external torpedo and bomb load of 670kg (1477lb)

Letov S 328

In 1920 Letov took over the Czech Military Air Arsenal and produced a series of single-engined biplanes for the Czech Air Force, culminating in the S 328 two-seat reconnaissance aircraft. The prototype S 328 was developed in 1932 from the earlier 28 reconnaissance biplane to a Finnish requirement, but no order was placed. The Czech Air Force revived interest in the aircraft and production of 445 examples of the S 328 began in 1934. This included 13 examples of the S 328N night-fighter model with four fixed and two trainable machine guns, and four examples of the S 328V twin-float seaplane for target-towing. Surviving aircraft were seized by Germany after its occupation of Czechoslovakia in March 1939. Most were retained as trainers, though some passed to allies such as Bulgaria and Slovakia. Slovak insurgents operated a few aircraft against the Germans in autumn 1944. The aircraft pictured was operated by the Slovak Insurgent Air Force from Tri Duby airfield in September 1944.

Country of origin:	Czechoslovakia
Type:	two-seat reconnaissance/observation aircraft
Powerplant:	one Walter-built 635hp (474kW) Bristol Pegasus II-M2 radial piston engine
Performance:	maximum speed 280km/h (174mph); service ceiling 7200m (23,620ft); range 700km (435 miles)
Weights:	empty 1680kg (3704lb); maximum take-off weight 2640kg (5820lb)
Dimensions:	span 13.71m (44ft 12in); length 10.36m (33ft 12in); height 3.4m (11ft 2in); wing area 39.4 sq m (424 sq ft)
Armament:	two fixed forward-firing 7.92mm machine guns; two 7.92mm machine guns on a Skoda pivot mount over the observer's cockpit; underwing racks with provision for up to 500kg (1102lb) of bombs

oré-et-Olivier LeO 20

uring World War I, the company of Fernand Lioré and Henri Olivier constructed
Nieuport, Morane-Saulnier and Sopwith designs under licence at Levallois-
ret, and in 1916 produced its first independent design, the LeO 4 reconnaissance
lane. LeO subsequently became the most important manufacturer of large French
itary aircraft, each of its designs a clear linear descendant of its predecessor. The
12 was a two-seat night-bomber, built to rival the Farman Goliath, with power
vided by 400hp (298kW) Lorraine engines. Re-engined with the vastly superior
stol Jupiter this became the Leo 122, which was built only in prototype form.
m this stemmed the LeO 20, the standard French heavy night-bomber between
28 and 1939. Some 320 of these four-seat aircraft were produced and many others
re trialled with various modifications. Despite its antiquated appearance the
craft remained in production up until the start of the World War II.

ountry of origin:	France
ype:	three/four-seat night-bomber
owerplant:	two 420hp (313kW) Gnome-Rhône 9Ady (license-built Bristol Jupiter) radial piston engines
erformance:	maximum speed 198km/h (123mph); service ceiling 5760m (18,900ft); range 1000km (621 miles)
Veights:	empty equipped 2725kg (6008lb); maximum take-off weight 5460kg (12,037lb)
imensions:	span 22.25m (73ft); length 13.81m (45ft 4in); height 4.26m (13ft 12in); wing area 105 sq m (1130 sq ft)
rmament:	two 7.7mm machine guns on pivoted mount in nose ; two 7.7mm machine guns in dorsal position; one 7.7mm machine gun in ventral bin; bomb racks for up to 500kg (1102lb) of bombs

Martin Model 130 China Clipper

Glenn L. Martin established the company that bore his name at Cleveland, Ohio in 1917, so ending his short association with the Wright Aeronautical Company. The Martin Model 130 China Clipper of 1934 was a classic long-range transoceanic flying-boat intended for service on Pacific and Far Eastern routes. The airframe incorporated a two-step all-metal hull powered by four Pratt & Whitney Twin Wasp radials, with accommodation for the crew of four and a complement of up to 48 passengers on short-haul routes. The first M-130s flew in December 1934, and all three were delivered late in 1935 to Pan American. Possessing excellent range, the M-130 could fly well in excess of the 4025km (2500 miles) demanded by Pan American on its San Francisco–Manila route. From April 1937 the route was extended to Hong Kong. China Clipper and Philippine Clipper were turned over to the US Navy in 1942, Hawaii Clipper having been lost at sea in 1938.

Country of origin:	USA
Type:	long-range commercial flying-boat
Powerplant:	four 830hp (619kW) Pratt & Whitney Twin Wasp radial piston engines
Performance:	cruising speed 252km/h (157mph); service ceiling 5180m (17,000ft); range 5150km (3200 miles)
Weights:	loaded 23,700kg (52,252lb)
Dimensions:	span 39.62m (130ft); length 27.69m (90ft 10in); height 7.49m (24ft 7in)

Martin PBM Mariner

The Martin PBM Mariner was of huge importance to the Allied war effort. It was designed in 1936 and proved by the quarter-scale Martin 162A. A full-size prototype was ordered in June 1937 followed by 20 production PBM-1 boats in December. The PBM was a very advanced design, with high wing loading and retractable stabilising floats built into the wing tips. A single XPBM-2 was built with increased fuel capacity and catapult-launching equipment. The most prolific variant was the PBM-3, which had its own subvariants. The PBM-3B (32 built) was supplied to the RAF under the Lend Lease Act as the Mariner Gr Mk I; the -3C (274) introduced greater armour protection and revised armament; the -3D (201) had more powerful engines, self-sealing fuel tanks, turreted armament and greater bomb-carrying capacity; the -3R (50) was a transport version without armament; and the -3s was a long-range anti-submarine version with ASW radar and reduced defensive armament.

Country of origin:	USA
Type:	nine-seat maritime patrol and anti-submarine flying-boat
Powerplant:	two 1900hp (1417kW) Wright R-2600-22 Cyclone radial piston engine
Performance:	maximum speed 340km/h (211mph); service ceiling 6035m (19,800ft); range 3605km (2240 miles)
Weights:	empty 15,048kg (33,175lb); maximum take-off weight 26,308kg (58,000lb)
Dimensions:	span 35.97m (118ft); length 24.33m (79ft 10in); height 8.38m (27ft 6in); wing area 130.80 sq m (1408 sq ft)
Armament:	two .5in Browning machine guns in nose turret; two .5in Browning machine guns in dorsal turret; two .5in Browning machine guns in tail turret; one .5in Browning machine gun in two ventral positions; provision for up to 3628kg (8000lb) of bombs or depth charges

Martin PBM-5 Mariner

M artin decided to improve the performance of the PBM by fitting more powerful 2100hp (1556kW) Pratt & Whitney R-2800-34 Double Wasps to produce the XPBM-5, which in other respects was similar to the PBM-3D. The production PBM-5 boats had R-800-22 engines and in this form were built to the extent of 631 boats, with six subvariants. The five PBM-5A aircraft for the US Coast Guard had retractable tricycle landing gear; PBM-5E was the designation given to PBM-5s equipped with an AN/APS-15 radar; PBM-5G was the redesignation of four PBM-5 boats supplied to the US Coast Guard. The single PBM-5M was used for missile testing and the PBM-S was the designation of a small number of PBM-5s equipped with special ASW equipment. Over 500 PBMs were still in service in the Korean War, in addition to the surplus aircraft that were supplied to Argentina, the Netherlands and Uruguay. Pictured is a Uruguayan PBM-5E, with armament deleted

Country of origin:	USA
Type:	nine-seat maritime patrol and anti-submarine flying-boat
Powerplant:	two 2100hp (1566kW) Wright R-2800-22 Double Wasp radial piston engines
Performance:	maximum speed 340km/h (211mph); service ceiling 6160m (20,200ft); range 4345km (2700 miles)
Weights:	empty 15,422kg (34,000lb); maximum take-off weight 27,216kg (60,000lb)
Dimensions:	span 35.97m (118ft); length 24.33m (79ft 10in); height 8.38m (27ft 6in); wing area 130.80 sq m (1408 sq ft)
Armament:	nacelle bays and underwing racks with provision for up to 3628kg (8,000lb) of bombs or depth charges

Martinsyde F.4 Buzzard

H P. Martin and George Handasyde formed a partnership in 1908 to design and construct aircraft, later renaming the company Martinsyde. Throughout World War I, Martinsyde supplied the RFC with a series of fine scouting aircraft. The F.1 and F.2 were prototypes for the F.3. Designed by George Handasyde and first flown in November 1917, this was an outstanding machine, but was dogged by the continual nagging of the Air Board for engineering changes, and by the scarcity of the specified Rolls Royce Falcon engine. After many modifications and with a 300hp (224kW) Hispano engine installed the aircraft was redesignated F.4, and in service had the official name Buzzard Mk I. The Buzzard was faster than any contemporary British fighter and judged 'superior to any other contemporary single-seat fighter'. Orders were placed for a total of 1700 aircraft from four contractors, and by the armistice 52 had been delivered. Many were later sold abroad.

Country of origin:	United Kingdom
Type:	single-seat fighter
Powerplant:	one 300hp (224kW) Hispano-Suiza 8-cylinder Vee piston engine
Performance:	maximum speed 233km/h (145mph); service ceiling 7620m (25,000ft); endurance 2hrs 30mins
Weights:	empty 776kg (1710lb); maximum take-off weight 1038kg (2289lb)
Dimensions:	span 10m (32ft 9in); length 7.77m (25ft 6in); height 3.15m (10ft 4in); wing area 29.73 sq m (320 sq ft)
Armament:	two fixed forward-firing .303in Vickers machine guns

Martinsyde Type A Mk II

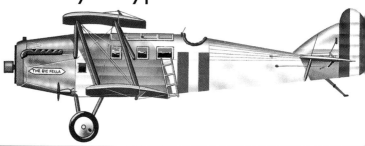

After World War I Martinsyde found itself with a stock of about 200 surplus F.4 Buzzards from a cancelled military order. Many of these were sold abroad to Portugal, Finland, Japan, Latvia, Ireland and Spain. Others were converted to various roles for civilian customers. Martinsyde developed two civil versions before going into liquidation in 1921; the F.4A was a two-seat tourer and the Type A Mk II had an enclosed four-seat cabin forward of the open cockpit. Only four of the latter were built, one of which had the distinction of being the first aircraft operated by the Irish Air Corps, established after the completion of the Anglo–Irish Treaty in December 1922. It was delivered during the truce in the summer of 1922 to Baldonnel. Named 'The Big Fella' for General Michael Collins, it was purchased to assist in his escape should the talks fail.

Country of origin:	United Kingdom
Type:	four-seat passenger transport
Powerplant:	one 300hp (224kW) Hispano-Suiza 8-cylinder Vee piston engine
Performance:	maximum speed 233km/h (145mph); service ceiling 7620m (25,000ft); endurance 2hrs 30mins
Weights:	empty 776kg (1710lb); maximum take-off weight 1038kg (2289lb)
Dimensions:	span 10m (32ft 9in); length 7.77m (25ft 6in); height 3.15m (10ft 4in); wing area 29.73 sq m (320 sq ft)

Naval Aircraft Factory N3N-1

esigned by the US Navy's Bureau of Aeronautics, this two-seat primary trainer was the NAF's most extensively built and enduring product, serving for 26 years th the US armed forces. The XN3N-1 prototype made its maiden flight in August 35, and 179 N3N-1 production aircraft were delivered from June 1936 with ovision for wheeled landing gear or float alighting gear. The first 159 had the 0hp (164kW) Wright R-790-8 radial engine, but later aircraft switched to the rated R-760-8. This unit was also used in the 816 examples of the N3N-3 delivered m 1938 with a vertical tail surface of revised shape, a modified main landing gear rangement with a single strut on each side, and an uncowled engine installation at was retrospectively adopted for the N3N-1 in 1941 and 1942. The N3N served th great utility throughout World War II, but most of the surviving aircraft were ter sold to civil operators. Pictured is an N3N-1, based at Pensacola in 1939.

Country of origin:	USA
Type:	two-seat primary flying trainer
Powerplant:	one 220hp (164kW) Wright J-5 Whirlwind 7-cylinder, single-row radial engine
Performance:	maximum speed 203 km/h (126mph); service ceiling 4635m (15,200ft); range 756km (470 miles)
Weights:	empty 948kg (2090lb); maximum take-off 1266kg (2792lb)
Dimensions:	span 10.36m (34ft); length 7.77m (25ft 6in); height 3.30m (10ft 10in); wing area 28.33 sq m (305 sq ft)

Nieuport 11

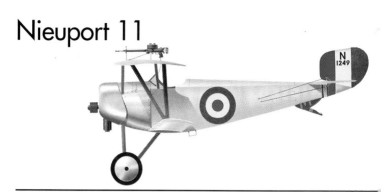

In January 1914 designer Gustave Delage joined the Etablissments Nieuport and started the series of aircraft that made him, and the company, famous. The first of these was the Nieuport 10, a small two-seat reconnaissance sesquiplane (with the lower wing much smaller than the upper). This aircraft was produced in two versions, one with the observer and gun in front of the pilot (10AV) and the other with the observer and gun behind (10AR). With only a Gnome-Rhône rotary engine to power them, the two-seaters proved underpowered and most were converted to single-seat scouts. A larger version was built as the Nieuport 12; production total for both types was 170. Concurrently with this programme, Delage designed and built the Nieuport Bébé for the Gordon-Bennett race, and developed this into the Type 11 scout. Hundreds were built for the RFC, RNAS, French and Belgian Aviation Militaire, and the Imperial Russian Air Service.

Country of origin:	France
Type:	single-seat fighting scout
Powerplant:	one 80hp (60kW) Le Rhône 9C 9-cylinder rotary engine
Performance:	maximum speed 155km/h (97mph); service ceiling 4500m (14,765ft); endurance 2hrs 30mins
Weights:	empty 350kg (772lb); maximum take-off weight 480kg (1058lb)
Dimensions:	span 7.55m (24ft 9in); length 5.8m (19ft); height 2.45m (8ft); wing area 13 sq m (140 sq ft)
Armament:	one fixed forward-firing .303in Vickers machine gun

Nieuport 17

The Nieuport 17 was unquestionably one of the finest Allied combat aircraft of World War I. It bore a close physical resemblance to the Type 16, but was slightly larger and, to avoid the problems with wing-twist that had afflicted the XI at high speeds, the lower wing was considerably stiffened. The aircraft first flew in January 1916 and the first deliveries were made in May, helping to end the 'Fokker scourge' of the previous months. The aircraft was highly manoeuvrable for its time, with a high rate of climb and good performance. Many hundreds were built for service with the RFC and RNAS, Aviation Militaire in France and Belgium, Russia, Holland, Italy, Finland and the USAAF. The fame of the Type 17 is due in no small part to the fact that it was the chosen mount of the Escadrille de Cicognes, Escadrille Lafayette and of the aces Nungesser, Guynemer, Ball and Bishop.

Country of origin:	France
Type:	single-seat fighting scout
Powerplant:	110hp (82kW) Le Rhône 9J rotary piston engine
Performance:	maximum speed 170km/h (106mph); service ceiling 1980m (6500ft); range 250km (155 miles)
Weights:	empty 374kg (825lb); maximum take-off weight 560kg (1235lb)
Dimensions:	span 8.2m (26ft 11in); length 5.96m (19ft 7in); height 2.44m (8ft); wing area 14.75 sq m (159 sq ft)
Armament:	one fixed forward-firing .303in Vickers machine gun

Nieuport 27

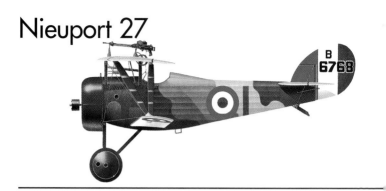

The most successful offshoot of the Type 17 was the Type 21, produced simply by substituting an 80hp (60kW) Le Rhône engine and enlarging the ailerons. Nearly 200 of these were produced, mostly for Russia and the USA, and in the years after the war it was the mount of a number of the barnstormers. A slightly heavier version was the Type 23 which had slightly enlarged tail surfaces and either an 80hp (60kW) or 120hp (89kW) Le Rhône engine. The Type 24 was yet another variant, with improved streamlining, fixed fin and a circular section fuselage, which was sold to the USA (124), Belgium, Italy and Japan. The Type 24-bis trainer had the original Type 17 tail unit, and the Type 25 was the Type 24 prototype fitted with the tailplane and skid seen on the Type 27. This had a 120hp (89kW) Le Rhône engine and was used by Sweden, the RFC and RNAS, and the USAAF. Pictured is a Nieuport 27 of No 1 Squadron, RFC, with French-style two-tone camouflage.

Country of origin:	France
Type:	single-seat fighting scout
Powerplant:	120hp (89kW) Le Rhône rotary piston engine
Performance:	maximum speed 185km/h (115mph); service ceiling 5550m (18,210ft); range 250km (155 miles)
Weights:	empty 380kg (838lb); maximum take-off weight 585kg (1289lb)
Dimensions	span 8.2m (26ft 11in); length 5.85m (19ft 2in); height 2.42m (7ft 11in); wing area 14.75 sq m (159 sq ft)
Armament:	one fixed forward-firing .303in Vickers machine gun; one fixed forward-firing .303in Lewis machine gun

Nieuport 28

I aving exhausted all the possibilities for variations to the Type 17 airframe, Nieuport produced a totally new aircraft which it designated the Type 28. This marked a break from the V-strut sesquiplane configuration of the earlier Nieuport outs, which was replaced by wings of almost equal proportion braced by parallel ruts. The rectangular section fuselage was superseded by one of circular section, ited around a new 160hp (119kW) Gnome-Le Rhône 9N engine. The Type 28 was dered into production almost off the drawing board, but in service from March 918 the Gnome engine proved to be its Achilles' heel, proving itself totally nreliable. A further failing was that at high speed any violent manoeuvre tended to p the fabric from the upper wing. Notwithstanding these problems, the Type 28 appened to be the only fighter readily available to the US Expeditionary Force, the ursuit Squadrons of which began arriving in France in early 1918.

Country of origin:	France
Type:	single-seat fighter
Powerplant:	one 160hp (119kW) Gnome-Le Rhône 9N rotary piston engine
Performance:	maximum speed 195km/h (121mph); service ceiling 5200m (17,060ft); range 400km (248 miles)
Weights:	empty 532kg (1172lb); maximum take-off weight 740kg (1631lb)
Dimensions:	span 8m (26ft 3in); length 6.2m (20ft 4in); height 2.48m (8ft 2in); wing area 20 sq m (215 sq ft)
Armament:	two fixed forward-firing .303in Vickers machine guns

Nieuport-Delage Ni-D 29

Nieuport's last wartime fighter was first flown in prototype form in August 1918 and subsequent flight-testing confirmed the soundness of Gustave Delage's design. All the performance parameters were met with the exception of ceiling, and so for the second prototype a wing of increased span was constructed. In this form the Nieuport Ni-D 29 was ordered into quantity production at the beginning of 1920. Initial deliveries of an eventual 250 aircraft to the French Aviation Militaire were made in 1922 and the order book was soon filled with orders from Spain and Belgium, which took 30 (10 license-built) and 108 (87 license-built) aircraft respectively. French-built machines were supplied to both Sweden and Argentina. Japan was by far the biggest customer; an aircraft was purchased and using this as pattern Nakajima built 608 for the Imperial Japanese Army as the Ko-4. Macchi in Italy built smaller numbers.

Country of origin:	France
Type:	single-seat fighter
Powerplant:	one 300hp (224kW) Hispano-Suiza 8Fb 8-cylinder Vee piston engine
Performance:	maximum speed 235km/h (146mph); service ceiling 8500m (27,885ft); range 580km (360 miles)
Weights:	empty 760kg (1675lb); maximum take-off weight 1150kg (2535lb)
Dimensions:	span 9.7m (31ft 10in); length 6.49m (21ft 3in); height 2.56m (8ft 5in); wing area 26.7 sq m (287 sq ft)
Armament:	two fixed forward-firing .303in Vickers machine guns

Nieuport-Delage Ni-D 52

ustave Delage's output before terminating his partnership with Nieuport in
1934 was prolific, evidenced by the fact that at the 1924 Paris Salon de
éronautique, Nieuport-Delage unveiled no less than three new designs at a time
en the military fighter market was severely depressed. Each of the designs bore
number 42, but each was quite different. One of the aircraft on display was one
wo Ni-D 42 racers built for the 1924 Coupe Beaumont contest. Displayed
ngside this was the Ni-D 42 C.1 single-seat and Ni-D 42 C.2 two-seat fighter. The
mer aircraft was operated in some numbers by the Aviation Militaire, and
wned a successful family of aircraft over the next decade. The Ni-D 52 of 1927
ctured in the Spanish Republican Air Force colours) closely resembled the Ni-D
but was constructed of metal instead of wood. First flown in 1927, it won the 1928
anish fighter competition and was built under licence by Hispano until 1936.

Country of origin:	France
Type:	single-seat fighter
Powerplant:	one 580hp (433kW) Hispano-Suiza 12Hb 12-cylinder Vee piston engine
Performance:	maximum speed 255km/h (158mph); service ceiling 7000m (2965ft); range 400km (249 miles)
Weights:	empty 1368kg (3016lb); maximum take-off weight 1837kg (4050lb)
Dimensions:	span 12m (39ft 4in); length 7.5m (24ft 7in); height 3m (9ft 10in); wing area 30.90 sq m (333 sq ft)
Armament:	two fixed forward-firing 7.62mm Vickers machine guns

North American Aviation Carrier Pigeon

Built by the Curtiss Aeroplane & Motor Company for a US Post Office mailplane competition, the Model 40 Carrier Pigeon was developed by Clement Key's North American Aviation after it bought out Curtiss in 1928. Shown here in its original form, this single-engined sesquiplane was constructed of wood, metal and fabric with wide track landing gear for rough field operations and a large mail hold for and aft of the pilot's open cockpit. Ten of the 15 Carrier Pigeons were built for National Air Transport, formed in 1925 to fly passenger services and from 1926 responsible for the Chicago–Dallas mail route. In May of that year one of the Carrier Pigeons inaugurated the latter route and from April 1927 the aircraft was on the New York–Chicago section of the Post Office's transcontinental route. In 1929 the Carrier Pigeon II entered service; this was virtually a new design and was powered by a geared 600hp (447kW) Curtiss G-IV-1570 Conqueror engine.

Country of origin:	USA
Type:	single-engined mailplane
Powerplant:	one 400hp (298kW) Liberty 12 inline piston engine
Performance:	maximum speed 201km/h (125mph); service ceiling 3900m (12,800ft); range 845km (525 miles)
Weights:	empty 1634kg (3603lb); maximum take-off weight 2549kg (5620lb)
Dimensions:	span 12.78m (41ft 11in); length 8.78m (28ft 9in); height 3.68m (12ft 1in); wing area 46.91 sq m (505 sq ft)

Northrop N-3PB

Norway, with its countless miles of coastline and myriad fjords and inland waterways, has always been a good market for seaplane manufacturers. The N-3PB single-engine floatplane ordered by the Norwegian Buying Commission from Northrop represented something of a departure for the company, which had previously built only landplanes. The Norwegian order covered 24 aircraft and only eight months after receiving the order the first prototype was flying, powered by a 1200hp (895kW) Wright Cyclone GR-1820 radial engine. All of the aircraft were delivered to the exiled Royal Norwegian Naval Air Service (RNNAS), operating as an RAF unit after the German invasion. The RNNAS operated its N-3PBs on anti-submarine patrol and convoy escort duties from coastal sites in Iceland, often in extremely harsh conditions. Although several were lost on landing in severe arctic weather, none were lost due to enemy action.

Country of origin:	USA
Type:	two-seat coastal patrol floatplane
Powerplant:	one 1200hp (895kW) Wright Cyclone GR-1820 radial engine
Performance:	maximum speed 414km/h (257mph); service ceiling 7315m (24,000ft); range 1609km (1000 miles)
Weights:	empty 2808kg (6190lb); maximum take-off weight 4808kg (10,600lb)
Dimensions:	span 14.91m (48ft 11in); length 10.97m (36ft); height 3.66m (12ft)
Armament:	four 0.5in fixed forward-firing machine guns in leading edges of wing, one 0.3in machine gun in rear of cockpit, and one 0.3in machine gun in ventral position, plus a load of 907kg (2000lb)

Pfalz D.III

The Pfalz Flugzeug-Werke GmbH began producing aircraft in 1913. At first it built Morane monoplanes and other types under licence. The D.III was a completely fresh design into which company designer Robert Thelen incorporated much experience gained in 1916-17 with the production of LFG-Roland fighters. Though fractionally inferior in performance to the best contemporary Albatros and Fokker scouts, the III and IIIa were strong and well-liked by pilots. The monocoque fuselage was well streamlined and owed much to Deperdussin construction principles. However production was delayed due to a lack of skilled workers. About 600 were built, the more powerful IIIa having rounded wings and tailplane, and the guns located on top of the nose to allow for easier maintenance. A single example of an experimental triplane version of the D.III was built, but this was never flown. Pictured is the D.III flown by Vzfw Hecht of Jasta 10 based near Courtrai.

Country of origin:	Germany
Type:	single-seat fighter
Powerplant:	one 180hp (134kW) Mercedes D.IIIa inline piston engine
Performance:	maximum speed 165km/h (103mph); service ceiling 5180m (17,000ft); range 350km (217 miles)
Weights:	empty 750kg (1,653lb); maximum take-off weight 935kg (2061lb)
Dimensions:	span 9.4m (30ft 10in); length 6.95m (22ft 9 1/2in); height 2.67m (8ft 9in); wing area 22.1sq m (237.89sq ft)
Armament:	two fixed forward-firing 7.92mm LMG 08/15 machine-guns

olikarpov I-15bis Chaika

ne might be forgiven for thinking that the I-15 biplanes were superseded by the
I-16 monoplane. In fact the I-16 flew before any of them. Early in 1933 Nikolai
likarpov began designing an aircraft to succeed his I-5 biplane fighter. The new
craft had a gulled upper wing (to improve the pilot's forward fields of vision) and
Wright R-1820-F Cyclone radial piston engine, a US unit being imported in limited
mbers pending the start of licensed production as the M-25. The I-15 (404 with the
0hp/358kW M-22 and 270 with the M-25 engine) entered service in 1934. It was
mplemented by I-15bis (or I-152) aircraft, many of which were still in limited
vice at the time of Germany's June 1941 invasion of the USSR. The I-15bis had
improved M-25V engine in a longer-chord cowling, a conventional upper wing,
ater fuel capacity, and doubled gunfire power. Pictured is an I-15bis aircraft
pplied to support Chinese Nationalist forces in Manchuria during 1937 and 1938.

Country of origin:	USSR
Type:	single-seat fighter
Powerplant:	one 750hp (559kW) M-25B 9-cylinder, single-row radial engine
Performance:	maximum speed 370km/h (230mph); service ceiling 9000m (29,530ft); range 530km (329 miles)
Weights:	empty 1310kg (2888lb); maximum take-off weight 1730kg (3814lb)
Dimensions:	span 10.20m (33ft 5in); length 6.33m (20ft 9in); height 2.19m (7ft 2in)
Armament:	four 7.62mm fixed forward-firing machine guns; plus external bomb load of 100kg (220lb)

Polikarpov I-153

Otherwise known as the I-15ter, the I-153 was first flown in 1938 as an attempt to modernise the I-15bis by reducing drag. In this capacity the two most important changes were a reversion to the type of gulled upper wing used on the I-15, and the introduction of manually operated retractable main landing gear units. Some 3437 aircraft of this type were constructed and entered service in time for participation in the border incident with Japan in the summer of 1939. The type was also heavily involved in the Russo–Finnish 'Winter War' of 1939–40, and in the first part of the German invasion of the USSR from June 1941. The surviving I-153 aircraft were relegated to training service from the middle of 1943, although Finland used captured aircraft as first-line fighters into 1944. The aircraft was flown with some degree of success by experienced pilots, but for less experienced aviators it could sometimes be a handful.

Country of origin:	USSR
Type:	single-seat fighter and fighter-bomber
Powerplant:	one 1000hp (746kW) Shvetsov M-62 9-cylinder single-row radial engine
Performance:	maximum speed 444km/h (276mph); service ceiling 35,105ft (10,700m); range 880km (547 miles)
Weights:	empty 1348kg (2972lb); maximum take-off weight 2110kg (4652lb)
Dimensions:	span 10m (32ft 9in); length 6.17m (20ft 2in); height 2.80m (9ft 2in)
Armament:	four fixed forward-firing 12.7mm machine guns; plus external bomb and rocket load of 200kg (441lb)

Potez 25 A.2

Before incorporation into SNCASE in 1935, Potez was among the largest French aircraft manufacturers. The giant Potez works at Meaulte was established in 1920 by Henri Potez and from it came a long and highly successful series of single-engine military and civil aircraft. The Potez 25 was one of the most famous and extensively built military aircraft of the interwar period. It was developed from the earlier Potez 24 A.2 prototype, designed by Louis Coroller and first flown in 1924. After modifications it was flown as the Potez 25. Two basic versions were offered, the A.2 two-seat fighter and B.2 two-seat bomber. In all, nearly 4100 were built in 87 different variants for domestic and foreign markets. Most came from the manufacturer, although 300 were license built in Poland, 200 in Yugoslavia, 70 in Romania and 27 in Portugal. Pictured is a Potez 25 A.2 of the 2do Escadron de Reconocimiento y Bombardio of the Paraguayan Air Force, during operations against Bolivia in 1933.

Country of origin:	France
Type:	two-seat general-purpose military aircraft
Powerplant:	one 450hp (335kW) Lorraine-Dietrich 12-cylinder Vee piston engine
Performance:	maximum speed 220km/h (137mph); service ceiling 7200m (23,620ft); range 660km (410 miles)
Weights:	empty equipped 1510kg (3329lb); maximum take-off weight 2500kg (5512lb)
Dimensions:	span 14.19m (46ft 7in); length 9.19m (30ft 2in); height 3.65m (11ft 11in); wing area 47 sq m (506 sq ft)
Armament:	one fixed forward-firing .303in Vickers machine gun; two .303in Lewis machine guns on TO 7 ring mounting over observer's cockpit; underwing racks with provision for 200kg (441lb) of bombs

Royal Aircraft Factory B.E.2c

His Majesty's Balloon Factory at Farnborough diversified into heavier-than-air machines in 1909. Under the direction of Mervyn O'Gorman, Geoffrey de Havilland and F. M. Green built the B.E.1 (Blériot Experimental) tractor biplane in 1911 from the airframe of a Voisin pusher biplane. The following B.E.2 retained the same basic airframe and was the first military aircraft to be built as such in Britain. By mid-1913 it equipped 13 RFC squadrons. Production gave way to the B.E.2a with unequal-span wings, and the B.E.2b with revised decking around the cockpits and different aileron instead of wing-warping controls. The B.E.2c introduced the 90hp (66kW) RAF 1a engine and was the first to be armed with a machine gun. In wartime service the B.E.2 was a fine reconnaissance platform, but its stability proved lethal in aerial combat and many were lost during the 'Fokker Scourge' of 1915–16. Production certainly exceeded the 3535 for which records survive.

Country of origin:	United Kingdom
Type:	two-seat reconnaissance/light bomber aircraft
Powerplant:	one 90hp (67kW) RAF 1a inline piston engine
Performance:	maximum speed 145km/h (90mph); service ceiling 2745m (9000ft); endurance 4hrs
Weights:	empty 649kg (1431lb); maximum take-off weight 953kg (2100lb)
Dimensions:	span 12.42m (40ft 9in); length 8.31m (27ft 3in); height 3.66m (12ft); wing area 33.44 sq m (360 sq ft)
Armament:	one .303in Vickers machine gun capable of being mounted on various upper centre wing and fuselage points

Royal Aircraft Factory F.E.2b

The first successful Fighter Experimental design from the Royal Aircraft Factory was ready to go into production in January 1914, and had it done so the RFC would have been able to match the Fokker monoplanes of the German Air Service on better terms. Instead, nearly a year elapsed after the first flight before a production order was even placed, and by this time the whole concept of a pusher biplane was rapidly becoming obsolete. The layout was due to the need to fire a machine gun, as in 1913 there was no way of safely firing ahead through a tractor propeller. The pilot therefore occupied the rear cockpit, although for night operations this was reversed. The first order for 12 F.E.2as was placed in August 1914, followed by the progressively more powerful F.E.2b and F.E.2c. Altogether some 1939 of these were built, as well as 386 long-span F.E.2d models.

Country of origin:	United Kingdom
Type:	two-seat fighter
Powerplant:	one 120hp (89kW) Beardmore inline piston engine
Performance:	maximum speed 129km/h (80mph); service ceiling 2745m (9000ft); endurance 3hrs
Weights:	empty 904kg (1993lb); maximum take-off weight 1347kg (2970lb)
Dimensions:	span 14.55m (47ft 9in); length 9.83m (32ft 3in); height 3.85m (12ft 7in); wing area 45.89 sq m (494 sq ft)
Armament:	one or two .303in Lewis machine guns; plus up to 159kg (350lb) of bombs

Royal Aircraft Factory R.E.8

The 'Harry Tate', as it was dubbed by the RFC's Cockney contingent, was designed to meet an RFC requirement for a two-seat reconnaissance/artillery spotting aircraft. It resembled a scaled-up version of the B.E.2 and shared the same staggered biplane wing configuration, but it had a far sturdier fuselage and more substantial armament. Early tests revealed good all-round handling, encouraging the RFC to place a large order. The first aircraft were delivered in autumn 1916 but these were grounded after a series of mysterious accidents. As a result the tail was redesigned and the mass production of an eventual 4077 aircraft was resumed. However, like the earlier B.E.2, the aircraft's inherent stability proved to be a major handicap in aerial combat, and among the rank and file it was never a really popular machine.

Country of origin:	United Kingdom
Type:	two-seat reconnaissance/artillery spotting aircraft
Powerplant:	one 150hp (112kW) RAF 4a 12-cylinder Vee piston engine
Performance:	maximum speed 164km/h (102mph); service ceiling 4115m (13,500ft); endurance 4hrs 15mins
Weights:	empty 717kg (1580lb); maximum take-off weight 1301kg (2869lb)
Dimensions:	span 12.98m (42ft 7in); length 6.38m (20ft 11in); height 2.9m (9ft 6in); wing area 22.67 sq m (444 sq ft)
Armament:	one fixed forward-firing .303in Vickers machine gun; one .303in Lewis machine gun on pivoted mounting over rear cockpit; plus a bomb load of up to 102kg (224lb)

Royal Aircraft Factory S.E.5a

Undoubtedly the best warplane to come from the Royal Aircraft Factory at Farnborough, the S.E.5 (Scout Experimental) was one of the great combat craft of World War I. It was designed around a new Hispano-Suiza engine (which somewhat ironically proved to be its lingering curse) by H. P. Folland with J. Kenworthy, and the first of three prototypes flew in November 1916. This and the second aircraft were lost in crashes. The third aircraft had a slightly modified radiator, cut-out in the upper wing, centre-section gravity tank, armament, and a windscreen that proved to be obstructive to the pilot's view. When the first S.E.5 aircraft were delivered to No 56 Squadron in March 1917 its pilots were dismayed to find that an even bigger screen had been added. Removal of these screens was expediently ordered before the unit was declared ready for combat. Pictured is one of the squadron's S.E.5a aircraft, built by the Austin Motor Company.

Country of origin:	United Kingdom
Type:	single-seat fighting scout
Powerplant:	one 150hp (112kW) Hispano-Suiza 8a 8-cylinder inline piston engine
Performance:	maximum speed 177km/h (110mph); service ceiling 5185m (17,000ft); range 483km (300 miles)
Weights:	empty 639kg (1410lb); maximum take-off weight 902kg (1988lb)
Dimensions:	span 8.11m (26ft 7in); length 6.38m (20ft 11in); height 2.89m (9ft 6in); wing area 22.67 sq m (444 sq ft)
Armament:	one fixed forward-firing .303in Vickers machine gun, one .303in Lewis machine gun on Foster mount on upper wing

Royal Aircraft Factory S.E.5a

Fewer than 60 150hp (112kW) S.E.5s were built, and these were dogged by the continuing unreliability of the Hispano-Suiza engine, which was replaced in the S.E.5a prototype by a 200hp (150kW) Hispano. Other alterations were a head fairing behind the cockpit, gravity-feed fuel and water tanks in the centre section of the upper wing, and short-span wings. Contracts for the new machine were placed in February 1917, and most of the subsequent aircraft were built at Vickers and Martinsyde. Some of the first S.E.5as were license-built (by Wolseley) versions with the Hispano engine – despite previous problems – and again there were problems in service. By the end of the year barely a quarter of the production order had been fulfilled, mainly because of the shortage and poor quality of the engines from both suppliers. Pictured is an aircraft of No 74 Squadron, which received its first S.E.5a in March 1918 and was the most successful operator of this aircraft.

Country of origin:	United Kingdom
Type:	single-seat fighting scout
Powerplant:	one 200hp (149kW) Wolseley (licence-built) Hispano-Suiza 8a 8-cylinder Vee piston engine
Performance:	maximum speed 222km/h (138mph); service ceiling 5185m (17,000ft); range 483km (300 miles)
Weights:	empty 639kg (1410lb); maximum take-off weight 902kg (1988lb)
Dimensions:	span 8.11m (26ft 7in); length 6.38m (20ft 11in); height 2.89m (9ft 6in); wing area 22.67 sq m (444 sq ft)
Armament:	one fixed forward-firing .303in Vickers machine gun; one .303in Lewis machine gun on Foster mount on upper wing

Royal Aircraft Factory S.E.5a

The engine problems of the S.E.5a were only fully resolved when Wolseley developed the Viper, a high-compression direct-drive version of the Hispano. There were further problems with the Constantinesco interrupter gear, but when all the shortcomings had been eliminated the true potential of the airframe was unleashed. The S.E.5a became increasingly popular with the aces of the day. Ball, who had first criticised the type, scored most of his victories on the aircraft, as did Beauchamp-Proctor, 'Billy' Bishop, Edward 'Mick' Mannock, and James McCudden. Some 5205 aircraft were built, including a small number of conversions as two-seat trainers. The Curtiss Aeroplane and Motor Company in the USA had plans to build 1000, and 56 kits of parts were sent to the there for assembly. The Armistice cut short these plans and only one 180hp (134kW) Wright-Martin engine was built. Pictured is an Austin-built S.E.5a of the 25th Squadron, US American Expeditionary Force.

Country of origin:	United Kingdom
Type:	single-seat fighting scout
Powerplant:	one 200hp (149kW) Wolseley W.4a 8-cylinder Vee piston engine
Performance:	maximum speed 222km/h (138mph); service ceiling 5185m (17,000ft); range 483km (300 miles)
Weights:	empty 639kg (1410lb); maximum take-off weight 902kg (1988lb)
Dimensions:	span 8.11m (26ft 7in); length 6.38m (20ft 11in); height 2.89m (9ft 6in); wing area 22.67 sq m (444 sq ft)
Armament:	one fixed forward-firing .303in Vickers machine gun; one .303in Lewis machine gun on Foster mount on upper wing

Royal Aircraft Factory S.E.5a

With the end of the war, the S.E.5a vanished fairly quickly from military service, although small numbers lingered on in Australia, Canada and South Africa. However, as unwanted fighters became available to the civil market, they were quickly bought and pressed into use in some unusual roles. Some of the best known aircraft were owned and operated by a former army major by the name of Jack Savage, who used his small fleet to pioneer the art of skywriting in the early 1920s. These had a special modification to the exhaust pipes; they were lengthened down the fuselage to a 'Y' junction at the sternpost, the rudder being divided to accommodate this. Into this the smoke-producing substance was introduced from a tank inside the fuselage, the flow being controlled by a small tap in the cockpit. The chemical would react due to the exhaust's heat, producing the highly-visible white smoke. The example pictured above served from 1928 to 1934.

Country of origin:	United Kingdom
Type:	single-seat biplane
Powerplant:	one 200hp (149kW) Wolseley W.4a 8-cylinder Vee piston engine
Performance:	maximum speed 222km/h (138mph); service ceiling 5185m (17,000ft); range 483km (300 miles)
Weights:	empty 639kg (1410lb); maximum take-off weight 902kg (1988lb)
Dimensions:	span 8.11m (26ft 7in); length 6.38m (20ft 11in); height 2.89m (9ft 6in); wing area 22.67 sq m (444 sq ft)

SPAD S.VII

Just prior to World War I, the Société Pour les Appareils Deperdussin (SPAD) was rescued from the mire of bankruptcy by the esteemed French aviator Louis Blériot, who renamed it as the Société Pour l'Aviation et ses Dérivés, retaining the initials SPAD. The new SPAD undertook the design and manufacture of one of the unremarkable 'A' series of two-seat fighters, prior to the development from early 1915 of the SPAD S.V tractor biplane. This was the company's first truly successful military aircraft and undisputedly one of the greatest single-seat scouts of the war. The key to the design was the new Vee engine designed in 1915 by Marc Birkgit, chief designer of Hispano-Suiza. This engine powered the prototype when it first flew in April 1916, prompting the French authorities to place an order for 268. The first of these began to arrive at the squadrons in September, with the service designation S.VII. Later aircraft had a more powerful 180hp (134kW) 8Ac engine.

Country of origin:	France
Type:	single-seat fighting scout
Powerplant:	one 150hp (112kW) Hispano-Suiza 8Aa 8-cylinder Vee piston engine
Performance:	maximum speed 192km/h (119mph); service ceiling 5334m (17,500ft); range 360km (225 miles)
Weights:	empty 510kg (1124lb); maximum take-off weight 740kg (1632lb)
Dimensions:	span 7.81m (25ft 8in); length 6.08m (19ft 11in); height 2.20m (7ft 2in); wing area 17.85 sq m (192 sq ft)
Armament:	one fixed forward-firing .303in Vickers machine gun

SPAD S.VII

In French service the SPAD S.VII proved to be a nimble and rugged fighter, with a respectable rate of climb and turn and the stability essential for accurate gun-laying. The first combat success with the new type was scored by Lieutenant Armand Pinsard of Escadrille No 26 on 23 August 1916. By the summer of 1917 the S.VII was in service with 50 *Escadrilles de chasse* (fighter squadrons) on the Western Front. Georges Félix Madon, Marcel Nogués and Armand de Turenee, and the famous Georges Guynemer all flew the aircraft with skill and élan. The bulk of the production total of 6000 aircraft was built by subcontractors, namely Blériot, Janoir, Kellner, de Marçay, Regy, Freres and Sommer. The RFC and RNAS took a large number of the aircraft. Pictured is an RFC S.VII of No 23 Squadron, flying from La Lovie aerodrome in France in the summer of 1917. The forward fuselage panelling apart, the rest of the aircraft was finished in natural doped fabric.

Country of origin:	France
Type:	single-seat fighting scout
Powerplant:	one 150hp (112kW) Hispano-Suiza 8Aa 8-cylinder Vee piston engine
Performance:	maximum speed 192km/h (119mph); service ceiling 5334m (17,500ft); range 360km (225 miles)
Weights:	empty 510kg (1124lb); maximum take-off weight 740kg (1632lb)
Dimensions:	span 7.81m (25ft 8in); length 6.08m (19ft 11in); height 2.20m (7ft 2in); wing area 17.85 sq m (192 sq ft)
Armament:	one fixed forward-firing .303in Vickers machine gun

PAD S.VII

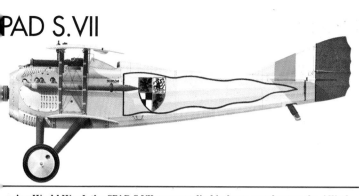

uring World War I, the SPAD S.VII was supplied in large numbers to the Allied forces. Italy took 214, the USA 189, Britain 185, Russia 43 and Belgium 15. After war surplus S.VIIs were sold off to Brazil, Czechoslovakia, Greece, Peru, Poland, tugal, Romania, Thailand and Yugoslavia, making it one of the most successful widely exported of contemporary French aircraft. Pictured is the personal int of the Commanding Officer of the XXIII Gruppo of the Italian Regia onautica, stationed at Lonade Pozzolo in 1924. The pennant-type insignia was nded to improve the appearance of Italy's aircraft after Mussolini created an ependent air arm in 1923. The shield on the fuselage side is made up of the gnia of the 74a, 75a, 76a and 91a *squadriglie* in the Gruppo. Of particular note e horse rampant at the lower left corner of the pennant, later adopted by Enzo rari (who had a family connection with 76a) for his motor cars.

ountry of origin:	France
pe:	single-seat fighting scout
owerplant:	one 180hp (134kW) Hispano-Suiza 8Ac 8-cylinder Vee piston engine
erformance:	maximum speed 192km/h (119mph); service ceiling 5334m (17,500ft); range 360km (225 miles)
Weights:	empty 510kg (1124lb); maximum take-off weight 740kg (1632lb)
imensions:	span 7.81m (25ft 8in); length 6.08m (19ft 11in); height 2.20m (7ft 2in); wing area 17.85 sq m (192 sq ft)
rmament:	one fixed forward-firing .303in Vickers machine gun

271

SPAD S.XIII

Boosted by the lobbying of Georges Guynemer and by the evolution of new German scouts, Louis Béchereau made strident efforts to improve the performance of the SPAD S.VII. The resulting SPAD S.XII Ca.1 was powered by a 200hp (134kW) Hispano-Suiza 8c engine and mounted a formidable 37mm Hotchkiss gun, fitted between the cylinder blocks and firing through the propeller block. Less than a hundred were built before production switched to the popular S.XIII, which had a 165hp (220kW) Hispano-Suiza 8Ba engine, twin Vickers machine guns, slightly larger wings, improved ailerons and an enlarged rudder. The prototype was first flown in April 1917 and series aircraft began entering service the end of May. The S.XIII soon replaced the S.VII in service and its popularity spread far and wide. Orders for some 10,000 aircraft were cancelled at the end of the war. Pictured is an S.XIII of No 23 Squadron, RFC.

Country of origin:	France
Type:	single-seat fighting scout
Powerplant:	one 220hp (164kW) Hispano-Suiza 8BEc 8-cylinder Vee piston engine
Performance:	maximum speed 224km/h (139mph); service ceiling 6650m (21,815ft); endurance 2hrs
Weights:	maximum take-off 845kg (1863lb)
Dimensions:	span 8.1m (26ft 7in); length 6.3m (20ft 8in); height 2.35m (7ft 8in)
Armament:	two fixed forward-firing .303in Vickers machine guns

Saro London Mk II

n 1928 A. V. Roe bought a large share of S. E. Saunders Ltd and the company subsequently built aircraft under the name of Saunders-Roe, more commonly own by the abbreviated form of Saro. The A.27 London coastal patrol flying-boat as built to Air Ministry Specification R.24/31 and was a development of the earlier 7 Severn. The A.27 was slightly smaller, but in all other respects very similar to e A.7, with two 875hp (652kW) Bristol Pegasus III radial engines. Ten aircraft were oduced for RAF Coastal Command as the Saro London Mk I, the first of them livered in 1936. The following 20 Mk IIs had up-rated powerplant in circular celles driving four-blade propellers, all Mk Is being modified subsequently to this andard. Pictured is one of the aircraft operated by No 240 Squadron, which erated from Stranraer under No 15 Group in 1940.

Country of origin:	United Kingdom
Type:	coastal patrol flying-boat
Powerplant:	two 1055hp (787kW) Bristol Pegasus X radial piston engines
Performance:	maximum speed 249km/h (155mph); service ceiling 6065m (19,900ft); range 1770km (1100 miles)
Weights:	empty 5035kg (11,100lb); maximum take-off weight 8346kg (18,400lb)
Dimensions:	span 24.38m (80ft); length 17.31m (56ft 9in); height 5.72m (18ft 9in); wing area 132.38 sq m (1425 sq ft)
Armament:	one .303in Lewis machine gun on pivoted mount in bow; one .303in Lewis machine gun on pivoted mount in each of two midships positions; underwing racks with provision for up to 907kg (2000lb) of bombs or depth charges

Saro Princess

G-ALUN

After World War II the most advanced aeronautical powers had grand visions for giant aircraft that it was confidently predicted would revolutionise commercial aviation. However, none of these projects went beyond the experimental stage – although each represented an amalgamation of advanced technologies, not one had any real commercial viability. The Saro SR.45 Princess was one of the foremost examples, conceived and developed during the war in the mistaken belief that in peacetime flying-boats would continue to operate on transatlantic routes. After an order for three prototypes in May 1946 by the British Overseas Airways Corporation the development programme ran into serious problems, mainly associated with the gearboxes of the turboprop engines, and soon fell behind schedule. In 1951, BOAC realised that landplanes could operate just as safely and more economically on this route and cancelled the programme.

Country of origin:	United Kingdom
Type:	220-seat transatlantic flying-boat
Powerplant:	ten 2500hp Bristol Proteus 600 turboprop engines
Performance:	maximum speed 576km/h (358mph); range 9720km (6040 miles)
Weights:	loaded 156,492kg (345,000lb)
Dimensions:	span 66.9m (219ft 6in); length 45.11m (148ft); height 16.99m (55ft 9in)

Savoia-Marchetti S.55SA

Despite its rather ungainly appearance (promulgated by its twin-catamaran hulls), the Savoia-Marchetti S.55 was one of the most advanced flying-boats of the interwar years and was an indispensable tool of the Regia Marina during the 1930s. It was designed in response to a request for a new multi-engine torpedo-bomber flying-boat, with the twin engines carried on a pylon above the thick cantilever wing carried at shoulder height on the twin-hulls. The centre wing section contained the pilot's cockpit, and extending from the rear of each hull was a boom to carry the tail unit, with two fins and three rudders. The prototype was flown in the summer of 1924, but military chiefs were critical of its unconventional design and limited performance. Savoia-Marchetti then developed a civil version as the S.55C. The military belatedly took an interest and ordered the first 14 S.55A aircraft in 1926. These were followed by the S.55M, S.55SA, and S.55X.

Country of origin:	Italy
Type:	(S.55X) long-range bomber-reconnaissance flying-boat
Powerplant:	two 880hp (656kW) Isotta-Fraschini Asso 750 Vee piston engines
Performance:	maximum speed 279km/h (173mph); service ceiling 5000m (16,405ft); range 3500km (2175 miles)
Weights:	empty equipped 5750kg (12,677lb); maximum take-off weight 8260kg (18,210lb)
Dimensions:	span 24m (78ft 9in); length 16.75m (54ft 11in); height 5m (16ft 5in); wing area 93 sq m (1001 sq ft)
Armament:	two 7.7mm machine guns in nose position in each of the hulls; plus one torpedo or 2000kg (4409lb) of bombs

Short 184

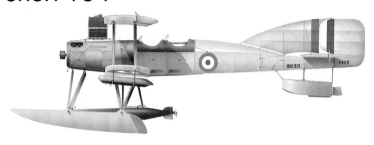

In 1908 Eustace and Oswald Short gained a licence to build the Wright Flyer, and at Leysdown on the Isle of Wight established the world's first factory for the construction of aircraft. The Type 184 was built in response to an Admiralty requirement for a torpedo-carrying seaplane and gave sterling service during World War I. Some 900 aircraft were built, with a variety of engines, but after achieving some spectacular early successes in its intended role the Type 184 was most commonly used for reconnaissance. The aircraft served in many theatres, from the Arctic Circle to the Indian Ocean. In 1916 one fitted with temporary wheels took off successfully from the seaplane-carrier *Campania*. Pictured is one of three aircraft attached to the famous seaplane-carrier HMS *Vindex*. The aircraft is shown here with a 14in torpedo. On 25 March 1916 this same aircraft was loaded with bombs and sent to attack the Zeppelin sheds at Tondern, but without success.

Country of origin:	United Kingdom
Type:	two-seat torpedo-bomber/reconnaissance floatplane
Powerplant:	one 260hp (194kW) Sunbeam Maori Vee piston engine
Performance:	maximum speed 142km/h (88mph); service ceiling 2745m (9000ft); endurance 2hrs 45mins
Weights:	empty 1680kg (3703lb); maximum take-off weight 2433kg (5363lb)
Dimensions:	span 19.36m (63ft 6in); length 12.38m (40ft 7in); height 4.11m (13ft 6in); wing area 63.92 sq m (688 sq ft)
Armament:	one .303in Lewis machine gun on pivoted mount in rear cockpit; plus one 14in torpedo or up to 236kg (520lb) of bombs

Short S.23 C-Class flying-boat

The S.23 of 1936 represented an important break from the biplane-type flying-boats Short had previously built. With four 920hp (686kW) Bristol Pegasus XC engines, a streamlined hull and high set cantilever wing, and of all-metal construction, the S.23 was some 37km/h (23mph) faster than the RAF's Bristol Bulldog fighters. The promising performance demonstrated during flight trials with the first aircraft prompted Imperial Airways to place an order for 28 for service on Empire mail routes. The first aircraft entered service in September 1936 and soon the S.23 was ranging far and wide to Australia, Bermuda, Durban, Egypt, Malaya, New York and East and South Africa. The S23 lacked sufficient range to fly non-stop to New York, prompting development of the S.30 (9 built). War halted any further development and several S.23s were pressed into service with the RAF. Of the 42 Empire-class aircraft built, only 13 outlasted the conflict.

Country of origin:	United Kingdom
Type:	passenger/mail flying-boat
Powerplant:	four 920hp (686kW) Bristol Pegasus XC radial piston engines
Performance:	maximum speed 322km/h (200mph); service ceiling 6095m (20,000ft); range 1223km (760 miles)
Weights:	empty 10,659kg (23,500lb); maximum take-off weight 18,370kg (40,500lb)
Dimensions:	span 34.75m (114ft); length 26.82m (88ft); height 9.7m (31ft 10in); wing area 139.35 sq m (1500 sq ft)

Short Singapore Mk III

The first of the Short flying-boats to bear the name Singapore was the S.5, but this was notable only for the fact that it was used by Sir Alan Cobham and his crew between 17 November 1927 and 31 May 1928 for the first circumnavigation and aerial survey of Africa – a distance of some 32,000km (20,000 miles). The S.12 Singapore Mk II of 1932 got no further than prototype stage, but the S.19 submitted to Air Ministry Specification R.3/33 attracted more interest, and four development aircraft were ordered. The first of these flew in July 1934 and after a series of successful tests at Felixstowe the type was ordered into series production as the Singapore Mk III, for delivery from March 1935. Attrition accounted for 14 of these aircraft, the remainder serving in the Middle and Far East until replaced by the Short Sunderland from mid-1941.

Country of origin:	United Kingdom
Type:	six-seat reconnaissance flying-boat
Powerplant:	four 560hp (418kW) Rolls-Royce Kestrel VIII/IX 12-cylinder Vee piston engines
Performance:	maximum speed 233km/h (145mph); service ceiling 4570m (15,000ft); range 1609km (1000 miles)
Weights:	empty 8355kg (18,420lb); maximum take-off weight 12,474kg (27,500lb)
Dimensions:	span 27.43m (90ft); length 23.16m (76ft); height 7.19m (23ft 7in); wing area 170.38 sq m (1834 sq ft)
Armament:	one .303in Lewis machine gun in nose position; one .303in Lewis machine gun in dorsal position; one .303in Lewis machine gun in tail position; plus up to 907kg (2000lb) of bombs

Short Sunderland Mk I

Short was one of two companies that responded to the requirement outlined in Air Ministry Specification R.2/33 for a modern four-engined monoplane flying-boat. In the S.23 'Empire' class of civil flying-boats it had an ideal starting point and the proven lineage was a factor that contributed to the Air Ministry's order for 21 production examples of the S.25 in March 1936, some 18 months before the first prototype made its maiden flight in October 1937. The initial production model was the Sunderland Mk I that entered service in the summer of 1938 with an initial two squadrons. By the time World War II started in September 1939, another two British-based squadrons had converted to the type, and the rising rate of production allowed another three to convert during the first months of the war. Sunderland Mk I production totalled 90 flying-boats, 15 of them by the Blackburn Aircraft Company, and all powered by 1010hp (753kW) Bristol Pegasus engines.

Country of origin:	United Kingdom
Type:	10-seat maritime reconnaissance flying-boat
Powerplant:	four 1010hp (753kW) Bristol Pegasus XXII 9-cylinder single-row radial engines
Performance:	maximum speed 336km/h (209mph); service ceiling 4570m (15,000ft); range 4023km (2500 miles)
Weights:	empty 13,875kg (30,589lb); maximum take-off weight 22,226kg (49,000lb)
Dimensions:	span 34.38m (112ft 9in); length 26m (85ft 3in); height 10.52m (34ft 6in)
Armament:	two 0.303in trainable forward-firing machine guns in bow turret; four 0.303in trainable rearward-firing machine guns in tail turret; one 0.303in trainable lateral-firing machine gun in each beam position; internal bomb, depth charge and mine load of 2000lb (907kg)

Short Sunderland Mk II

The Sunderland Mk II first flew in August 1941 as a Mk I development with four 1050hp (783kW) Bristol Pegasus XVIII radial engines fitted with two-speed superchargers. Later in the production run of 58 such flying-boats came improved armament in the twin Browning nose turret, two more Brownings in an FN.7 dorsal turret on the right side of the hull at the trailing edge (replacing the single machine guns in the manually operated waist positions), four Brownings in an FN.4A tail turret with armament doubled to 1000 rpg, and the addition of air-to-surface search radar. Only 43 such aircraft were produced, 15 of them at the Short & Harland facility in Belfast. Pictured is a Mk II of No 210 Squadron. Note the spinners on the propellers and flame-damping exhausts, the latter adopted in an attempt to disguise the aircraft from U-boats at night.

Country of origin:	United Kingdom
Type:	10-seat maritime reconnaissance flying-boat
Powerplant:	four 1065hp (794kW) Bristol Pegasus XVII 9-cylinder, single-row radial engines
Performance:	maximum speed 336km/h (209mph); service ceiling 4570m (15,000ft); range 4023km (2500 miles)
Weights:	empty 13,875kg (30,589lb); maximum take-off weight 22,226kg (49,000lb)
Dimensions:	span 34.38m (112ft 9in); length 26m (85ft 3in); height 10.52m (34ft 6in)
Armament:	two 0.303in trainable forward-firing machine guns in bow turret; two 0.303in trainable forward-firing machine guns in dorsal turret; four 0.303in trainable rearward-firing machine guns in tail turret, internal bomb, depth charge and mine load of 2000lb (907kg)

Short Sunderland Mk III

First flown in June 1942, the Sunderland Mk III was the first major production model of the family and was in essence a late-production Sunderland Mk II with revised planing bottom. Production of the 407 Mk IIIs lasted to late 1943. The Mk I was also converted for use as a long-range passenger aircraft and operated by British Overseas Airways Corporation from March 1943 on gradually extending routes. Operating alongside radar-equipped Catalinas, the RAF Short Sunderlands were extremely active in hunting for U-boats over the North Atlantic. When the latter received Metox passive receivers tuned to ASV Mk II they received ample warning of the presence of British aircraft and kills dropped dramatically. In response the RAF introduced the ASV Mk III, operating in the radar band well below 10cm (20in) and with the aerials neatly faired into blisters under the outer wings. When thus fitted the Sunderland became a Mk IIIa, of which 54 were built.

Country of origin:	United Kingdom
Type:	10-seat maritime reconnaissance flying-boat
Powerplant:	four 1065hp (794kW) Bristol Pegasus XVII 9-cylinder, single-row radial engines
Performance:	maximum speed 336km/h (209mph); service ceiling 4570m (15,000ft); range 4023km (2500 miles)
Weights:	empty 13,875kg (30,589lb); maximum take-off weight 22,226kg (49,000lb)
Dimensions:	span 34.38m (112ft 9in); length 26m (85ft 3in); height 10.52m (34ft 6in)
Armament:	two 0.303in trainable forward-firing machine guns in bow turret; two 0.303in trainable forward-firing machine guns in dorsal turret; four 0.303in trainable rearward-firing machine guns in tail turret; internal bomb, depth charge and mine load of 2000lb (907kg)

Short Sunderland GR.5

As the war in the Pacific hotted up Coastal Command began to discover the limits of its current generation of Sunderland aircraft, underlining the need for a more powerful long-range flying-boat. This was outlined in Specification R.8/42, to which Short Brothers submitted a proposal for a Bristol Hercules engined version the Sunderland, designated the Mk IV. This eventually grew into a very different aircraft from the Sunderland and it was decided instead to simply re-engine the Mk III with Pratt & Whitney R-1830-90B Twin Wasp engines that were already in widespread service on the Catalina and Dakota. After trials with this engine in March 1944, Short Brothers installed better armament and made other detail modifications. This new version was adopted as the Sunderland GR.Mk V, of which 143 were completed up until June 1946. Pictured is a GR.Mk V of No 23 Squadron, South African Air Force.

Country of origin:	United Kingdom
Type:	10-seat maritime reconnaissance flying-boat
Powerplant:	four 1200hp (895kW) Pratt & Whitney R-1830-90B Twin Wasp 14-cylinder, two-row radial engines
Performance:	maximum speed 343km/h (213mph); service ceiling 5455m (17,900ft); range 2980 miles (4796km)
Weights:	empty 16,738kg (36,900lb); maximum take-off weight 27,216kg (60,000lb)
Dimensions:	span 34.38m (112ft 9in); length 26m (85ft 3in); height 10.52m (34ft 6in)
Armament:	two 0.303in machine guns in bow turret; four 0.303in machine guns on sides of bow; two 0.303in machine guns in dorsal turret; four 0.303in machine guns in tail turret; one 0.5in machine gun in beam positions; internal bomb, depth charge and mine load of 4960lb (2250kg)

Siemens-Schukert D.III

Siemens-Schukert Werke, a subsidiary of the vast Siemens electrical firm, began building experimental aircraft at the turn of the century and later, in 1916, built small numbers of the D.I, a copy of the French Nieuport 17. In 1917 the sister firm Siemens und Halske produced the remarkable Sh.III engine and this was installed in the various prototype D.II airframes of different span designed by Siemens-Schukert Werke's Chief Engineer Harald Wolff. The engine showed considerable promise, but suffered from imperfect development. The mid-span prototype went into production as the D.III, and demonstrated outstanding speed, climb and manoeuvrability. Service deliveries began in January 1918. However, the engine proved to be so troublesome that the entire fleet was withdrawn and re-engined with the Sh.IIIa, with the lower cowl cut away to improve cooling. Those aircraft that made to the front mostly served with Jasta 15 of Jagdgeschwader II.

Country of origin:	Germany
Type:	single-seat fighting scout
Powerplant:	one 200hp (150kW) Siemens und Halske Sh.IIIa rotary piston engine
Performance:	maximum speed 180km/h (112mph); service ceiling 8000m (26,245ft); endurance 2hrs
Weights:	empty 534kg (1177lb); maximum take-off weight 725kg (1598lb)
Dimensions:	span 8.43m (27ft 8in); length 6.7m (18ft 8in); height 2.8m (9ft 2in); wing area 203.44 sq m (19 sq ft)
Armament:	two fixed forward-firing 7.92mm LMG 08/15 machine guns

Sikorsky S-42

Igor Sikorsky left Russia after the October 1917 revolution and in March 1923 he established the small Sikorsky Aircraft company in the USA, starting with the S-29A twin-engine transport. His first truly successful design was the S-30, bought in some numbers by Pan American, which remained faithful to Sikorsky's designs and in August 1931 issued a requirement for a long-range transatlantic flying-boat able to carry a crew of four and a complement of 12 passengers over 4023km (2500 miles) at a cruising speed of 233km/h (145mph). Martin and Sikorsky both submitted designs and were awarded production contracts late 1932. The first S-42 was delivered to Pan Am's Dinner Key base in August 1934 and inaugurated the Miami–Rio route the same month. By the end of 1935 S-42s were making staged crossings of the Pacific from California to Manila. In all three S-42s, three more powerful S-42As with longer span wings, and four S-42Bs with aerodynamic refinements.

Country of origin:	USA
Type:	passenger flying-boat
Powerplant:	four 700hp (522kW) Pratt & Whitney Hornet S51DG 9-cylinder radial piston engines
Performance:	cruising speed 267km/h (166mph); service ceiling 5790m (19,000ft); range 1250km (775 miles)
Weights:	empty equipped 17,237kg (38,000lb)
Dimensions:	span 34.79m (114ft 2in); length 21.08m (69ft 2in); height 5.28m (17ft 4 in)

Sopwith Camel F.1

The Triplane had only been in service for six months when its replacement, the Sopwith Camel, began to arrive in service. Perhaps the most famous aircraft of World War I, the Camel was so-called because of its distinctive 'humped' back, and between June 1917 and November 1918 it destroyed at least 3000 enemy aircraft, a greater total than that attained by any other aircraft. The Camel was a clear linear descendant of the Pup and Triplane, but its combat performance was achieved at some cost to the peerless handling of the earlier types. In inexperienced hands the Camel could bite, and the engine's torque was such that it had a nasty tendency to drop suddenly to the left on take off. Casualties among trainee pilots were high, but once mastered it was a superb dogfighter. Total production was in the order of 5490 aircraft, many of which served with foreign air arms.

Country of origin:	United Kingdom
Type:	single-seat fighting scout
Powerplant:	one 130hp (97kW) Clerget rotary piston engine
Performance:	maximum speed 185km/h (115mph); service ceiling 5790m (19,000ft); endurance 2hrs 30mins
Weights:	empty 421kg (929lb); maximum take-off weight 659kg (1453lb)
Dimensions:	span 8.53m (28ft); length 5.72m (18ft 9in); height 2.59m (8ft 6in); wing area 21.46 sq m (231 sq ft)
Armament:	two fixed forward-firing .303in Vickers machine guns; plus up to four 11.3kg (25lb) bombs carried on fuselage sides

Sopwith Camel F.1

The designation F.1 covered Camels fitted with numerous different engine and armament fits. Engines in the 100–150hp (75–112kW) range by Bentley, Clerget, Gnome and Le Rhône were fitted to production machines, and the Camel was also fitted with a 150hp (112kW) Le Rhône and a 180hp (134kW) Gnome Monosoupape. There was also a night-fighter version with a pair of Lewis guns on a double Foster mounting above the top-wing centre section, and the cockpit moved about 30cm (12in) aft to allow the pilot to operate the guns. Exhaust flame dampers and navigation lights were also fitted. This version was introduced with Home Defence units, and turned the tide of the battle against the German Gotha bombers. An experimental trench-fighter version was built by Nieuport & General as the TF.1 with two downward firing Lewis guns and a third on the upper wing section. Pictured is a Camel F.1, in post-war markings, built by Boulton & Paul.

Country of origin:	United Kingdom
Type:	single-seat fighting scout
Powerplant:	one 130hp (97kW) Clerget rotary piston engine
Performance:	maximum speed 185km/h (115mph); service ceiling 5790m (19,000ft); endurance 2hrs 30mins
Weights:	empty 421kg (929lb); maximum take-off weight 659kg (1453lb)
Dimensions:	span 8.53m (28ft); length 5.72m (18ft 9in); height 2.59m (8ft 6in); wing area 21.46 sq m (231 sq ft)
Armament:	two fixed forward-firing .303in Vickers machine guns; plus up to four 11.3kg (25lb) bombs carried on fuselage sides

Sopwith Camel 2F.1

The final production version of the Camel was the 2F.1, a shipboard fighter with slightly reduced wingspan, jettisonable steel-tube landing gear and detachable rear fuselage (for compact carrier stowage). At the time of the Armistice the Royal Air Force (newly formed from the Royal Flying Corps and Royal Naval Air Service) had some 129 2F.1 Camels on charge, 112 of which were with the Grand Fleet. As well as being flown from the aircraft carriers HMS *Furious* and HMS *Pegasus*, they were catapulted from platforms erected on the gun turrets and forecastles of many other warships. Some aircraft remained in service at sea after the end of the war. Pictured is a Sopwith-built Camel 2F.1 flown by Canadian ace Bill Alexander, with 'A' Flight, No 10 (Naval) Squadron, RNAS, at Treizennes. This unit became No 210 Squadron, RAF, on 1 April 1918.

Country of origin:	United Kingdom
Type:	single-seat fighting scout
Powerplant:	one 130hp (97kW) Clerget rotary piston engine
Performance:	maximum speed 185km/h (115mph); service ceiling 5790m (19,000ft); endurance 2hrs 30mins
Weights:	empty 421kg (929lb); maximum take-off weight 659kg (1453lb)
Dimensions:	span 8.2m (26ft 11in); length 5.72m (18ft 9in); height 2.59m (8ft 6in)
Armament:	one fixed forward-firing .303in Vickers machine gun; one .303in Lewis machine gun; plus (on some) two 22.7kg (50lb) bombs carried on fuselage sides

Sopwith Pup

The Pup got its abiding nickname from its likeness to a scaled-down 1½ Strutter. was first flown in February 1916 with an 80hp (60kW) Le Rhône rotary engine Given the relatively small power output of this engine, the fact that the Pup was such a pleasure to fly speaks volumes of its design and construction. It was very small, simple and reliable, and its generous wing area gave it excellent performance at height. With only 80hp (60kW) on tap it soon became underpowered for combat with the more powerful Albatros and Halberstadt scout though compared with an Albatros it could turn twice for a single turn by the enemy. Sopwith built 170 Pups for the RNAS, and another 1600 were built for the RFC. Because of their exceptional time-to-height performance, many Pups were assigned to home defence units to counter the German bombing threat.

Country of origin:	United Kingdom
Type:	single-seat fighting scout
Powerplant:	one 80hp (60kW) Le Rhône rotary piston engine
Performance:	maximum speed 179km/h (112mph); service ceiling 5334m (17,500ft); range 500km (310 miles)
Weights:	empty 358kg (790lb); maximum take-off weight 556kg (1225lb)
Dimensions:	span 8.08m (26ft 6in); length 5.89m (19ft 4in); height 2.87m (9ft 5in); wing area 23.60 sq m (254 sq ft)
Armament:	one fixed forward-firing .303in Vickers machine gun or one .303in Lewis aimed obliquely through cut-out in centre section of upper wing; anti-airship armament usually eight Le Prieur rockets launched from interplane struts

Sopwith Snipe

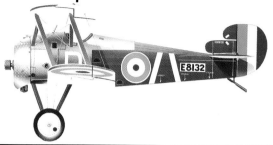

Designed as a successor to the Camel, the Snipe had a protracted development spanning six prototypes during which it was subjected to meticulous testing against such machines as the Bobolink and Nieuport B.N.1, before the Air Ministry finally decided to order it into production. All this was very much different from the experience of the Tabloid some four years previously, but in those four years much had been learned and the Snipe faced a horde of competitors. The Mk I had twin Vickers, the Lewis previously mounted on the upper plane having been found too difficult to aim, and electric heating and pilot oxygen for high-altitude flying. Deliveries to units in France began only eight weeks before the Armistice, but in the few aerial combats with the enemy the Snipe gave ample demonstration of its quality. Of the 4,515 ordered only 100 had been delivered by the Armistice; post-war production brought the total to 497, some remaining in front-line service until 1926.

Country of origin:	United Kingdom
Type:	single-seat fighting scout
Powerplant:	one 230hp (172kW) Bentley B.R.2 rotary piston engine
Performance:	maximum speed 195km/h (121mph); service ceiling 5945m (19,500ft); endurance 3 hours
Weights:	empty 595kg (1,312lb); maximum take-off weight 916kg (2,020lb)
Dimensions:	span 9.17m (30ft 1in); length 6.02m (19ft 9in); height 2.67m (8ft 9in); wing area 25.08sq m (270sq ft)
Armament:	two fixed forward firing synchronised .303in Vickers machine-guns, plus up to four 11.3kg (25lb) of bombs on external racks

Sopwith 1½ Strutter

Deriving its nickname – by which it became universally known – from the '1½' sets of struts attaching the upper wing, the 1½ Strutter was the first military aircraft to be designed from the outset with a synchronised gun, and (apart from the Russian Sikorsky IM series) the first to equip a strategic bombing force. It included such unexpected features as a variable-incidence tailplane and airbrakes on the lower wing. The two-seat prototype was first flown in December 1915, and service deliveries of the first of an eventual 1513 machines were in April 1916. Most of the later versions were single-seat 9700 bombers and 'Ship Strutters' for the new Royal Navy aircraft carriers. About 4000 were built in France, and the aircraft was also operated with the air arms of Belgium, France, Japan, Latvia, Romania, and Russia, and with the American Expeditionary Force.

Country of origin:	United Kingdom
Type:	two-seat multi-role combat aircraft
Powerplant:	one 130hp (97kW) Clerget rotary piston engine
Performance:	maximum speed 164km/h (102mph); service ceiling 3960m (13,000ft); range 565km (350 miles)
Weights:	empty 570kg (1260lb); maximum take-off weight 975kg (2149lb)
Dimensions:	span 10.21m (33ft 6in); length 7.7m (25ft 3in); height 3.12m (10ft 3in); wing area 32.14 sq m (346 sq ft)
Armament:	one fixed forward-firing .303in Vickers machine gun; plus up to four 25kg (56lb) bombs or an equivalent weight of smaller bombs

Sopwith Tabloid

In the summer of 1913 young T. O. M. (Tommy) Sopwith bought the lease on a former ice-skating rink in Kingston-upon-Thames, and set up the Sopwith Aviation & Engineering Company. He had hired Fred Sigrist to look after his yacht and now involved him in the design of aircraft, while Harry Hawker was taken on as a pilot and manager of the growing staff. From this came thousands of the greatest combat aircraft of World War I. One of the first to be built at the Sopwith works was a racing biplane, so small it was called the Tabloid. After Hawker had completed initial tests at Brooklands it was flown to Farnborough where it astonished everyone by reaching 148km/h (92mph) with a passenger and reaching 647m (1200ft) in one minute after leaving the ground. Thirty-six were subsequently built for the RFC and RNAS; RNAS machines mounted a series of famous attacks on the Zeppelin sheds in winter 1914. A float-equipped version was built as the Sopwith Schneider.

Country of origin:	United Kingdom
Type:	single-seat maritime patrol and attack seaplane
Powerplant:	one 100hp (74.5kW) Gnow Monosoupape 9-cylinder rotary piston engine
Performance:	maximum speed 148km/h (92mph); service ceiling 4600m (15,000ft); range 510km (315 miles)
Weights:	empty 545kg (1200lb); maximum take-off weight 717kg (1580lb)
Dimensions:	span 7.77m (25ft 6in); length 7.02m (23ft); height 3.05m (10ft)
Armament:	Royal Naval Air Service seaplanes had one .303in Lewis machine gun

Sopwith Triplane

The lessons from early aerial combats over the Western Front emphasised the need for the highest possible rate of climb and manoeuvrability and, by fitting three slender planes to an airframe derived from the Pup, Sopwith designer Herbert Smith sought to exceed even this aircraft in these respects. The prototype flew in May 1916, and demonstrated an exceptional rate of climb, at only a small cost to manoeuvrability. The first aircraft entered service in November 1916 and over the following six months the Triplane gained almost complete ascendancy over enemy fighters. The German aircraft industry was launched into frenetic activity and by early 1917 almost every company was designing a triplane that could match it. Pictured here is the aircraft of Flight Lieutenant R. A. Little, No 8 (Naval) Squadron, RNAS, based in northern France in the spring of 1917.

Country of origin:	United Kingdom
Type:	single-seat fighting scout
Powerplant:	one 130hp (97kW) Clerget 9B 9-cylinder rotary piston engine
Performance:	maximum speed 188km/h (117mph); service ceiling 6250m (20,500ft); endurance 2hrs 45mins
Weights:	empty 499kg (1101lb); maximum take-off weight 699kg (1541lb)
Dimensions:	span 8.08m (26ft 6in); length 5.74m (18ft 10in); height 3.2m (10ft 6in); wing area 21.46 sq m (231 sq ft)
Armament:	one or two fixed forward-firing .303in Vickers machine guns

Supermarine S.5

Noel Pemberton-Billing founded the company which became the Supermarine Aviation Works in 1916. Its early designs were for flying-boats, however it competed unsuccessfully in the 1919 Schneider Trophy race, not returning until 1922, when the Supermarine Sea Lion was flown into first place at Naples. In 1927 two new S.5 seaplanes were entered for the contest at Venice, this superbly streamlined all-metal aircraft taking first (pictured) and second place respectively. In the penultimate contest in 1929 the S.6, powered by a 1900hp (1417kW) Rolls-Royce 'R' engine, came first. Only the timely intervention of Lady Houston, who provided funding after the withdrawal of government support, allowed Britain to field an entrant in the final contest of 1931. With no time to develop a new airframe, R.J. Mitchell could only shoehorn a 2350hp (1752kW) version of the Rolls-Royce engine into the airframe. The resulting S.6B won the Trophy permanently for Britain.

Country of origin:	United Kingdom
Type:	racing seaplane
Powerplant:	one 875hp (652kW) Napier Lion VIIB 12-cylinder Vee Piston engine
Performance:	maximum speed 514.29km/h (319mph)
Weights:	loaded 1470kg (3242lb)
Dimensions:	span 8.15m (26ft 9in); length 7.4m (24ft 3in); height 3.38m (11ft 1in)

Supermarine Southampton Mk I

In addition to its military aircraft designs, Supermarine produced a small number of commercial passenger-carrying amphibian flying-boats. The most successful of these was the single-engine Sea Eagle biplane of 1923, three of which were built for the British Marine Air Navigation company for service on its Southampton–Channel Islands routes. These were complemented in 1926 by a Supermarine Swan, from which was developed the elegant Southampton, designed by R. J. Mitchell. This five crew biplane flying-boat first flew in March 1925 and deliveries began to the RAF a few months later. The Mk II had a Duralumin hull, which represented a considerable weight saving over the wooden-hulled Mk I. Production total was 68 aircraft. T he example pictured here is a Mk I of No 480 (Coastal Reconnaissance) Flight, RAF, based at Calshot during the mid-1920s.

Country of origin:	United Kingdom
Type:	(Mk II) general reconnaissance flying-boat
Powerplant:	two 500hp (373kW) Napier Lion VA W-12 piston engines
Performance:	maximum speed 174km/h (108mph); service ceiling 4265m (14,000ft); range 1497km (930 miles)
Weights:	empty 4082kg (9000lb); maximum take-off weight 6895kg (15,200lb)
Dimensions:	span 22.86m (75ft); length 15.58m (51ft 1in); height 6.82m (22ft 4in); wing area 134.61 sq m (1449 sq ft)
Armament:	one .303in Lewis gun on pivoted mount in nose position; one .303in Lewis gun on pivoted mount in each of two midships positions, plus up to 499kg (1100lb) of bombs

Supermarine Walrus Mk I

The Walrus began life as the Supermarine Seagull, a three-man deck landing amphibian for RAF use as a fleet spotter from Royal Navy aircraft carriers which came into service in the early 1920s. The prototype Mk V version of the Seagull was fitted with a Bristol Pegasus engine in a pusher configuration and after evaluation by the Fleet Air Arm this was adopted under the name Walrus Mk I. Production began in 1936 of an eventual 746 boats, this total including 191 Walrus Mk IIs with Saro wooden hulls and Bristol Pegasus VI engine. The Walrus was stressed for catapult-launching and saw service with the Australian, British and New Zealand navies in practically every theatre of war. Known universally as the 'Shagbat', the Supermarine Walrus was also used in the air-sea rescue role, ensuring it a place in the hearts of many aircrew. Pictured above is a Walrus Mk I based on HMS *Belfast* in the early 1940s.

Country of origin:	United Kingdom
Type:	four-seat spotter-reconnaissance amphibian
Powerplant:	one 750hp (559kW) Bristol Pegasus VI radial piston engine
Performance:	maximum speed 217km/h (135mph); service ceiling 5210m (17,100ft); range 966km (600 miles)
Weights:	empty 2223kg (4900lb); maximum take-off weight 3266kg (7200lb)
Dimensions:	span 13.97m (45ft 10in); length 11.35m (37ft 3in); height 4.65m (15ft 3in); wing area 56.67 sq m (610 sq ft)
Armament:	one .303in Vickers 'K' gun in bow; one or two .303in Vickers 'K' guns in midships positions; underwing racks with provision for up to 272kg (600lb) of bombs, or two Mk VIII depth charges

Vickers Valentia

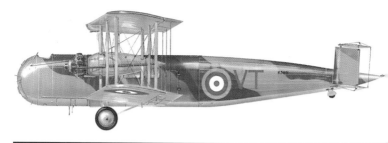

Vickers derived a military transport aircraft for the Royal Air Force from the Vickers Virginia bomber. The new aircraft, which first flew in 1922, shared the biplane wing and tail unit of its predecessor but had a completely new large-capacity fuselage with accommodation for two crew in an open cockpit and up to 23 fully-equipped troops in an enclosed cabin. A further three prototypes were flown, followed by the first largescale production version, the Type 169 Victoria Mk V, which had swept outer wing panels and Napier Lion VIIIB engines, and all moving rudders. The Victoria Mk VI spawned the Type 264 Valentia, which had Bristol Pegasus IIL3 engines. Some 97 Victorias were built and 28 newbuild Valentias, although 54 Victorias were later converted to Valentia standard. The Valentia served with the RAF in the Middle East until 1944.

Country of origin:	United Kingdom
Type:	troop transport
Powerplant:	two 622hp (464kW) Bristol Pegasus IIL3 radial piston engine
Performance:	maximum speed 193km/h (120mph); service ceiling 4955m (16,250ft); range 1287km (800 miles)
Weights:	empty 4964kg (10,944lb); maximum take-off weight 8845kg (19,500lb)
Dimensions:	span 26.62m (87ft 4in); length 18.14m (59ft 6in); height 5.41m (17ft 9in); wing area 202.34 sq m (2178 sq ft)
Armament:	provision to fit underwing racks for 998kg (2200lb) bomb load

Vickers Vildebeest Mk III

In 1927 the British Air Ministry began its search for a new light bomber to replace the Hawker Horsley torpedo/day bomber, which entered service that year. The Vickers Vildebeest was designed to this requirement, and was flown as the Type 132 prototype in April 1928. Development with a number of engines was followed by the initial Mk I production model with Bristol Pegasus I for service delivery in April 1933. The Mk II had the Pegasus IIM3, the Mk III had a revised rear cockpit for a third crew member. Production of the first three series amounted to 152 aircraft. In December 1937 the last of 57 Mk IVs, the last production series, was delivered. About 100 Vildebeest were still serving at the outbreak of World War II, and were used operationally in the Far East. Pictured is a Mk III of No 273 Squadron, Royal Air Force, stationed at China Bay in Ceylon in 1939. The squadron re-equipped with the Fairey Fulmar in March 1942.

Country of origin:	United Kingdom
Type:	three-seat general-purpose aircraft
Powerplant:	one 660hp (492kW) Bristol Pegasus IIM3 sleeve-valve radial piston engine
Performance:	maximum speed 230km/h (142mph); service ceiling 5182m (17,000ft); range 2500km (1553 miles)
Weights:	empty 1918kg (4229lb); maximum take-off weight 3674kg (8100lb)
Dimensions:	span 14.94m (49ft in); length 11.17m (36ft 8in); height 5.42m (17ft 9in)
Armament:	one fixed forward-firing .303in Vickers machine gun; one .303in Lewis machine gun on pivoted mount in rear cockpit

Vickers Vimy Mk I

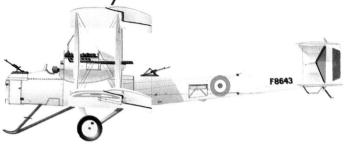

Vickers was already a large, well-established company when in 1911 it diversified into aircraft production. The F.B two-seat fighter/reconnaissance aircraft were used in large numbers, and in the closing stages of World War I Vickers produced a large biplane aircraft designed with the express purpose of attacking Berlin. The F.B.27 Vimy was designed by Rex Pierson to meet the same criteria as the Handley-Page V/1500 and de Havilland D.H.10 Amiens, and it too was ordered into largescale production for the newly formed Independent Bombing Force. By comparison with these two aircraft the Vimy was quite compact, and demonstrated exceptional handling qualities when flight-tested at Martlesham Heath during 1918 (lifting a greater load than the Handley-Page 0/400 on half the power). Production began of the Vimy Mk I but by the end of October 1918, the RAF had only three aircraft in service. Pictured is a Morgan-built Mk I of No 70 Squadron, based at Heliopolis in 1921.

Country of origin:	United Kingdom
Type:	(Mk I) heavy bomber
Powerplant:	two 360hp (269kW) Rolls Royce Eagle VIII 12-cylinder Vee piston engines
Performance:	maximum speed 166km/h (103mph); service ceiling 2135m (7000ft); range 1464km (910 miles)
Weights:	empty 3221kg (7101lb); maximum take-off weight 5670kg (12,500lb)
Dimensions:	span 20.75m (68ft 1in); length 13.27m (43ft 6in); height 4.76m (15ft 7in); wing area 123.56 sq m (1330 sq ft)
Armament:	one .303in Lewis Mk III machine gun on pivoted mount in nose; one .303in Lewis Mk III machine gun on pivoted mount in dorsal position; one .303in Lewis Mk III machine gun on pivoted mount in ventral or each of two beam positions; internal bomb cells and underwing racks with provision for up to 2179kg (4804lb) of bombs

Vickers Vimy Mk I

Production of the Vimy only really got underway after World War I, and by June of 1919 the Mk I was in full RAF service. The aircraft achieved fame through two of the most significant record-breaking flights of the 1920s. The first of these was staged in a company-owned Vimy Mk I with all the military equipment removed and extra fuel tankage installed, increasing capacity to 3932 litres (865 gallons). On 14 June 1919 Messrs Alcock and Brown took off from Newfoundland and at 8.40am the next day landed in a peat bog in Ireland, marking the first successful non-stop transatlantic crossing by air. At the end of the year another remarkable flight was undertaken, in a Vimy Mk I registered as G-EAOU. Between 12 November and 10 December two Australian brothers, Captain Ross Smith and Lieutenant Keith Smith, accompanied by Sergeants W. H. Shiers and J. M. Bennett, flew the 17,912km (11,130 miles) to Darwin in Northern Australia.

Country of origin:	United Kingdom
Type:	heavy bomber
Powerplant:	two 360hp (269kW) Rolls Royce Eagle VIII 12-cylinder Vee piston engines
Performance:	maximum speed 166km/h (103mph); service ceiling 2135m (7000ft); range 1464km (910 miles)
Weights:	empty 3221kg (7101lb); maximum take-off weight 5670kg (12,500lb)
Dimensions:	span 20.75m (68ft 1in); length 13.27m (43ft 6in); height 4.76m (15ft 7in); wing area 123.56 sq m (1330 sq ft)

Vickers Vimy Mk I

Service in the hot climes of the Middle East was taxing on both men and machines. By the late 1920s it was proving increasingly difficult to achieve acceptable levels of serviceability with the water-cooled Rolls-Royce Eagle engines fitted to the Vimys still in service with the flying training schools and parachute training schools, and it was decided to re-engine the survivors with 420hp (313kW) Armstrong Siddeley Jupiter engines, or 460hp (343kW) Bristol Jupiter radial engines. The aircraft pictured was built by Vickers at Weybridge in Surrey as a Mk I Vimy bomber before being modified with dual controls. It was one of the four Mk Is to be re-engined with the Jupiter IV in the late 1920s while on the charge of No 4 Flying Training School at Abu Sueir, Egypt. The last remaining military Vimy was retired from service by this unit in 1933.

Country of origin:	United Kingdom
Type:	multi-engine trainer
Powerplant:	two 420hp (313kW) Bristol Jupiter IV 9-cylinder radial piston engines
Performance:	maximum speed 166km/h (103mph); service ceiling 2135m (7000ft); range 1464km (910 miles)
Weights:	empty 3221kg (7101lb); maximum take-off weight 5670kg (12,500lb)
Dimensions:	span 20.75m (68ft 1in); length 13.27m (43ft 6in); height 4.76m (15ft 7in); wing area 123.56 sq m (1330 sq ft)

Vickers Vimy Mk II

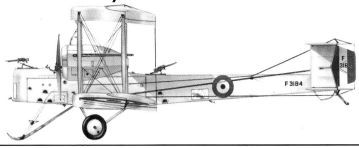

S ome 158 Vimys were completed to Mk I standard and there followed 74 other variants, and 55 variants of the Vickers Vernon. The Vimy Mk III (10 built by RAE at Farnborough) and Mk IV (25 built by Westland) had Rolls Royce Eagle engines and minor detail changes. The designation Vimy Mk II is most confusing, as it appears to have been given to many different types. To confuse matters further, the Mk III and Mk IV were redesignated Mk II in 1923, in an attempt to introduce some clarity! What is certain is that the Vimy was the standard heavy bomber of the RAF from 1919 to 1930, after which it began to be replaced by the Vickers Victoria. Most of the RAF aircraft were sent overseas to act as a tool of the RAF's air policing operations in the Middle East, where Nos 45, 58, 70 and 216 Sqns and No 4 Flying Training School were operating. The aircraft pictured served with No 70 Squadron in Egypt.

Country of origin:	United Kingdom
Type:	heavy bomber
Powerplant:	two 360hp (269kW) Rolls Royce Eagle VIII 12-cylinder Vee piston engines
Performance:	maximum speed 166km/h (103mph); service ceiling 2135m (7000ft); range 1464km (910 miles)
Weights:	empty 3221kg (7101lb); maximum take-off weight 5670kg (12,500lb)
Dimensions:	span 20.75m (68ft 1in); length 13.27m (43ft 6in); height 4.76m (15ft 7in); wing area 123.56 sq m (1330 sq ft)
Armament:	one .303in Lewis Mk III machine gun on pivoted mount in nose; one .303in Lewis Mk III machine gun on pivoted mount in dorsal position; one .303in Lewis Mk III machine gun on pivoted mount in ventral or each of two beam positions; internal bomb cells and underwing racks with provision for up to 2179kg (4804lb) of bombs

Vickers Vimy Mk IV

Vickers built a prototype Vimy Mk II during World War I, and an order was placed for 75. However, the order was cancelled at the war's end as the new Royal Air Force retrenched in the face of large cuts in funding. In 1923 the RAF ordered 10 of these Mk IIs, but because of the attempts at rationalisation they were sometimes referred to as Mk IVs. It had been planned to use the American Liberty engine for the Mk II, but all of them were completed by Vickers with the Rolls-Royce Eagle engine. Another 15 were built to the Mk II standard in 1923–4, some of which were later re-engined with the Jupiter or Jaguar radial. The aircraft shown here is a Westland-built Mk IV, the second of a batch of 25 completed by the company. All were later redesignated Mk II. Note the drab olive camouflage, which was applied to aircraft that operated from Britain.

Country of origin:	United Kingdom
Type:	heavy bomber
Powerplant:	two 360hp (269kW) Rolls Royce Eagle VIII 12-cylinder Vee piston engines
Performance:	maximum speed 166km/h (103mph); service ceiling 2135m (7000ft); range 1464km (910 miles)
Weights:	empty 3221kg (7101lb); maximum take-off weight 5670kg (12,500lb)
Dimensions:	span 20.75m (68ft 1in); length 13.27m (43ft 6in); height 4.76m (15ft 7in); wing area 123.56 sq m (1330 sq ft)
Armament:	one .303in Lewis Mk III machine gun on pivoted mount in nose; one .303in Lewis Mk III machine gun on pivoted mount in dorsal position; one .303in Lewis Mk III machine gun on pivoted mount in ventral or each of two beam positions; internal bomb cells and underwing racks with provision for up to 2179kg (4804lb) of bombs

Vickers Vimy Ambulance

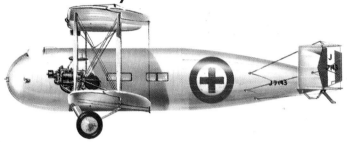

The final two versions in the Vimy family were the Napier-Lion-powered Vimy Ambulance and the Vickers Vernon bomber/transport. The Vimy Ambulance was generally similar to the Commercial but with a nose loading door to provide access for the four stretchers or eight sitting patients, plus two medical attendants. The Vickers Vernon bomber/transport was used extensively by the RAF during operations against insurgent tribesmen in Iraq during 1921. The Vimy Ambulance was built to the extent of four aircraft, and the Vernon was built in three variants; the 20 Mk Is had Rolls Royce Eagle VIII engines, the 25 Vernon Mk IIs had the Napier Lion, and the 10 Mk IIIs had high-compression Lion II engines and additional wing tanks. All Vernons served with Nos 45 and 70 Squadrons in the Middle East, between March 1922 and January 1927.

Country of origin:	United Kingdom
Type:	air ambulance
Powerplant:	two 450hp (336kW) Napier Lion inline piston engines
Performance:	cruising speed 135km/h (84mph); service ceiling 3200m (10,500ft); range 724km (450 miles)
Weights:	take-off weight 5670kg (12,500lb)
Dimensions:	span 20.47m (67ft 2in); length 13m (42ft 8in); height 4.76m (15ft 7in); wing area 123.56 sq m (1330 sq ft)

Vickers Vimy Commercial

In January 1919 Vickers began development of a commercial transport version of the Vimy, designated the Vimy Commercial. The prototype was first flown in April 1919, with the tail, wings, landing gear and powerplant of the bomber, but with an all-new large-diameter fuselage to provide a cabin for ten passengers. The *Daily Mail* had offered a £10,000 prize to the crew who could complete a non-stop flight from Cairo to Cape Town, and as a publicity stunt the prototype Vimy Commercial, sponsored by the *The Times* and piloted by two Vickers test pilots, Captains S. Cockerell and F. C. G. Broome, attempted the journey. Registered as G-EAAR, the aircraft crashed as it was taking off from Tangora in Tanganyika. The loss of the prototype did not affect an order placed by the Chinese Government for 40 aircraft. Three others were built, the most famous of them undoubtedly the G-EASI City of London, which operated almost continually between Croydon and Brussels from 1920 to 1934.

Country of origin:	United Kingdom
Type:	commercial transport aircraft
Powerplant:	two 360hp (269kW) Rolls Royce Eagle VIII 12-cylinder Vee piston engines
Performance:	cruising speed 135km/h (84mph); service ceiling 3200m (10,500ft); range 724km (450 miles)
Weights:	take-off weight 5670kg (12,500lb)
Dimensions:	span 20.47m (67ft 2in); length 13m (42ft 8in); height 4.76m (15ft 7in); wing area 123.56 sq m (1330 sq ft)

Vickers Vincent

The Royal Air Force selected a modified version of the Vildebeest that it called the Type 266 Vincent to supersede the Fairey IIIF and Westland Wapiti in the army cooperation role. The prototype for this aircraft was a converted Mk I Vildebeest; and although derived directly from the Mk III Vildebeest, the Vincent differed by having an extra fuel tank in place of a torpedo and message retrieval equipment to allow communication with ground forces. The Vincent entered RAF service in late 1934 and was extensively used in Aden, Egypt, India, Iraq, Kenya and the Sudan. Production total was 197, and at the outbreak of World War II about half of these remained in service with the RAF. The last was retired from service in Iraq in 1941. Pictured is one of a small number of aircraft that were supplied to the Royal New Zealand Air Force.

Country of origin:	United Kingdom
Type:	three-seat general purpose aircraft
Powerplant:	one 825hp (615kW) Bristol Perseus VIII sleeve-valve radial piston engine
Performance:	maximum speed 230km/h (142mph); service ceiling 5182m (17,000ft); range 2500km (1553 miles)
Weights:	empty 1918kg (4,229lb); maximum take-off weight 3674kg (8,100lb)
Dimensions:	span 14.94m (49ft in); length 11.17m (36ft 8in); height 5.42m (17ft 9in)
Armament:	one fixed forward firing .303in Vickers machine gun, one.303in Lewis machine gun on pivoted mount in rear cockpit

Vickers Virginia Mk VII

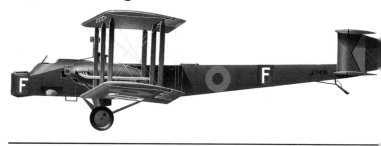

Designed to replace the Vimy, from 1924 until 1937 the Vickers Virginia was the standard heavy bomber of the Royal Air Force. The prototype first flew in November 1922. It was large and heavy, and was constructed in much the same way as its predecessor, but in the event this proved something of a blessing as the aircraft's service career was progressively stretched far beyond its expected retirement date. The first major production version after a convoluted development programme was the Mk V, which had 468hp (349kW) Napier Lion II engines and a third (central) rudder in the tail unit to distinguish it. Some 114 newbuild aircraft followed, built to various standards. As each new type was introduced earlier aircraft were upgraded. Stealth was an unknown concept at this time, and the wooden screws driven by direct-drive Napier Lion engines could be heard from far and wide.

Country of origin:	United Kingdom
Type:	heavy night-bomber
Powerplant:	two 580hp Napier Lion VB W-12 piston engines
Performance:	maximum speed 174km/h (108mph); service ceiling 4725m (15,500ft); range 1585km (985 miles)
Weights:	empty 4377kg (9650lb); maximum take-off weight 7983kg (17,600lb)
Dimensions:	span 26.72m (87ft 8in); length 18.97m (62ft 3in); height 5.54m (18ft 2in); wing area 202.34 sq m (2178 sq ft)
Armament:	one .303in Lewis machine gun in nose position; twin .303in Lewis machine guns in dorsal position; plus up to 1361kg (93,000lb) of bombs

Voisin-Farman I

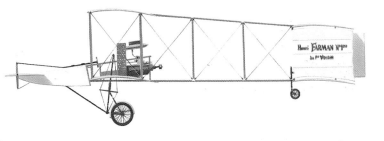

The French brothers Charles and Gabriel Voisin began to experiment with kite-making at the end of the nineteenth century. In 1906 they established Les Frères Voisin at Billancourt, where they built two biplanes with a boxkite tail structure, incorporating a rudder and using a pusher configuration. Although neither of these attempts were particularly successful, the brothers were commissioned by Henry Farman to build an aircraft for him. The Voisin-Farman I was a far better aircraft, powered by a 50hp (37kW) Antoinette engine. Its first flight in October 1907 was 771m (2530ft). On 13 January 1908 Farman piloted the aircraft on a circular flight of 1km (0.62 miles), the first person to do so in Europe. Unfortunately the brothers' successes encouraged them to develop the same basic airframe, which quickly became obsolescent. Henry Farman later went into business for himself as an aircraft designer, after breaking further European aviation records.

Country of origin:	France
Type:	single-seat biplane
Powerplant:	one 50hp (37kW) Antoinette engine
Performance:	estimated maximum speed 105km/h (65mph); range 1km (0.62 miles)
Weights:	maximum take-off weight 500kg (1102lb)
Dimensions:	span 10m (32ft 10in)

Vought OS2U Kingfisher

Vought built the VS-310 Kingfisher floatplane reconnaissance aircraft to replace the O3U Corsair in service with the US Navy. It was first flown in prototype form in landplane configuration in March 1938 and underwent sea trials with float gear in May. A production order for the OS2U-1 Kingfisher followed, and the first of these entered service in August 1940. This was the first catapult-launched monoplane to enter service with the US Navy, and was a valuable asset to both the carrier air wings and the US Navy's inshore patrol squadrons. The type was also used by the Royal Navy as the Kingfisher Mk I, 100 being supplied under the Lend Lease Act. Eighteen of the 24 aircraft that were en route to the Dutch East Indies in 1942 were seconded to the Royal Australian Air Force. Pictured is a Mk I of the Antarctic Flight, Royal Australian Air Force, during 1947.

Country of origin:	USA
Type:	two-seat observation floatplane
Powerplant:	one 450hp (336kW) Pratt & Whitney R-985-4 radial piston engine
Performance:	maximum speed 264km/h (164mph); service ceiling 3960m (13,000ft); range 1296km (805 miles)
Weights:	empty 1870kg (4123lb); maximum take-off weight 2722kg (6000lb)
Dimensions:	span 10.95m (35ft 11in); length 10.31m (33ft 10in); height 4.61m (15ft 1in); wing area 24.34 sq m (262 sq ft)
Armament:	one fixed forward-firing .3in Browning machine gun; one .3in Browning machine gun on pivoted mount in rear cockpit; underwing racks with provision for two 45kg (100lb) or 147kg (325lb) bombs

Vought-Sikorsky VS-44 Excalibur

The flying-boat which had been such a successful means of transport in the 1930s had another short lease of life immediately after the war, before the new generation of landplanes with sufficient range to span the oceans condemned it to history. In the USA the last large commercial flying-boat built was the Vought-Sikorsky VS-44A. Only three of these four-engine flying-boats were produced, the first making its maiden flight in January 1942. During the World War II they operated a New York–Foynes service, and were also used as transatlantic military transports for the Naval Air Transport Service, but under the jurisdiction of American Export Airlines. The three aircraft were Excalibur, Excambia and Exeter. Only Excambia was used commercially to any extent after the war, operated first by Avalon Air Transport and then with Antilles Air Boats.

Country of origin:	USA
Type:	passenger flying-boat
Powerplant:	four 1200hp (895kW) Pratt & Whitney R-1830-S1C3-G engines
Performance:	cruising speed 257km/h (160mph); range 6116km (3800 miles)
Weights:	maximum take-off weight 26,082kg (57,500lb)
Dimensions:	span 37.79m (124ft); length 24.15m (79ft 3in); height 8.41m (27ft 7.25in)

Westland Wapiti Mk IA

During World War I the Westland Aircraft Works at Yeovil delivered 390 D.H.9A bombers, and over the next 10 years derived its main income from reconditioning them for arduous service with the RAF overseas. In 1926 the Air Ministry issued a specification for a D.H.9A replacement, carrying a bigger bomb load with better reliability but using as many D.H.9 parts as possible. The winner of the competition was the Wapiti, one of the most hard-used and well-loved aircraft to serve with the RAF, which took a total of 512 aircraft. Another 500 were built for foreign customers and many more were built in South Africa. The Mk II had a metal structure and the army-cooperation version had a long fuselage, message hook, brakes and tailwheel. There were also arctic, long-range, float and ski versions. About 80 were still serving in India in 1942.

Country of origin:	United Kingdom
Type:	two-seat general-purpose aircraft
Powerplant:	one 480hp (358kW) Bristol Jupiter VIIIF radial engine
Performance:	maximum speed 225km/h (140mph); service ceiling 6280m (20,600ft); range 853km (530 miles)
Weights:	empty 1728kg (3810lb); maximum take-off weight 2449kg (5400lb)
Dimensions:	span 14.15m (46ft 5in); length 9.65m (31ft 8in); height 3.61m (11ft 10in); wing area 43.48 sq m (468 sq ft)
Armament:	one fixed forward-firing .303in Vickers machine gun; one .303in Lewis machine gun on Scarff ring over rear cockpit; plus up to 263kg (580lb) of bombs

Wright Flyer III

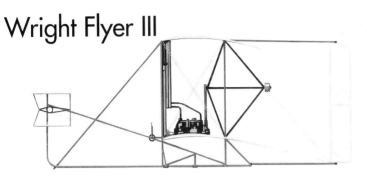

Brothers Orville and Wilbur Wright began experimenting with unmanned gliders at the turn of the century, gaining the experience to build the Flyer, which Orville piloted for the world's first powered, manned, controlled and sustained flight at Kill Devil Hill, Kitty Hawk, North Carolina on 17 December 1903. The Wright brothers developed this aircraft as the Flyer II with modified wings and engine tuned to deliver 15hp (11kW), but this was not a success. The following Flyer III was the first truly practical machine. It shared the engine and propellers of the Flyer II but had a more complex control system, and was first flown on 23 January 1905. The first 10 flights lasted no longer than 10 seconds, which the brothers attributed to their inexperience of the more advanced control system, but in October Wilbur Wright achieved a flight of 39 minutes 23 seconds, covering a distance of 38.9km (24 miles).

Country of origin:	USA
Type:	experimental biplane
Powerplant:	one 20hp (15kW) Wright 4-cylinder inline engine
Performance:	maximum speed 56km/h (35mph)
Weights:	388 kg (855lb)
Dimensions:	span 12.34m (40ft 6in); length 8.53m (28ft); height 2.44m (8ft); wing area 46.73 sq m (503 sq ft)

Zeppelin-Staaken R-series

The largest aircraft used in World War I were the sluggish but capable *Riesenflugzeug* (giant aeroplane) series produced by the Zeppelin Werke Staaken. Originally this organisation had been Gotha, where the V.G.O.1 weighing 9000kg (19,850lb) first flew in April 1915 on the power of three 240hp (179kW) engines. Via several other one-off bombers, with three, four or five engines and different schemes of defensive armament, the design team of Baumann, Hirth and Klein eventually produced R.VI. Except for the V.G.O.I, which was lost in a crash, all of the giant bombers were used on the Eastern Front or against Britain. The VI went into production, one being built by the Staaken works, six by Aviatik, four by OAW, and seven by Schütte-Lanz. Three of the Aviatik machines had different noses, tails and Maybach engines. The VI was followed by an assortment of derivatives, mainly powered by five Maybach engines, with varied airframes.

Country of origin:	Germany
Type:	heavy bomber
Powerplant:	four 245hp Maybach Mb.IV 6-cylinder inline piston engines
Performance:	maximum speed 130km/h (81mph); service ceiling 3800m (12,500ft); range 800km (500 miles)
Weights:	empty 7350kg (16,200lb); maximum take-off weight 11,460kg (25,265lb)
Dimensions:	span 42.2m (138ft 6in); length 22.1m (72ft 6in); height 6.3m (20ft 8in)
Armament:	one or two 7.92mm Parabellum machine guns in nose position; one or two 7.92mm Parabellum machine guns in dorsal cockpit; one 7.92mm Parabellum machine gun in rear position; internal bay with provision for up to 18 100kg (220lb) or one 1000kg (2205lb) bomb carried in semi-recessed position, up to a maximum load of 2000kg (4409lb)

Index

Note: Page numbers in **bold** refer to main entries.